BEIHEFTE ZUR
ZEITSCHRIFT FÜR ROMANISCHE PHILOLOGIE

BEGRÜNDET VON GUSTAV GRÖBER
FORTGEFÜHRT VON WALTHER VON WARTBURG
HERAUSGEGEBEN VON KURT BALDINGER

Band 150

LENORA D. WOLFGANG

BLIOCADRAN

A Prologue to the
Perceval of Chrétien de Troyes
Edition and Critical Study

MAX NIEMEYER VERLAG TÜBINGEN
1976

CIP-Kurztitelaufnahme der Deutschen Bibliothek

[Bliocadran]
Bliocadran : a prologue to the Perceval of Chrétien de Troyes ; ed. and critic.
study / Lenora D. Wolfgang. – 1. Aufl. – Tübingen : Niemeyer, 1976.
   (Zeitschrift für romanische Philologie : Beih. ; Bd. 150)
   ISBN 3–484–52055–8
NE : Wolfgang , Lenora D. [Bearb.] ; Crestien ‹de Troyes› : Perceval

ISBN 3-484-52055-8

To my husband

MARVIN E. WOLFGANG

TABLE OF CONTENTS

PREFACE

The *Bliocadran* is an 800-verse prologue to the *Perceval* of Chrétien de Troyes preserved in two Old French manuscripts of the thirteenth century and in a prose version printed in 1530. Ever since Potvin first published the *Bliocadran* in 1863 from the one manuscript then known to contain it, the Prologue has often been mentioned in studies of *Perceval* romances, but it has never been considered in its own right as a poem.

The only other edition of the work was by Hilka, in an appendix to his *Percevalroman,* based on manuscript *L* and on Potvin's 1865 printing of manuscript *P*. The shortcomings of Hilka's edition have often been indicated. The present edition, therefore, accompanied by the traditional critical apparatus, endeavors first of all to provide an accurate and reliable text using both manuscripts of the poem.

The Introduction provides a summary of previous scholarship and a reevaluation of the work. In several controversies, particularly about the extent of Chrétien's authorship, the origins of the *Perceval* stories, and the relationships among the various romances that contain *Perceval* enfances, the *Bliocadran* has been used as evidence without, however, a thorough understanding of the poem itself. Because of this, many distorted conclusions, as well as actual misstatements, are to be found in the critical literature, and the work has too often been summarily dismissed.

Previous scholarship that has drawn attention to the discrepancies between narrative details in the Prologue and those in the mother's speech to her departing son in Chrétien's poem, and that has drawn attention to the seeming failure of the *Bliocadran* author to appreciate the provocative beginning of the *Perceval,* has heretofore condemned the *Bliocadran* on structural and aesthetic grounds. By choosing, however, a different point of view, by interpreting the narrative *theme* that relates the Prologue to the beginning of Chrétien's poem rather than the narrative *details* that separate the two works, I have tried to demonstrate that the *Bliocadran* makes an excellent beginning to Chrétien's *Perceval,* and one that is not unlike the beginnings of his other romances.

Other questions that have been raised about the *Bliocadran* are treated in the Introduction: how is the Prologue related to Celtic sources, to the Didot-*Perceval* and the *Perlesvaus,* and to Wolfram; what is the origin of this name for Perceval's father; what can be learned from tracing the other names for Perceval's father in the romances? Previous scholarship which has assembled lists of analogous or contradictory narrative details, or which has concentrated on the manuscript tradition alone, has proved inconclusive. Again, a more fruitful approach has been to consider the narrative themes for which details have been borrowed or altered. This approach is particularly illuminating in the case of the relationships among Chrétien, the Prologue and Wolfram, and between the Prologue and the *Perlesvaus*. The study of the various names and rôles assigned to Perceval's father in the romances sheds light on the poetic practices of those medieval authors and is useful for tracing the shifting rôles assigned to Perceval from Chrétien to the Vulgate Cycle.

This edition was originally submitted as a doctoral thesis at the University of Pennsylvania. It was prepared under the guidance and close supervision of Professor William Roach to whom I owe immeasurable gratitude, both for my first introduction to medieval studies and for the continuing support and encouragement that he has generously shown me since the inception of this study. It is to him that I dedicate whatever merits this edition may contain.

I wish to express special gratitude to Emeritus Professor Albert W. Thompson of Washington State University, whose articles about the *Bliocadran* originally initiated my interest in this little work, and who generously gave of his time to read the finished manuscript and to send me a lengthy critique offering many suggestions for its improvement.

It is also a pleasure to acknowledge my indebtedness to Professors Ruth J. Dean and Frank Paul Bowman who read the original manuscript and offered invaluable critiques that saved me particularly from many infelicities of expression.

To Selma Pastor who typed the manuscript, to my husband Marvin who read the Introduction with the practiced eye of a published author, and to my daughters Karen and Nina who respected their mother's needs for periods of concerted effort, and who lightened her heart with their pride, I express a gratitude no less profound for being brief.

And finally, I offer my sincere gratitude to the Department of Romance Languages of the University of Pennsylvania for helping to defray part of the costs of printing this study, and to Professor Dr. Kurt Baldinger, for according me the honor of appearing in so illustrious a series of publications.

L. D. W.

INTRODUCTION

1. THE *BLIOCADRAN* AS PROLOGUE TO CHRETIEN'S *PERCEVAL*

In six significant passages of Chrétien's *Perceval* the identity and mission of Perceval are gradually revealed[1]. His precise kinship relations present problems in the *Perceval*[2], but he emerges nonetheless as the sole male heir of a disappearing family of former renown. He is the son of a widow and the only survivor of three brothers[3]. He is the cousin of a mutilated or wounded king who has no issue. This Fisher King must have had a brother or sister, whose line, however, ends in a female, a niece, who sends the sword destined for Perceval to the Grail Castle[4]. The »germaine cousine«, who upbraids Perceval in the wood after his failure at the Grail Castle, is of uncertain parentage, but she also represents the end of a family line. Else-

---

[1] Editions of the *Perceval*: Charles Potvin, *Chrestien de Troyes. Perceval le Gallois*, 6 vols. (Mons, 1865–71), vol. I (1865) and vol. III (1866) [In some printings of Potvin's edition vol. I (1866) contains *Le Roman en Prose (Perlesvaus)* and the *Perceval* is in vols. II and III.]; Gottfried Baist, *Crestien's von Troyes Contes del Graal (Percevaus li galois)* (1909, 1912); Alfons Hilka, *Der Percevalroman (Li Contes del Graal)* (Halle, 1932); William Roach, *Le Roman de Perceval ou Le Conte du Graal*, 2nd ed. (Geneva, Paris, 1959). Most quotations are from Hilka's standard edition of 1932.
The passages that reveal the identity of Perceval are Hilka, *Perceval*, 1932, verses 407–488 (the mother's speech), verses 1039–43 (the laughing damsel), verses 3145–70 (Perceval receives the sword sent by the Fisher King's niece), verses 3507–3622 (Perceval meets the *cousine germaine*), verses 4646–83 (the Hideous Damsel and her challenges), verses 6415–19 (Perceval with his Hermit Uncle).

[2] Perceval is now considered to be the cousin, not the nephew, of the Fisher King. See William A. Nitze and T. Atkinson Jenkins, *Le Haut Livre du Graal, Perlesvaus*, vol. II (Chicago, 1937), pp. 190–191; Jean Frappier, *Chrétien de Troyes* (Paris, 1957), p. 184; G. D. West, *Grail Problems II: The Grail Family in the Old French Verse Romances*, RPh, XXV (1971), 55–56.

[3] For a summary of Perceval's relatives in the Grail romances see G. D. West, *op. cit.*, pp. 53–73. I do not agree with his conclusions about the *Bliocadran* (pp. 71–72); see below p. 8.

[4] See Hilka, *Perceval*, verses 3145–70.

where, this cousin is represented as a sister[5]. Of two known uncles, one is a hermit and the other, father of the Fisher King, is barely alive, surviving on a host, brought to him in the Grail. Perceval's family, however ambiguous certain details may be, is obviously in a state of dissolution. The anger and disappointment Perceval experiences from various characters illustrate the urgency of their need for him to assume the functions and rôles that only gradually become apparent. Perceval is by inheritance a great knight, the last of his line and, by implication, the only possible future Grail King.

From the first episode of the romance, Perceval's encounter with the Five Knights in the forest, the reader is aware that the rôle of chivalry is being called into question. The young hero is mysteriously unaware of the Arthurian world, whereas even the field laborers appreciate the meaning of their young lord's first encounter with knights. At the mention of the word »knights« the mother faints, only to arise with an eighty-two line speech of anxiety and revelation of the situation that fails to impress her son. The speech reveals her fear of chivalry, the causes of that fear and its effects on her life: dishonor, poverty and deaths of sons and husband. Her passionate intention is to disenchant her son from what he has just seen and heard and to keep him at home. Perceval has experienced none of these ancient griefs and does not even know he is poor. Dazzled, Perceval will leave. Nothing more is revealed in the *Perceval* about Perceval's father and brothers or about the conditions that led to the downfall of »Li jantil home aprés la mort / Uterpandragon qui rois fu« (vv. 444–445). The mother's speech is dramatic, provocative, and, unfortunately, never elucidated. Because of its vague character, other writers will develop some of the implications they find there.

It is not my purpose to discuss Chrétien's skill as a storyteller. The negative tone in regard to chivalry established at the beginning of the *Conte* does not recur after Perceval's departure from home although there is a contrast within the *Perceval* between worldly chivalry and chivalry with a high or holy purpose. Both the unfinished state of Chrétien's work and its undeveloped implications inspired a great body of continuations, rationalizations, elaborations and elucidations. The *Bliocadran Prologue* is one small part of this vast corpus. My concern in this study is to trace what subsequent authors did with the material found in Chrétien concerning the Grail family and how they may have combined their own elaborations with other sources. The unknown author of the *Bliocadran* set about answering the immediate

---

[5] Perceval has a sister in the Second Continuation, the *Perlesvaus,* Didot-*Perceval* and in Gerbert's Continuation. For these editions: Nitze, *op. cit.;* William Roach, *The Didot-Perceval, According to the Manuscripts of Modena and Paris* (Philadelphia, 1941); Mary Williams, *Gerbert de Montreuil. La Continuation de Perceval,* 2 vols. (Paris, 1922–25, CFMA, nos. 28 and 50).

questions posed by the text: who was Perceval's father, and why was Perceval hidden away in a wilderness?

The *Bliocadran Prologue,* which might be more accurately called a prelude, introduction or elucidation, was perhaps inspired by two motives: to create a background for Perceval's father and to rationalize the abrupt beginning of the *Perceval.* The author of the *Bliocadran* was confronted by a narrative technique in the *Perceval* unlike that of Chrétien's other romances: it begins without a familiar setting or any warning by the author that the reader must be patient until things begin to fall into place. It is curious that three of Chrétien's *romans* open at Arthur's court[6]:

> Au jor de Pasque, au tans novel,
> a Quaradigan, son chastel,
> ot li rois Artus cort tenue;   *(Erec,* 27–29)

> Et dit qu'a une Acensïon
> li rois Artus cort tenue ot,
> riche et bele tant con lui plot,   *(Charrete,* 30–32)

> Artus, li boens rois de Bretaingne
> la cui proesce nos enseigne
> que nos soiens preu et cortois,
> tint cort si riche come rois
> a cele feste qui tant coste,
> qu'an doit clamer la Pantecoste.
> Li rois fu a Carduel en Gales;   *(Chevalier au Lion,* 1–7)

With this kind of beginning the reader knows all he needs to about the setting. He is immediately oriented and prepared for any kind of adventure to present itself. Anyone can come to the court and any adventure may be announced with the reassuring background and guarantee of that court. In one other romance, however, the *Cligés,* Chrétien does not begin at Arthur's court, so he feels obliged to explain things in advance:

> Un novel conte rancomance
> D'un vaslet qui an Grece fu
> Del linage le roi Artu.
> Mes ainz que de lui rien vos die,
> Orroiz de son pere la vie,
> Dom il fu, et de quel linage.
> Tant fu preuz et de fier corage
> Que por pris et por los conquerre
> Ala de Grece en Engleterre,
> Qui lors estoit Bretaigne dite.   *(Cligés,* 8–17)

---

[6] Editions from which these quotations are taken: Mario Roques, *Les Romans de Chrétien de Troyes, édités d'après la copie de Guiot,* vol. I., *Erec et Enide,* vol. III., *Le Chevalier de la Charrete,* vol. IV., *Le Chevalier au Lion (Yvain)* (Paris, 1952–60, CFMA, nos. 80, 86, 89. Reprinted 1963–65); and Alexandre Micha, *Les Romans de Chrétien de Troyes ...* vol. II., *Cligés* (Paris, 1957, CFMA, no. 84. Reprinted 1965).

The *Perceval* alone of the five Arthurian romances of Chrétien begins *in medias res*. In light of Chrétien's other romances, the *Bliocadran Prologue* supplies what Chrétien did for them, especially for the *Cligés*, an introduction and a setting. It »explains in advance«. Frappier[7] continued to quote and agree with Fourquet's harsh criticism of the Prologue for »spoiling« Chrétien's brilliant beginning to the *Perceval*:

> C'est là un jeu ingénieux que seul pouvait se permettre un conteur très écouté. Il demande un au ditoire capable d'apprécier la fantaisie souveraine de l'auteur, qui accumule les mystères, déroute l'imagination, pour donner soudain une explication imprévue et simple. Tous les auditoires n'étaient pas préparés à ce jeu, fait pour une cour très cultivée. Le début devait paraître inintelligible; on n'avait pas la patience d'attendre l'explication. Il était fatal qu'un remanieur éprouvât le besoin de tout expliquer *d'avance*[8].

This condemnation has become one of the major issues among the critics who are eager to dispense quickly with the Prologue as unworthy of serious consideration. But the *Bliocadran Prologue* does not »tout expliquer *d'avance*«. It is primarily concerned with Perceval's father, who is subsequently not explained in the *Perceval* and then, only in the last 52 (of 800) verses, does the *Bliocadran* author rework material borrowed from Chrétien in order to prepare the scene with the five knights. When Perceval's mother, at the end of the *Bliocadran*, warns him against »men covered with iron« whom he may encounter in the woods this arouses anticipation and detracts nothing from the scene when it takes place. Anticipation fulfilled is as valid a literary experience as surprise. The general opinion that the *Bliocadran* is an inferior approach, aimed at an unsophisticated reader, fails to consider that Chrétien used more conventional beginnings for his other romances, nor does it take into consideration the fact that no less a poet than Wolfram will create a prelude and explain a great many things in advance. It is modern criticism that looks for progression in techniques and seems to find it in the beginning of Chrétien's last *roman*, whereas there may be other reasons for such a beginning. If, as the Celticists contend, Perceval owes his existence to a variety of Irish and Welsh heroes whose stories were circulating at the time, then it may be that the multiplicity of conflicting and varying versions of these tales led Chrétien to hesitate about making a choice among them at the outset of his poem. He may have sought to create his own hero before giving him a background that might conflict with these »well-known« tales. By alluding only vaguely to Perceval's unnamed father, perhaps intending

---

[7] Jean Frappier, *Cours de Sorbonne, Perceval* (Paris, 1953, 1966), pp. 18–19, and the same author's *Chrétien de Troyes et le mythe du Graal* (Paris, 1972), pp. 44–45.
[8] J. Fourquet, *Wolfram d'Eschenbach et le Conte del Graal* (Paris, 1938, 2nd ed., 1966), pp. 106–107. The chapter dealing with the *Bliocadran* in Fourquet's second edition of 1966 (pp. 81–90) is identical to that of the first edition.

to come back and fill in details, he was free to create his own hero. After he had selected his details and re-created his Perceval, whatever background he would have chosen could no longer contradict what might have been known about any particular hero. The *Bliocadran Prologue* does not explain everything in advance, nor does the conventionality of its form condemn it any more than the conventionality of the beginnings of Chrétien's other four Arthurian romances can be said to condemn them.

The modern reader is, perhaps, more concerned than the medieval with linear development and with coherence or precision of detail. The medieval author or reader sought, rather, variety of material and attractiveness of detail. The many so-called blunders and contradictions unearthed by modern criticism were perhaps not even noticed by a reader of, for example, a cyclic manuscript of the Vulgate Cycle or the Prose *Tristan*. The *Bliocadran Prologue* contains several glaring contradictions of detail with the *Perceval*, which are all the more disconcerting because in the two manuscripts that contain the work a mere 407 verses separate the *Bliocadran* from the mother's speech to her son. The contradictions are as follows:

Chrétien	Bliocadran
Perceval's father had been wounded and ruined. He fled with his wife, two older sons and Perceval, about two years old, to a manor he already had in a waste forest. The father, sometime thereafter[9], died of grief upon learning that both the older sons were killed shortly after they had been knighted and were on their way home.	Perceval's father, Bliocadran, died in a tournament when Perceval, his only son, was born. The wife and the young son fled to the forest. Eleven brothers of the father had also died in tournaments. These deaths at arms motivated the flight of the mother and son to a hidden place where she chose a site and built a manor.
No brothers of Perceval's father are mentioned.	

The immediate question is how, with such seemingly glaring contradictions in detail, can the *Bliocadran* be justified as an elucidation of the *Conte du Graal?*

This poem of 800 verses[10] was first discussed in 1857 and was first printed in 1863[11]. Paul Meyer reviewed Potvin's edition of 1865 in 1866[12] and said,

---

9 The father must have died shortly thereafter since Perceval has no memory of his father or of any brothers.

10 There are 798 verses in MS *P*. See below pp. 81–83 for »Summary of Episodes«.

11 Wilhelm Ludwig Holland, *Über eine Handschrift von Crestiens Gedichte Li Contes del Graal*, Germania, II (1857), 426–427. Holland first found a notice about the manuscript in the Archiv der Gesellschaft für ältere deutsche Geschichtskunde, VIII (1843), p. 474, by Bethmann. See the last part of my Introduction, »Manuscripts and Editions«, for further discussion. Holland printed verses 1–23 of the *Bliocadran*. Charles Potvin first printed the text in *Bibliographie de Chrestien de Troyes* (Brussels, Leipzig, Ghent, Paris, 1863), pp. 89–118.

12 Paul Meyer, Revue Critique d'Histoire et de Littérature, I (1866), 129–137.

somewhat surprisingly, ». . . je reconnais qu'il est bien dans le style de Chrestien«. The early controversy centered on which was the real prologue to the *Perceval* and whether Chrétien was the author of either or both. Birch-Hirschfeld[13] denied Chrétien's authorship of the *Bliocadran* convincingly; Newell[14] called the authentic prologue »vulgar nonsense«; Bruce[15] called the *Bliocadran* »the invention of a third-rate poet«; Lot called it a work »d'une naïve platitude«[16]. This first cycle of opinion was related to the question of authorship. Once it was proved that Chrétien was not the author, the work seemed to have no merit whatever. A renewed interest in the Prologue had to await the appearance of a critical edition of the *Perceval* since what could be said about it depended in part on whether all the manuscripts did indeed contain the revelations of the mother's speech. A second controversy involved the relationship of the *Bliocadran* to Wolfram's *Parzival*. Miss Weston[17] was the first to outline parallels between these two works. After the publication of Hilka's critical edition of the *Perceval* in 1932, two scholars, Sister M. A. Rachbauer[18] and Fourquet[19] took up again detailed comparisons of the *Bliocadran* and Books I and II of the *Parzival*, arriving at opposite conclusions. A recent comment on this line of investigation by Springer[20] acknowledges divided opinion about whether Wolfram knew and used the Prologue. A third approach to the *Bliocadran*, in studies by Loomis and Miss Newstead, is to consider the possible common, lost sources of Chrétien, *Bliocadran* and Gahmuret in Celtic prototypes[21]. There has been

---

[13] Adolf Birch-Hirschfeld, *Die Sage vom Gral* (Leipzig, 1877), pp. 69–74. Gaston Paris [HLF, XXX (1888), pp. 27, 187, note 2] also refuted as Chrétien's the first 1282 verses of Potvin's text.

[14] William Wells Newell, *The Legend of the Holy Grail, Part VIII*, JAF, XV (1902), 54–55.

[15] James Douglas Bruce, *The Evolution of Arthurian Romance*, vol. II, 2nd ed. (Baltimore, 1928), p. 90.

[16] Ferdinand Lot, *Les Auteurs du Conte du Graal*, Romania, LVII (1931), 135. This is in part a review of Maurice Wilmotte, *Le Poème du Gral et ses auteurs* (Paris, 1930). Wilmotte, in his translations and adaptations of parts of the Perceval romances in verse, *Le Roman du Gral* (Paris, 1930), includes his translation of the *Bliocadran Prologue*, pp. 71–81.

[17] Jessie L. Weston, *The Legend of Sir Perceval*, vol. I (London, 1906), pp. 76–101, esp. p. 93.

[18] Sister M. A. Rachbauer, *Wolfram von Eschenbach*, a study of the relation of the content of Books III–VI and IX of the *Parzival* to the Crestien manuscripts (Washington, 1934).

[19] J. Fourquet, *Wolfram d'Eschenbach et le Conte del Graal* (Paris, 1938, 2nd ed., 1966).

[20] Otto Springer, Wolfram's *Parzival*, in Roger Sherman Loomis, ed., *Arthurian Literature in the Middle Ages, a Collaborative History* (Oxford, 1959, 1961), pp. 218–250. (This work will hereafter be referred to as *ALMA*.)

[21] Roger Sherman Loomis, *Arthurian Tradition and Chrétien de Troyes* (New York, 1949), pp. 193, 243, 347–355, 479; Helaine Newstead, *Perceval's Father and Welsh Tradition*, RR, XXXVI (1945), 3–31.

no detailed study of the *Bliocadran* other than Brugger's[22], and it was concerned primarily with the etymology of the name. Nitze[23] was also concerned with parallels among Perceval *enfances* and briefly alludes to the *Bliocadran* in his edition of the *Perlesvaus*[24].

I shall return to problems discussed by these and other scholars, but I wish here to point out that the *Bliocadran* has been used for many scholarly purposes without ever having been satisfactorily edited or thoroughly considered in its own right. It was A.W.Thompson, editor of the other »spurious« prologue, the *Elucidation,* who pointed out in 1931, 1955 and again in 1959 that the *Bliocadran* deserves specific consideration: »The *Bliocadran* has never been studied for its own sake, but always incidentally, tangentially. In the present state of our knowledge it would be rash to conclude that its author had access to other versions of the original story. It may well be, as some have thought, simply an invention of its author to give a more adequate introduction to Chrétien's poem, with no knowledge of Perceval except what he found there«[25]. In the same chapter Thompson speaks in its favor: »Scholars have often made disdainful remarks about the literary quality of the composition. To be sure it lacks the sparkle of Chrétien's verse. On the other hand it is a straightforward narration, coherent and well motivated. Human emotions are sympathetically described, and feudal customs are well portrayed. It is more realistic than most medieval romances and bears no overt traces of folk-lore. In most respects the *Bliocadran* is an excellent beginning to Chrétien's poem«[26].

It is the aim of this study to present a satisfactory edition based on the two manuscripts containing the *Bliocadran* and to study it »for its own sake«. There is in most remarks a note of impending disappointment: if the *Bliocadran* is »simply an invention of its author« and it cannot be proved to contain elements from other »traditions« or to have influenced other works, such as the *Parzival,* then there seems to be very little value in the work at all. Even if Chrétien was the only source of the *Bliocadran,* which I shall attempt to disprove, and even if it had no subsequent influences, which I believe also to be false, there is still a value in studying the work: to discover how a medieval author viewed the *Perceval,* what his version, in terms of

---

22 Ernst Brugger, Bliocadran, the Father of Perceval, in *Medieval Studies in Memory of Gertrude Schoepperle Loomis* (Paris and New York, 1927), pp. 147–174.
23 William Nitze, *The Sister's Son and the Conte del Graal,* MPh, IX (1911–12), 291–322; Nitze, *Perceval and the Holy Grail* (Univ. of Cal. Pub. in Mod. Phil., vol. 28, no. 5, 1949).
24 Nitze, *Perlesvaus,* II, p. 191.
25 Albert Wilder Thompson, Additions to Chrétien's *Perceval* – Prologues and Continuations, in *ALMA,* pp. 211–212. See also, Thompson, *The Elucidation* (New York, 1931); Thompson, *The Text of the Bliocadran,* RPh, IX (1955–56), 205–209.
26 Thompson, Additions to Chrétien's *Perceval, ALMA,* p. 209.

additions, omissions or elaborations, can tell us about poetic practices in general, and about the handling of Arthurian material in particular. I shall of course investigate the possibility that Wolfram had access to a manuscript of the *Perceval* that contained the *Bliocadran*, that the motif of the eleven brothers of Perceval's father, first in Robert de Boron and then in the *Perlesvaus*, is an essential one in the early stages of the development of Grail material and try to discover whether the name for Perceval's father furthers in any way the theories of Celtic prototypes.

It is curious that in a very recent study (1971), a scholar as widely familiar with Arthurian material as G. D. West could misinterpret Perceval's position in the *Bliocadran*. West's article assembles material concerning the »Grail Family« in the poetic texts. He says that in the *Bliocadran* the poet »gives prominence to P.'s father, and shows a tendency to adhere to elements of tradition in which the hero is a member of the Grail Family through the paternal line, whereas in Chrétien's poem P. belongs to the family through his mother, and his father is a character of comparatively minor importance«[27]. This conclusion does not seem justified. In the Prologue, Bliocadran is one of twelve brothers, eleven of whom are already dead. When Bliocadran is killed there is no male left on his side of the family. If Perceval is to meet later in the story a Hermit Uncle and a Grail King Uncle, they can only be on the mother's side. The opposite tradition, that Perceval descends from the male line of the Grail Family is in Robert de Boron. The *Bliocadran* poet is not so much giving prominence to a tradition in which Perceval descends through his father from the Grail Family as he is trying to account for the identity of that knight. West is here concerned with the genealogical issues of the Grail poems, which are indeed complex, and has somehow forced a conclusion not supported by the text. The *Bliocadran* text has been the victim of other mistakes that I shall discuss as the occasion arises[28].

2. NARRATIVE THEME AND NARRATIVE DETAIL IN THE *PERCEVAL* AND THE *BLIOCADRAN PROLOGUE*

As I have already mentioned, once it was discovered that all the manuscripts of the *Perceval* do contain the mother's speech (vv. 407–488), there seemed to be no way of reconciling the clash of narrative details presented by the *Bliocadran Prologue* with those in that speech. The only explanation for what seem to be glaring contradictions between the texts is not that the *Bliocadran* author did not know what was in the *Conte*, but that he did not have a chapter-and-verse attitude toward the information he found

---

[27] G. D. West, *Grail Problems, II: The Grail Family in Old French Verse Romances*, RPh, XXV (1971–72), p. 72.
[28] See particularly below, Introduction, 5. »Bliocadran, the name«, pp. 38–46.

8

there, an attitude that has distorted most of the scholarship on the subject. The *Bliocadran* author felt free to elaborate, alter, or even to eliminate the details he found in the mother's speech. The modern critic tends to dismiss the *Bliocadran* in favor of that speech. This latter, however, is not among the best of Chrétien's inventions, as I shall discuss below.

The names for Perceval's father are many and varied: Alain, Alain le Gros, Guellans Guenelaus, Gales li Caus, Pellinor or, as in the Manessier Continuation of the *Perceval,* announced as unknown (v. 44751)[29]. I shall return to these names for Perceval's father when discussing the romances that use them, but it is important to note here that contradictions concerning specific details, such as the names of Perceval's father, or of his mother, sisters, uncles, cousins, and so on, have not been used as a basis for evaluating the works that contain these details. Similar contradictions should not, therefore, be the basis, as has been the case, for evaluating the *Bliocadran Prologue.*

The *Bliocadran* poet has elaborated a theme suggested by the *Perceval* and in so doing has produced a good, if not a better, introduction to the *Perceval* than the material given in vv. 407–488. What I propose is that the *Bliocadran* author retained the same narrative theme as that in the mother's speech in the *Perceval* and that he changed Chrétien's narrative details in order to make a stronger case for that theme. What the *Bliocadran* author saw in the mother's speech was a way of rearranging, eliminating and inventing details, so that the theme – her great fear of the destruction wrought by knightly activity, which led to isolation in a waste forest – is more directly motivated. In the *Bliocadran,* all tragic events precede and culminate in the flight to the forest. The underlying theme is that the chivalric practice of the tournament can be a brutal and destructive activity. This was a contemporary concern. The Church at times bitterly condemned the tournament in some of its more brutal and more materialistic manifestations. This narrative theme, which I believe has been obscured by the more obvious concern with narrative detail in vv. 407–488 of the *Perceval,* was seized upon by the *Bliocadran* author. His manner of using it is typical of a medieval author; he choses his material and elaborates it into episodes that illustrate the narrative theme so that apparent contradictions of details are of secondary consideration. Miss Bogdanow[30], following Vinaver[31], has recently demonstrated how fruitful this approach can be for the study of a medieval work. In the detailed comparison which follows of the *Perceval* and the *Bliocadran Prologue* I hope to demonstrate that both works illustrate

---

[29] Potvin, *Perceval le Gallois,* vol. VI. Manessier's Continuation is in vol. V (1870) and vol. VI (1871) of this edition.

[30] Fanni Bogdanow, *The Romance of the Grail* (Manchester, 1966), p. 194.

[31] Eugène Vinaver, *King Arthur's Sword, or the Making of a Medieval Romance,* BJRL, XL (1957–58), 513–526.

9

the same narrative theme, and that narrative details are of secondary importance.

The mothers's outburst against chivalry and the havoc it has wrought occupies eighty-two verses in the *Perceval*. The very word »Chevalier« pronounced by her son causes her to swoon. The practice of arms, she laments to him, has cursed her life, brought crippling wounds, misery, porverty, isolation, grief and death. It is a bristling, fiery speech, worthy of the pulpit. Perceval, however, never knew his father or his long-dead brothers. If he had had any memory of them, his indifference to his mother's speech would be entirely repulsive. It is clear he is hearing this narrative for the first time. It explains Perceval's ignorance of the world of knighthood while revealing a lineage that destines him for that world. It is significant, however, that every detail of family history is explained only as it has been affected by knightly activity. The father was a great knight; father and mother were descended from great knights; the two older sons were made knights by kings and almost immediately died »as armes«. The mother's previous silence was intended to hide knighthood from her son, her present passion is directed only against this activity. Has Chrétien put his own attitude toward some forms of chivalric practices into the mouth of the mother? Within the circumstances of the story, the mother's diatribe is justified. She has lost a husband and two sons and she naturally hates the institution which has occasioned her loss. But might Chrétien who wrote these lines so convincingly for a mother's rôle have intended to reveal his own general principles? It is a long and relentless speech; the theme never specifically reappears and has no effect upon Perceval or the action of the story. It is not an uncommon motif for an infant hero to be hidden away from threatening enemies until the time comes for him to return to the world and to assume his preordained rôle. Chrétien, I believe, has used this motif to suit a specific purpose: the hero is not being hidden from a particular enemy or safeguarded (as was Arthur) until manhood, but he is being shielded from a way of life. Chrétien is condemning the pursuit of arms.

It should not be any more startling to find a critique of chivalry in a courtly romance than to find a critique of courtly love, such as occurs in the *Erec* or the *Charrete*. Léon Gautier[32] and Sidney Painter[33] pointed out that the Church condemned tournaments as early as 1130. In that year the Council of Clermont considered tourneys »homicidal contests and [the Church] refused burial in consecrated ground to anyone killed in them. This decree was confirmed by the Lateran councils of 1139 and 1179. The ban on tournaments appeared in the canon law among the *Decretals* of Pope

---

[32] Léon Gautier, *La Chevalerie* (Paris, 1895), pp. 673–766.
[33] Sidney Painter, *French Chivalry* (Baltimore, 1940. Reprinted 1957, Cornell University Press), pp. 149–172.

Gregory IX«[34]. Thus the tournament at the time Chrétien was writing was a live and serious issue. During certain periods the Church relented: »In fact the Avignon Popes who lived under the dominance of the chivalrous kings of the Valois line felt obliged to rescind their predecessors' decrees against this form of knightly sport«[35]. Gautier's chapter on the twelfth and thirteenth-century tournament describes indeed a vicious, predatory and brutal sport[36]. As a probable cleric, Chrétien would naturally have shared the view of the Church. The Crusader »who was not supposed to tilt«[37] fell outside this consideration as did the knight with the high moral purpose of the Arthurian code. The attack is directed against a brutal sport or the practice of arms as a means of winning booty.

The *Bliocadran* author has taken the same theme, but has chosen different details to illustrate it, and has employed a different method of illustration. There is a curiously realistic and non-fictional tone in the mother's speech. A great knight in a romance is not usually permanently wounded in a battle or a tournament so that he is crippled and falls into ruin or goes into exile. If he is wounded, he recovers fully or he dies. It is not correct to say that the Fisher King and Perceval's father are doubles, for the Fisher King is not living in poverty nor are such material considerations even an issue in the latter's case. Perceval's father was the victim of a way of life, as were his two older sons who died by the sword. There is no glorification of the practice of arms nor even the usual substitute for it, an explanation. The best were fallen low, the good were ruined and »a tort«. The *Bliocadran* author took this brief mention of past events and recast it into a series of episodes.

Both narratives are concerned with the deaths of Perceval's male kin which have left him a sole survivor. It makes no difference to the story whether he had two brothers or eleven uncles. They existed only to motivate the mother's terror of chivalry in either account. It was not their existence that mattered, but the manner of their deaths. Perceval's father in Chrétien arouses sympathy: he suffered not only wounding, crippling, exile and poverty, but fatal grief for his sons. The *Bliocadran* author has dispensed with this particular complexity and made a compulsive knight errant of Bliocadran. Bliocadran has lately suffered the loss of eleven brothers but he is eager to set out for a tournament. He at first consents not to go, but once he is assured of an heir, he cannot be detained any longer. It is not a war or an invasion that draws him away, but knightly sport. The two combats he engages in are senseless, mercenary and brutal. In the first joust he captures

---

[34] Ibid., p. 155.
[35] Ibid., p. 89; Gautier, *Chevalerie*, pp. 681, 673–704.
[36] Gautier, *Chevalerie*, pp. 673–704.
[37] K. G. T. Webster, The Twelfth-Century Tourney, in *Anniversary Papers by Colleagues and Pupils of George Lyman Kittredge* (New York, 1913), p. 230.

booty and in the second he engages in a brutal combat with a total stranger and dies. Narrative detail differs in the two accounts, but narrative theme is the same. In neither account is the practice of arms justified. The *Bliocadran* is more direct in its attack than the *Perceval*. The speech of the mother combines past griefs with present fears, particularizing an attitude toward tournaments, whereas the direct presentation of Bliocadran's disregarding the deaths of his brothers, the pleas of his people and his wife, and the descriptions of the frankly brutal combats, allow no such ambiguity. That the verse is commonplace and the jousts conventionally presented tend to obscure the fact that the author has, by illustrating the narrative theme in such scenes, revealed his less than positive attitude toward the tournament.

In both the *Bliocadran* and the *Perceval* the story of Perceval's father has been invented in order to motivate hiding the hero away. In Chrétien the flight to the forest takes place after the wounding and ruin of the father but before the death of Perceval's two older brothers. In the *Bliocadran* the flight to the woods was directly correlated with the father's death and all tragic events preceded this action. In this manner the flight is directly caused by tragic circumstances, whereas in Chrétien the two stages of tragedy diffuse somewhat the effect of the drastic decision to flee civilization. In Chrétien there is some ambiguity about the circumstances of the father's wounding. We are not told it was in a tournament or in a war. The *Bliocadran* author chose to make the circumstance a tournament, thereby underlining the theme unambiguously as well as motivating the flight directly. The author has rearranged the order of the material he found in Chrétien (all tragic events precede flight), altered narrative detail (eleven uncles substituted for two brothers), and eliminated ambiguity about the theme (the more vague relationship of father and brothers to knightly activity is made explicit by depicting a fatal tournament directly).

The mother's speech to her son creates an awkward scene. I have said that Perceval's indifference can be partly justified by the fact that it all seems like so much »ancient history« to him, that he has no personal memory of the people or events described and that, dazzled by the five knights, he does not really listen. All the justifications of this scene in terms of theme and motivation do not erase the fact that it seems improbable that a son could be so indifferent to the story of the death and destruction of his family. But medieval material cannot be judged in this manner. Wolfram, it should be noted, although quite closely following Chrétien in this material, does eliminate any story of Perceval's father from the mother's speeches to the departing Parzival, and so avoids the awkwardness. The *Bliocadran* author may have been aware of the awkwardness of the mother's speech and may have wanted to eliminate it altogether and to replace it with his prologue. The main motive of the mother's speech in the *Perceval* is to explain why her grief is so great that she dies upon Perceval's departure for knightly activity. What the *Bliocadran* author has avoided by recounting events in a prologue is the necessity of Perceval's hearing and then being indifferent to her story.

In the *Bliocadran* the mother's grief and distress are elaborated in the central and longest episode of the work, Episode IV (213 verses)[38]. We are told of the great fears of Bliocadran's knights concerning the revelation of his death to his wife. Four days (MS *P*) or three days (MS *L*) after Bliocadran left for the tournament he is dead and his son is born. A messenger is sent out to him with the good news only to learn of the tragedy. The knights order the messenger to go back and say nothing about Bliocadran's death; rather he is to invent a story that they have all gone to the king's castle and will return in a week. The messenger announces this to the lady while the knights set about devising a way of breaking the real news to her. Their concern has already been well motivated. In Episodes I and II we witnessed the lady's begging Bliocadran to stay, supported by the townspeople. The circumstances now could not be worse. She must learn at the worst possible moment that what she feared the most has happened. Her great joy in the birth of a long-desired son must be turned into a moment of the greatest grief. The knights are aware that, if the news is not broken to her properly, she could die of grief. Dying of grief is, of course, what Perceval's mother is destined to do. This will happen because of the sudden and brutal manner of Perceval's leaving, i.e., she was not treated with the great delicacy and concern being shown her by the knights in the *Bliocadran*. The problem for the author is how to show the lady in violent grief and yet not have her die of it prematurely. The knights decide to go to an abbot and persuade him to announce the tragedy as comfortingly and as gently as possible. In twenty-three carefully prepared lines the abbot leads up to his revelation. Then follow the usual monologues and descriptions of grief. Masses are sung, the abbot departs and the mourning widow turns to her son for consolation. In this manner one purpose of the mother's speech is served: we are made to witness the extent of her grief not only in the act of mourning but through the actions of those who surround her, who are aware, as were the harrowers in Chrétien, that the lady has cause for great sorrow.

In Episode V, which is the second longest of the seven composing the romance, the author concerns himself with depicting the seriousness of the flight to the waste forest. For seven months the widow had been considering what to do. She has by now secretly packed up her belongings and decided to leave. It is taken as a matter of course in the *Perceval*, in the *Parzival* and in other stories of Perceval, that as a child he had been hidden away or is simply living unknown in a secluded place. The *Bliocadran* author, in order to underscore the seriousness of the step undertaken, elaborates in detail the

---

38 For an outline of all the Episodes, see below, pp. 81–83. Episode I, 53 verses; Episodes II, 108 verses; Episode III, 82 verses; Episode IV, 213 verses; Episode V, 199 verses; Episode VI, 69 verses; Episode VII, 76 verses.

method whereby the mother accomplishes her will. The widow's steward (*maior*) counsels her to proceed very carefully. She must pretend to be taking the child on a pilgrimage to Saint Brendan of Scotland and she must guarantee that her country will be held in trust by a nephew against Perceval's future return. The plan is wise, cautious and deliberate and is therefore successful.

It seems undeniable that the rash folly of Bliocadran's actions is being contrasted to the sensible and logical actions of the other characters in the story. It cannot be mere coincidence that the steward has twelve healthy children safe from the dangers of knighthood whereas the lady has twelve dead family members and fears for the life of her only child, or that Bliocadran, except for the conventional conversation of courtesy extended to the messenger who brings news of the tournament, is heard only gruffly, in two lines, silencing his wife as he goes off to that tournament. The theme against knight – errantry is well served. All other persons in the romance are logical, reasonable, careful, except Bliocadran.

Episode VI describes the journey of the mother and her followers. It takes more than fifteen days of swift travel, with only overnight stops, to arrive at a sufficiently isolated spot in a vast forest. The spot is chosen for its beauty, its running water and because there is no one to be seen for miles around.

As I previously mentioned, Episode VII, the final one, is the one attacked most by the critics. Only in these last verses does our author rework material directly borrowed from Chrétien's *Perceval*. The attack against this section was on aesthetic grounds. In Episode VII Perceval is now fifteen, a young hunter with the javelins. One day his mother warns him that if he should see people covered with iron in the forest they are devils who would devour him. He is to run away immediately, cross himself and say his credo, and he will be safe. Perceval promises he will do what she has said, God willing. The next day he goes hunting and encounters neither game nor men. The mother questions him about what he found and he reports that he found nothing. Here the *Bliocadran* ends. This scene in the *Bliocadran* creates anticipation for the famous scene with the five knights; it does not destroy the surprise of the scene. The pleasure is in watching the inevitable unfold. Knowing in advance has never spoiled the pleasure of a well-told tale. The author of the *Bliocadran* is doing at least two things in Episode VII: he is paying tribute to Chrétien's famous scene by anticipating it and he is making a very logical transition to the opening of the *Perceval*. The manner in which Fourquet blamed the *Bliocadran* author for spoiling the surprise in Chrétien really takes into consideration only a first reading of the *Perceval*[39]. Any prior knowledge of its contents only increases the pleasure of anticipation.

Apart from the eleven brothers of Perceval's father and the name Blio-

---

[39] See p. 4 above.

cadran, there is nothing in the Prologue to indicate any other source than the *Conte du Graal*. The name is not to be found elsewhere[40], but neither is the theme, with the possible exception of the *Parzival*. When the Grail theme dominates Arthurian romance, knights are judged according to their relative merits and a critique of chivalric practice as such is not developed again. This critique would have had little meaning after the development of such works as the Didot-*Perceval* or the *Perlesvaus*. I am inclined, at this point, to situate the composition of the *Bliocadran* somewhat before the *Perlesvaus*, but the author probably had some knowledge of the work of Robert de Boron. A fuller discussion of the date will be given when these works are considered in detail. The logical time of composition for the Prologue would be one when there is an awareness of the »tradition« of the eleven brothers of Perceval's father but before any particular name had become attached to him, and perhaps before a wide dissemination of the *Perceval* itself. It is what the *Perlesvaus* may owe to the *Bliocadran* that is of the greatest importance.

3. PERCEVAL'S FATHER
IN OTHER ARTHURIAN ROMANCES

There are fifteen manuscripts that contain the *Conte du Graal*. Of these, eleven contain at least one continuation. The two manuscripts that contain the *Bliocadran* also contain the First Continuation (C[1]) and the Second Continuation (C[2]). Manuscript *P* contains more »parts« of the compilation than any other single manuscript: the *Elucidation*, the *Bliocadran*, *Perceval*, C[1], C[2] and Manessier's Continuation. Not included in MS *P* are Chrétien's Prologue and the Gerbert interpolation. I propose that one imagine a reader of this manuscript. There is no name for Perceval's father other than Bliocadran in some 45,000 lines of verse[41]. In the Manessier Continuation, Perceval admits: »Ne sai coment ot nom mes pere« (Potvin, VI, 44751). A summary of who is Perceval's father in those manuscripts containing at least one continuation of the *Perceval* is in the following list. There are two manuscripts that contain the Gerbert Continuation. Gerbert should be considered separately in that he developed a set of names for Perceval's family, calling the father Gales li Caus[42].

---

[40] See G. D. West, *An Index of Proper Names in French Arthurian Verse Romances, 1150–1300* (Toronto, 1969), »Bliocadran«; Brugger, Bliocadran, in *Studies G. S. Loomis*, pp. 147–174.

[41] For text of the First and Second Continuations see William Roach, *The Continuations of the Old French Perceval of Chrétien de Troyes*, 4 vols. (Philadelphia, 1949–71). For the text of Manessier see note 29 above.

[42] For text of Gerbert see Mary Williams, *Gerbert de Montreuil. La Continuation de Perceval*, 2 vols. (Paris, 1922–25) (CFMA, nos. 28, 50, to verse 14078); for index of names see Amida Stanton, Gerbert de Montreuil as a writer of Grail Romance (Diss. University of Chicago, 1939), pp. 184–209.

A Contains the *Perceval*, C¹, and part of C². Perceval's father is referred to as Gulle Genelax (C¹, v. 7633).
E Contains *Perceval*, C¹ and C² and Manessier. There is no name for Perceval's father.
L Contains *Bliocadran, Perceval*, C¹ and C². Perceval's father is Guellans Guenelaus (C¹, v. 7671) and Bliocadran in the Prologue.
M Contains *Perceval*, C¹, C² and Manessier. Perceval of the family of Greloguevaus (C¹, v. 17741).
P Contains *Elucidation, Bliocadran, Perceval*, C¹, C², Manessier. Perceval's father is Bliocadran in the Prologue.
Q Contains *Perceval*, C¹, C² and Manessier. Perceval of the family of Galozgrenax (C¹, v. 17741).
R Contains *Perceval* and C¹ (fragment). No name for Perceval's father.
S Contains *Perceval*, C¹, C², Manessier. There is no name for Perceval's father.
T Contains *Perceval*, C¹, C², Gerbert, Manessier. Perceval's father is Gales li Caus in Gerbert.
U Contains *Perceval*, C¹, C², Manessier. Perceval of the family of Grelogrenaus (C¹, v. 17741).
V Contains *Perceval*, C¹, C², Gerbert, Manessier (the last three are parts or fragments). Perceval's father is Gales li Caus in Gerbert.
K Contains C² and Special Conclusion. Perceval's father is Alain le Gros in the Conclusion[43].

The puzzling name Gulle Genelax, and variant, for Perceval's father, mentioned only one time each in two (of eleven) First Continuation manuscripts, is perhaps a garbled reminiscence or rationalization of the names in *Erec*. There is in the *Erec* not only the Galez li Chaus mentioned by West, but Gaudeluz (v. 1681), Galerïez (1695) and Galegantins li Galois (1706)[44]. In the *Perlesvaus* Perceval's paternal grandfather is Gais or Glais li Gros and two of his uncles are Gosgallians and Galeriens. I have reserved for a separate chapter (»Bliocadran, the name«) a detailed discussion of some of these names, their possible origins and how they may have been derived from each other. It is rather amazing, when one considers the thousands of verses devoted to continuing the *Perceval*, that there is only to be found (apart from Gales li Caus) in a single suspect line the name Guellans Guenelaus or Gulle Genelax, a name of no consequence within the corpus. As late at 1230 Manessier, the third continuator, maintained Chrétien's original reticence

---

43 For text and discussion see William Roach, The Conclusion of the *Perceval* Continuation in Bern MS. 113, in *Studies in Medieval Literature in Honor of Albert Croll Baugh*, ed. MacEdward Leach (Philadelphia, 1961), pp. 245–254; text also in Roach, *Continuations*, IV, pp. 591–592.
44 G. D. West, *Grail Family*, RPh, XXV (1971–72), p. 64. Names from *Erec* cited from Roques, *Erec* (Paris, 1952). Galez li chaus is in verse 1696. Cf. Wendelin Foerster, ed., *Erec und Enide* (Halle, 1890, 1896, 1909, 1934), verses 1726, 1701, 1725, 1738. The name Galegantins li Galois occurs (with variations) in a list of knights in MS *A* of the First Continuation, v. 3782. Cf. *L* 3582 Gaila li gentius Galois, and *E* 12942, *T* 4672. But he is not said to be the father of Perceval.

about the hero's father. Thus the *Bliocadran* author and Gerbert, whose independent versions have been attached to the manuscripts of the *Perceval* and First and Second Continuations, were as completely free to invent a name or story for Perceval's father as any of the authors of the prose romances. The name Alain le Gros which occurs only in the special conclusion to MS *K* ties the *Perceval* and its Continuations to a »tradition« concerning Perceval's father. The mention of this name leads to a consideration of the work of Robert de Boron.

Alain or Alain le Gros is the name implied as Perceval's father in Robert de Boron's verse and prose *Joseph*[45]. In the Didot-*Perceval*[46], the *Perlesvaus*, the Bern conclusion to the Second Continuation and in the *Chevalier aux deux épées*[47] Alain le Gros is named as Perceval's father. There is a remnant of this tradition of Alain as Perceval's father in one manuscript of the Prose *Tristan*[48].

With the work of Robert de Boron the genealogy of Perceval becomes of major importance. It is Robert who makes the Grail a relic of the Last Supper and of the Crucifixion. The Biblical Joseph of Arimathea is the first »Grail Keeper«. In order to establish a »Grail Family« Joseph is given a sister, Enygeus, who is married to Bron (Hebron), the first »Rich Fisher«. The worthiest of their twelve sons, Alain, is the leader of his eleven brothers and their wives who are to travel to the West, but not with the Grail. Two other separate journeys are made. Petrus, a very holy member of the Grail Company (not Family) goes to the West to the »vaus d'avaron« to await »Le fil Alein« (Verse *Joseph*, line 3128) or, in seven manuscripts of the Prose *Joseph*, »le fil del fil Alaine« (line 1626). The third journey is to be by Bron, now called the Rich Fisher. Joseph gives him the Grail and entrusts him with its secrets. He is to go to the West »En quelque liu que il vourra« (Verse *Joseph*, 3359) and »Il atendra le fil sen fil« (Verse *Joseph*, 3365) (these directions announced by an angel). Joseph is to remain »En la terre lau il fu nez« (Verse *Joseph*, 3459). Robert promises to tell what happened and why he separated his story into several parts (last line Verse and Prose).

Now there are several elements in the story that guided future stories about the Grail, its guardians and Family, as well as elements that allowed in-

---

45 Verse *Joseph:* William A. Nitze, *Le Roman de l'Estoire dou Graal* (Paris, 1927, CFMA, no. 57); for the Prose *Joseph:* William Roach, *The Modena Text of the Prose Joseph d'Arimathie*, RPh, IX (1955–56), 313–342; Richard O'Gorman, An Edition of the Prose Version of Robert de Boron's *Joseph d'Arimathie* (Diss. University of Pennsylvania, 1962); Georg Weidner, *Der Prosaroman von Joseph von Arimathia* (Oppeln, 1881).
46 William Roach, *The Didot-Perceval, according to the Manuscripts of Modena and Paris* (Philadelphia, 1941).
47 Wendelin Foerster, *Li Chevaliers as deus espees* (Halle, 1877), verses 2604–05.
48 See Roach, *Didot-Perceval*, p. 7 and note 3; p. 8 and notes 1–4; and the relevant text, pp. 309–313.

dividual interpretations. Alain was the chosen one because he was the son who desired not to marry. This is what an angel had told Joseph. The choice of the nephew was to be made this way. However, Joseph prays again and receives final instructions from a »voice« in which the son of Alain is specifically mentioned, and the name Alain is given for the first time (Verse *Joseph*, 3128). Thus Alain is not to remain chaste; it was only his desire to be so that caused him to be chosen as the leader of his brothers and their wives. The second half of this poem (as divided by O'Gorman at v. 2307, with the introduction of Enygeus) seems devoted more to mystification than to explanation. There is a great deal of suggestion and half-revelation about future rôles and destinations. Perceval is never mentioned, nor is it ever said that the son of Alain is to be anything but »awaited«[49].

The Didot-*Perceval* is the first romance in which Bron is specifically the Fisher King, Grail Keeper and grandfather of Perceval, and Alain is the father of Perceval. Roach describes the romance as »a much-interpolated and rewritten version of a fairly faithful prose rendering of Robert's original ›branches‹ dealing with Perceval and the last days of Arthur«[50]. The *remanieur* who is responsible for the text as it stands incorporated material from Chrétien and the Second Continuator. Because the text must be considered in its two very different redactions and in relationship to three other branches, the *Joseph, Merlin,* and *Mort Artu,* as well as in its relationship to Chrétien and the Second Continuation, there are many problems of narrative detail. Alain exists only briefly in the story. In the version of MS *E*, Alain tells Perceval that when he is grown he must go to the famous court of

---

[49] The Grail Family problems are in the very first texts, Chrétien's *Perceval* and Robert's Verse and Prose *Joseph*. Perhaps the scarcity of names and abundance of third person pronouns leads to some confusions in the *Joseph* texts. In the Verse *Joseph* Petrus, when he will arrive in the West, »Le fil Alein atendra« (verse 3128), and Bron, when he will arrive in the West, »Il attendra le fil sen fil« (verse 3363). In the Prose *Joseph*, however, Petrus »il atende le fil del fil Alaine« (O'Gorman 1626, Weidner 1334). In other cases the Prose *Joseph* tried to clarify the Verse, especially about the females in Alain's group. In the Verse *Joseph* the voice tells Joseph that his nephew »La garde de ses freres eit Et de ses sereurs ensement« (verses 3098–99), and the Prose *Joseph* clarifies, »la garde de ses freres et de ses serors en la loi« (O'Gorman 1611–12, Weidner 1323). This same sort of distinction is made when Joseph addresses »Mi fil, mes filles, estes tuit« (verse 3238), but, »Vos estes tuit mi fil et mes filles en loi« (O'Gorman 1685, Weidner 1380–81). The verse says of Alain »En estranges terres ala Avec lui ses freres mena« (verses 3263–64), whereas the corresponding prose does not forget the wives also went, »Et ainsi *les* en mena en estranges terres« (O'Gorman 1698–1699, Weidner 1391–92) where *les* refers to »li home et les fames« of 1697 (1390). See further studies by O'Gorman, *The Prose Version of Robert de Boron's Joseph d'Arimathie*, RPh, XXII (1969–70), 449–461, and *La Tradition manuscrite du Joseph d'Arimathie en prose de Robert de Boron*, Revue de l'Histoire des textes, I (1971), 145–181.

[50] Roach, *Didot-Perceval*, p. 16.

18

Arthur. Alain then promptly dies (line 16) and Perceval sets out. In the version of MS *D*, the voice of the Holy Spirit reminds Alain of Joseph, Bron and the Grail. Bron cannot be healed and then die until Perceval finds him and learns the secrets of the Grail. The voice tells Alain to send his son to Arthur's court. Alain tells him to go and then dies (line 17)[51]. Alain in the Didot-*Perceval* is nothing more than a genealogical link in the Grail Family. His function seems to be merely that of initiating Perceval's departure for Arthur's court.

This beginning uses only one element from Chrétien, and that only in the redaction of MS *E* – that the mother, when she hears that Perceval has gone, is so fearful that he might be eaten by the wild beasts of the forest that she dies. Gone from the story is any notion that Perceval is hidden away in a forest safe from worldly chivalry. When Perceval sits in the vacant seat at the Round Table, a voice announces the history of the Grail, the enchantments of Britain, the asking of the question and the curing of the Fisher King[52]. It is MS *E* that allows the voice to associate Bron, Perceval's grandfather, with the Fisher King, goal of the quest, but does not quite let Perceval know he is the predestined knight[53]. Each time a voice has »appeared« to give a brief résumé of the story of the Grail, Joseph, Bron, and Alain, there is something missing: the other brothers of Alain. Just as in the *Joseph* the great task of the second half of the work seemed to be a painfully drawn division of duties toward the Grail and voyages toward the West, the beginning of the Didot-*Perceval* seems devoted to a piecemeal yielding of information so that not too much is known by Perceval at any given time, in order to keep the story in motion. Perceval wanders about for three years unable to find the Fisher King. It is not until he returns home that he finds out why. Both his sister and his uncle, the Hermit, tell the story of the Grail, Joseph, Bron, and Alain again. The sister's version in the redaction of MS *D* finally makes an allusion to the missing brothers of Alain. She is telling Perceval her story (and refers to seven brothers of her own in MS *D*, line 623) and includes a version of what the voice said to her father before he died: »Et sachiez que Brons vostre pere est [en] cest païs, et si ne savez ou, et il vos dona la guarde de voz freres par aider et por conseillier en loi . . .« (*D*, 630–632).

When Perceval reveals to his sister who he is, they both go to the Hermit, clearly referred to in both MSS *D* and *E* as the brother of Alain and their uncle. He sounds like one of the missing brothers of Alain from the *Joseph*. Now this relative is the subject of much discussion by Roach. In explaining the beginning of the text he says: »It is possible that Episode B originally gave an account of the eleven brothers of Alain, since all eleven are said to

---

[51] Ibid., pp. 139–140. See p. 35 for a discussion of the death of Alain in Episode B of MS *D*.

[52] Ibid., pp. 46, 150–151.

[53] Ibid., pp. 46–47.

have died in combat in the service of Christ in the *Perlesvaus* (52–54)«[54].
In a detailed discussion of Episode F, Perceval's visit to his sister and to his
Hermit Uncle, Roach asserts that the Hermit Uncle is a remodeling of Petrus
(another figure misplaced from the *Joseph*), but borrowed as a paternal uncle
from the Second Continuation[55]. The Hermit was an uncle in Chrétien too,
but a maternal uncle. The *remanieur*, I believe, faced with two texts in which
the hermit is an uncle, made Petrus, the only likely candidate for a hermit in
the *Joseph*, into the Hermit Uncle and retained the relationship as paternal
uncle not only because of this relationship in the Second Continuation, but
because of a reminiscence of the eleven brothers of Alain. This conclusion
still leaves at least ten brothers »missing«. What I intend to show is that
this lot of uncles is an embarrassing detail that the *remanieur* probably
wanted to eliminate from the text, but he did not quite succeed in doing so.
I quoted above a brief allusion by the sister in MS *D* (630–632) to Alain's
brothers. In the *Merlin* sections of these two manuscripts there is an excellent
illustration of the difficulties the redactors had with these brothers. It is
Merlin who is speaking and informing Arthur about the Grail, directly after
Arthur's coronation:

> Or si saces que li Graaus fu bailliés a Joseph, et aprés se fin le laissa a son
> serorge, qui avoit non Bron. Et cil Bron si a doze fils; si en est li uns només
> Alains li Gros; et li commanda li Rois Peschiere la garde de ses freres. Cil Alains
> est venus en ceste terre de Judee, si com nostre Sire l'a commandé, en ces illes
> vers Occidant, / et sont arivé en cest païs. Et li Rois Peschiere si converse en
> ces illes d'Irlande en un des plus biaus lius del monde . . .

The corresponding section in MS *D* is as follows:

> Or sachez qui le Graaus qui fust bailliez a Josep est en ce païs et en la guarde
> au riche Roi Pecheor, a qui Joseph le bailla par le comendement nostre Seygnor
> quant il dut fenir. Et cil Rois Pecheors est en grant enfermetez . . .[56]

When one compares these two parallel passages from the *Merlin* section of
MSS *E* and *D* there are two possible interpretations: either the redactor of
MS *D* deliberately discarded reference to the twelve sons of Bron or he inadvertently did so. Because the information in the version of MS *E* is accurate (not the grammar: *Cil Alains est venus . . . et sont arivé*) it is more
likely that the redactor of MS *D* decided to eliminate this specific reference,
as the eleven brothers are nowhere else accounted for. When Roach says, »It
is possible that Episode B originally gave an account of the eleven brothers of
Alain, since all eleven are said to have died in combat in the service of
Christ in the *Perlesvaus*«, he says that Brugger »argues plausibly that the

---

[54] Ibid., p. 34.
[55] Ibid., pp. 58–66.
[56] Ibid., pp. 305–306.

fate of the eleven brothers of Alain was originally described in Episode B as the motivation for Alain's retirement to the forest, where Perceval was brought up in ignorance of chivalry. As all his brothers had been killed in combat, Alain would have wished to keep his son from the same fate. However, the voice of the Holy Ghost which spoke to him at his death announced that it was God's will that Perceval should go to the court«[57]. It is at this point that I believe the *Bliocadran* can be used as evidence. The evidence of the *Merlin* sections of the Didot-*Perceval* and of Episode F shows that the *remanieurs* were trying to eliminate the eleven brothers of Alain but that reference to them still remained in the texts. Now if Robert's original story for Episode B had contained a convenient killing off of these brothers this solution would have retained some of the harmony of the original cycle, as Robert would have had to account for the brothers he created. A second possibility is that the brothers of Alain were merely mentioned several times, for we do find them in the text, and that nothing was devised to account for their fate. I propose that if Robert's original did include a recounting of the deaths of Alain's brothers then the *Bliocadran* can be presented as evidence that this version existed. There is nothing in the Didot-*Perceval* in its present state to suggest what Brugger proposes so plausibly, that »the fate of the eleven brothers of Alain was originally described in Episode B as the motivation« for Alain's retirement to the forest«. These narrative details, however, do sound like the *Bliocadran*.

There is in fact evidence to suggest that such a theme, retirement to the forest after knightly deaths, is contrary to the spirit of the Didot-*Perceval*. Alain in both redactions sends his son to Arthur's court. Merlin, in his explanation to Arthur about the Grail, tells him that the Fisher King cannot die »desci adont que uns cevaliers qui serra a la Table Reonde ait tant fait d'armes et de cevalerie, en tornois et par querre aventures, que il sera li plus alosés del monde«[58]. What is striking is that the narrative details postulated as having been in Robert's original are in fact in the *Bliocadran*. It is also possible that Robert simply announced that these brothers had died and the *remanieur*, finding no use even to mention their existence, tried to expunge all references to their existence. If this were the case and the author of the *Bliocadran* had access to a version of the Didot-*Perceval* in which the brothers were simply mentioned as dead, or to a version like the redactions of MSS *E* or *D* such as they exist, he would have been even freer to do as he wished with those elusive brothers of Perceval's father: to invent a story about their deaths.

---

[57] Ibid., p. 34 and note 3.
[58] Ibid., p. 306. The version in MS *D* (lines 323–325) is similar here to the version in MS *E* (lines 494–495) concerning the positive rôle of knightly exploits in the development of the hero.

In the »old« part of the Huth *Merlin*[59] there is evidence of this same vagueness about Alain and his brothers. When Merlin tells Blaise the story he is to write, he refers to »Alain et de sa compaignie«, and not to any brothers[60]. Later, when Merlin is explaining the Round Table to Uther, even Alain is suppressed. It seems, then, that even in this version of the »old« *Merlin*, Alain is being gradually eliminated to make way for Pellinor as Perceval's father[61]. Alain and his brothers, created by Robert, will reappear in the Vulgate Cycle. There they will not be a burden to Perceval's story, as some nine generations will have been invented to separate Joseph and his companions from Perceval and his contemporary family.

The *Perlesvaus*, unlike the *Didot-Perceval*, is quite explicit about the Grail Family. There are no scattered, vague references to Alain's brothers, but a decisive outline of Perceval's lineage for both the father and the mother, placed at the beginning of the romance. The brothers of Alain are listed one after the other and named. The mother, Iglais, is niece to Joseph of Arimathea, and she is sister to the Fisher King and to the Hermit, as in Chrétien. The father, Alain (Julain) le Gros des Vax de Kamaalot, descends from Nicodemus and had eleven brothers:

> ...molt buens chevaliers autressi com il fu, e ne vesqui chascuns que .xii. anz chevaliers, e morurent tuit a armes par leur grant ardement e por avancier la loi qui renovelee estoit. Il furent .xii. frere: Julains li Gros fu li ainz nez, Gosgallians fu aprés, Bruns Brandalis fu li tierz, Bertolés li Chaus fu li carz, Brandalus de Gales fu li quinz, Elinanz d'Escavalons fu li sistes, Calobritius li semes, Meralis du Pré du Palés li witimes, Fortunés de la Vermeille Lande li nuevimes, Meliarmans d'Albanie li .x., Galerians de la Blanche Tor li .xi., Alibans de la Gaste Cité li doziemes. Tuit cist morurent a armes o service du Saint Prophete qui avoit renovelee la Loi par sa mort, e plessierent ses ennemis a leur pooir. De cez .ii. manieres de gent dont vos avez oïz les nons e le recort, nos raconte Josephes li buens clers que cist buens chevaliers fu estrez, dont vos orroiz le non e la maniere[62].

The sister was also given a name, Dandrane[63]. All of these genealogies were set forth in tables by Nitze, showing how they diverge from and correspond to Chrétien and Robert[64].

The immediate effect of this exposition in *Perlesvaus* is one of relief. The author of the *Perlesvaus* has tried to form a coherent, logical narrative from disparate materials. A great many of the sources of the *Perlesvaus* have been

---

[59] Gaston Paris and Jacob Ulrich, *Merlin, roman en prose du XIIIe siècle* (Paris, SATF, 1886), vol. I, to p. 146.
[60] Ibid., p. 31.
[61] Ibid., Merlin to Uther, p. 98.
[62] Nitze, *Perlesvaus*, I, pp. 24–25, lines 44–57.
[63] Ibid., p. 24, line 41.
[64] Ibid., vol. II, pp. 190–191.

traced and I propose that the *Bliocadran* is one of them[65]. It is undeniable that Robert had promised in the *Joseph* to account for Petrus, Bron and Alain and his future heir. However rationalized or remodeled these personages may be, they are in some way accounted for before the *Perlesvaus*, except for the awkward material of eleven paternal uncles for Perceval. The Didot-*Perceval* showed a clumsy attempt to combine Chrétien, the First and Second Continuations and the work of Robert de Boron. As I have tried to show, the knightly death in combat of these brothers, postulated as having been in Robert's original, cannot be proved to have been in the work. There is thus only one real account of these brothers and that is in the *Bliocadran*. I propose that this work was composed in the spirit of Chrétien with some knowledge of Robert but before the *Perlesvaus*. In his genealogies, the author of the *Perlesvaus* has not so much invented as he has harmonized and accounted for sources that he must have believed could not be ignored, Chrétien and Robert. In the same manner that he named the sister derived from the Second Continuation, the Hermit Uncle and the mother, he gave names to the eleven brothers of the *Bliocadran*. The author of the *Bliocadran* may have known the name Alain, but using it would have meant going into the whole story of Joseph, et al., all of which had no place in Chrétien's story. In fact, Alain cannot be mentioned without the name's carrying with it all the burdens of Joseph and Bron. The whole tone of the beginning of the *Perlesvaus* is that whatever is known about Perceval's family is being assembled, not invented, so that the story can proceed without the awkwardness of wondering who is who at every stage. Twice the author of the *Perlesvaus* announces that the eleven brothers died to advance the New Law, once before and once after the list. This deliberateness seems to suggest that, for whatever reason they may have died in other stories, the present author wants the reader to know his interpretations. The subject here is chivalry in the service of God, without any ambiguity about frivolous tournaments. It is this use of previously existing material for its own symbolic purposes that everywhere seems to characterize the *Perlesvaus*.

Nitze acknowledges the possibility that the *Bliocadran* might have been known to his author: »There are also twelve brothers in the Bliocadran Prologue, but Alain is not one of them, and the date of the Prologue is quite uncertain, though it may have been included in one of the manuscripts known to our author«[66]. Elsewhere Nitze adds: »The preceding are the established sources of *P[erlesvaus]*, which the author presumably knew from one text, similar, it seems, to Hilka's MS *L*. In this regard, his work offers an analogy to the so-called *Elucidation*, which Thompson (p. 84) concludes, ›is based on Chrétien, Pseudo-Wauchier, and Wauchier‹. Out of this he built the frame-

---

[65] Ibid., pp. 90–156.
[66] Ibid., p. 123, note 39.

work of his romance, weaving the rest of this plot, together with its conclusion, from scattered material culled partly from wide reading and partly from local tradition«[67]. Finally, »Since the Bliocadran Prologue is found in MS. B.M. Add. 36614, which is closer to *P* than any other extant manuscript of Chrétien, it is always possible *P* was also influenced by it«[68]. It is unlikely that the manuscript tradition is of any use here since MS *L* was copied later than the composition of the *Perlesvaus* and the *Bliocadran* was added afterward. This situation does not rule out, however, the possibility that the manuscript from which MS *L* was copied was contemporaneous with (if not later than) the manuscript from which the addition of the *Bliocadran* to MS *L* was made. Loomis, in an article about additional sources of the *Perlesvaus* observes that its author »was remarkably familiar also with Arthurian romances«. »But it is reasonable«, he adds, »to infer that he must have known four or five lost Arthurian texts, and if we add them to the French romances which Nitze regarded as furnishing him with material, then we can hardly envisage him working in a monastic cell or scriptorium. Rather we should place him in the castle of an amateur of the *Matière de Bretagne*, where he might have served as a chaplain or secretary«[69]. I propose that one of these »lost« Arthurian texts is the *Bliocadran*. Nitze remarks in several places how well-knit, deliberately built-up, and unified the plot of *Perlesvaus* is[70]. It is this insistence on coherent narrative and the use of a wide variety of texts that suggests that the *Perlesvaus* author utilized material he found in the *Bliocadran*.

There is a passage at the beginning of the *Perlesvaus* in which Perceval's sister is telling her story to Arthur, without knowing to whom she is speaking. In this passage one can see how details from various sources have been reused to fit a very different theme: »The beau ideal of chivalry is to be, not the practice of courtly love nor the quest of mere adventure, but the militant service of Christianity. The knight who craves glory shall fight for his faith and shall convert the heathen. Thus the quest of the Grail will be the success of a war waged for the church«[71]. In the following passage the author of the *Perlesvaus* uses Perceval's ignorance of chivalry as a pretext to praise the practice of it. The eleven brothers here mentioned as having died in arms have already been praised for their high purpose. The mother does not die of grief when Perceval leaves to become a knight. The father is mentioned as having died, shortly after this passage, without any particular story attached to his death. What emerges is a systematic reuse of Perceval's ignorance

---

[67] Ibid., pp. 103–104; cf. pp. 95–96.
[68] Ibid., p. 191, note to Table V.
[69] Roger Sherman Loomis, *Some Additional Sources of Perlesvaus*, Romania, LXXXI (1960), 498–499.
[70] Nitze, *Perlesvaus*, II, pp. 157–172.
[71] Ibid., I, p. 16.

of chivalry and the deaths of his uncles to serve a new narrative theme as compared to the one suggested at the beginning of the *Perceval* and in the *Bliocadran.*

> Qant li vallez oï ainsi parler son pere, il demanda que chevaliers estoit. ›Biax filz, fist la mere, vos le devriez bien savoir par lignage.‹ Ele dist au vallet q'il avoit .xi. oncles eü de par son pere qi avoient esté tuit ocis a armes, e ne vesqi chascuns que .xii. anz chevaliers. Sire, fet ele au roi, li valez respondi que ce ne demandoit il mie, mes comfet chevalier estoient; e li peres li respondi que ce estoient cil du monde o il avoit plus de valeur. Aprés li dist: ›Biax filz, il ont hauberz de fer vestiz por leur cors garantir, e hiaumes laciez, e escuz e glaives, e espees çaintes por ex deffendre‹[72].

Not only is the mother's long tirade against chivalry from the *Perceval* absent here, but it is she, together with the father, who praises the knightly calling.

What the *Perlesvaus* has accomplished, then, is to account finally for the eleven uncles of Perceval. The name of the father is Alain and not Bliocadran for the latter implies only the naming of Chrétien's nameless chevalier, whereas Alain means a descendant of Joseph of Arimathea. In subsequent texts, specifically in the Vulgate Cycle, Alain and his brothers will appear again, but they will be chronologically historical Grail ancestors and, in most texts, Perceval's father will be Pellinor. Perceval is himself set aside for a new Grail Hero, Galaad.

It seems highly unlikely that the *Bliocadran* romance would have been composed after the *Perlesvaus* (*terminus ad quem* 1212)[73]. Although the ending of the *Perceval* was still occupying Gerbert and Manessier as late as 1230, and they could ignore the new genealogies for Perceval introduced by the Vulgate Cycle and other romances, it seems unlikely that an author concerned with the father of Perceval would have been uninfluenced by the tradition of Alain, or have felt that an introduction to the *Perceval* was even necessary at such a late date. This speculation, however, has another support, the evidence of Wolfram, to which I shall return.

The Grail Family in the romances that constitute the Vulgate Cycle[74] is both complex and confusing. Perceval's father, the Grail King, the Maimed King,

---

[72] Ibid., pp. 42–43.
[73] Ibid., II, p. 89.
[74] Heinrich Oskar Sommer, *The Vulgate Version of the Arthurian Romances*, 7 vols. (Washington, 1908–16. Reprinted 1967); Gweneth Hutchings, *Le Roman en prose de Lancelot du Lac* (Paris, 1938); Albert Pauphilet, *La Queste del Saint Graal* (Paris, 1923, 1949, CFMA, no. 33); James Douglas Bruce, *Mort Artu* (Halle, 1910); Jean Frappier, *La Mort le Roi Artu* (Paris, 1936); Studies: Ferdinand Lot, *Etude sur le Lancelot en Prose* (Paris, 1918. Reprinted 1954 with additions by M. Lot-Borodine); Albert Pauphilet, *Etudes sur la Queste del Saint Graal* (Paris, 1921); Jean Frappier, *Etude sur la Mort le Roi Artu* (Paris, 1936, 2nd ed., 1961); J. Neale Carman, *A Study of the Pseudo-Map Cycle of Arthurian Romance* (Kansas, 1973).

the Fisher King and the Hermit begin to »contaminate« each other. There are many key passages that illustrate the confusing character of these texts, but perhaps one from the *Queste* is most illustrative. The Maimed King is referred to in one passage as Parlan (3 MSS), Pelles (2 MSS), Pelehan (1 MS) and Pellinor (2 MSS)[75]. Pauphilet uses Parlan in his text. Pellinor is, of course, in other texts, considered Perceval's father. There is another Maimed King in the *Queste*, Mordrain, who survives from the time of Joseph of Arimathea, despite the fact that nine generations have passed. In the *Queste*, and here only, Perceval's sister names Pellehen as Perceval's father[76]. One has only to consult Sommer's *Index of Names and Places* of the Vulgate to realize that a great deal of duplication of names and rôles has taken place. Elsewhere in the Vulgate, Pelles, Alain and Pellinor will be called brothers and the second two are »malades«. And there is more than one Pellinor, one of whom is considered to be Perceval's father. In trying to determine who is Perceval's father, one must really consider each of these romances individually. It is Lot who pointed out that the Vulgate authors are deliberately obscure about Perceval's father:

> Jamais les origines de ce personnage et ses rapports de parenté avec Lancelot et Galaad ne seront pas (sic) nettement définis – et ils ne pouvaient pas l'être sans danger... Mais un silence profond et intentionnel s'étend au cours de toute l'œuvre sur la ɼ ɪrenté de ce héros embarrassant... En effet Perceval était représenté comme né de la fille de Pellès, Helizabel... Sur le père du héros du graal un compet silence était observé. Evidemment l'auteur avait une idée de derrière la tête. Laquelle? c'est ce qu'il est impossible de savoir, ses intentions ayant changé en cours de route et Galaad ayant été substitué à Perceval[77].

In the beginning of the *Lancelot* proper[78] there is graphic proof of the beginning of the shift of Grail Hero from Perceval to Galaad. Later in this same branch[79] there are references to the Perceval story as »another« story to be told about the Grail. It now becomes clear that when Perceval is displaced as the main Grail hero, he must also be divorced from Alain, whose main identity has been Father of the Grail Hero.

Because the *Lancelot* was the first composed of the Vulgate Cycle romances, I shall compare other texts to it, keeping in mind the above remarks by Lot about obscurity. Perceval, in the first major episode assigned to him, comes

---

[75] Sommer, VI, p. 150; Pauphilet, *Queste*, p. 209, line 9 and note to this line, p. 288. Sommer uses Pellinor in his text.

[76] Sommer, VI, p. 144; Pauphilet, *Queste*, p. 201, lines 23–24 and note to line 24, p. 287.

[77] Lot, *Etude Lancelot*, pp. 122, 222.

[78] Sommer, III, p. 29. This is the passage where one MS shows the name Perceval crossed out and replaced by Galaad. See J. Neale Carman, *Prose Lancelot, III,29*, RPh, VI (1952–53), 179–186.

[79] Sommer, III, p. 429, note 7.

to court identified only as the brother of Agloval[80]. He is one of nine knights sent to seek Lancelot and, during this episode, he has a vision of the Grail with Hector. Perceval has many chances during this episode to identity himself when challenged to do so. His only answer is that he is Agloval's brother or a knight of Arthur's.

There are several young knights introduced into the Vulgate who at first sound as if they are going to turn out to be Perceval. In the *Merlin* volume[81] »Pelles' son« is introduced with a long series of adventures and characteristics that duplicate what one would expect of Perceval. He turns out to be Eliezer. Nasciens, a young cousin of Perceval's also duplicates him[82]. In fact, all of these young heroes, Eliezer, Nasciens, Agloval and Galaad himself are not always clearly distinct from Perceval.

Pelles, Pellinor and Pellean (Pellehen) are all at some time in the seven volumes of the *Vulgate Version* identified as Perceval's father[83]. In each case there is confusion, corruption, contradiction or deliberate reticence in the texts. The Pellinor whom Sommer puts in the Index as Perceval's father is really only the Pellinor of the *Livre d'Artus*. In the *Merlin* volume, the Pellinor who is brother to Pelles and Alain is not the same Pellinor, but a cousin. Perceval is thus vaguely related to an Alain, but never as a son[84]. Nor is there any longer a Hermit Uncle to Perceval. Much of the scholarship concerning the Vulgate Cycle has been concerned with the Maimed and Fisher Kings, mentioning Perceval's father only incidentally[85].

At least three factors seem to explain the genealogical contradictions in the Vulgate Cycle: (1) the shift of the main Grail Hero from Perceval to Galaad; (2) the invention of an elaborate prehistory of approximately nine generations from the time of Joseph of Arimathea to that of Galaad; and (3) the desire of the Vulgate authors and compilers to include Grail material from as many sources as possible[86]. In the Vulgate *Estoire*[87] there are many genealogies, and Galaad's is very clear and more than once given. Perceval is of

---

[80] Sommer, V, pp. 383–393, 404–407.

[81] Sommer, II, pp. 346–349; 353–359; 360, 371, 388, 396.

[82] Sommer, II, p. 221.

[83] Pellinor: Sommer, VII (*Livre d'Artus*); Pellehen: Sommer, VI, p. 144. On Pelles, see note 92 below.

[84] Sommer, II, p. 125 and Sommer, *Galahad and Perceval*, MPh, V (1907–08), p. 305. In the latter, Sommer quotes MS. B.N. fr. 747, where Pelles, Pellinor and Alain are clearly brothers.

[85] This is Bruce's focus in his article, *Pelles, Pellinor and Pellean*, MPh, XVI (1918–19), 113–128; 337–350.

[86] Lot, *Etude Lancelot*, p. 123: »... nous saisissons notre homme dans le pénible travail d'élaboration de matériaux de toute provenance, disparates et peu cohérents qu'il avait à sa disposition. Des remanieurs, des ›réviseurs‹ auraient fait disparaître contradictions et disparates.« For another opinion about the formation of the cycle see Carman, *A Study of the Pseudo-Map Cycle of Arthurian Romance*, pp. 97–131.

[87] Sommer, I, pp. 280–296.

a vague »parenté« to the ancient founders of the Grail Family. Bron is no longer the brother-in-law of preceding romances. He speaks of his sons to Joseph as »tous vos parens prochains« (pp. 247, 249). Alain le Gros is the twelfth son (p. 251) who becomes the Rich Fisher instead of Bron (p. 252). Another of the twelve sons, Josué, is first the unmarried one (p. 286), but he then marries (p. 288) the daughter of the King who, converted because cured of leprosy, builds Corbenic to house the Grail. Although Alain is here called the first Fisher, it is the line of Josué that is to lead to the Rich Fisher, contemporary of Arthur, Pellehen. By another curious switching Pellehen becomes a Maimed King, but his son, Pelles, assumes the title Rich Fisher. It is Pelles' daughter who is the future mother of Galaad. It is not even entirely clear that Pelles is the son of Pellehen (p. 290, lines 28–33). Because the *Estoire* was written after the *Lancelot-Queste-Mort-Artu,* some of whose confusions I have mentioned, it is not surprising that the prehistory has curious lapses and silences. There are at least three Alains: Alain, the first Fisher, contemporary of Joseph and son of Bron; an Alain le Gros in the genealogy of Lancelot (Sommer, I, p. 293); and an Alain, brother to Pelles and Pellinor, related to but not father of Perceval. As I have said, Alain as father to Perceval specifically designates Perceval as the main Grail Hero. An Alain now appears in the *Estoire* genealogy as an ancestor of Galaad. Pellehen, who in the *Estoire* is a Fisher King, elsewhere considered a Maimed King, is somehow, in the *Queste,* called Perceval's father. What is implied, but not specifically stated until the *Livre d'Artus* does so, is that Agloval of the many brothers in the *Lancelot* is the son of Pellinor of the many sons (Sommer, II, p. 359).

Typical of a complex passage showing genealogy is the following one in the *Merlin* for Nasciens, a young hero of Arthur's war with Rion:

> Mais sour tous les autres le fist bien vns damoisiaus dont li contes doit moult bien parler car il ne fait mie a trespasser ains fait moult bien a rementeuoir dont il fu & comment il ot non. Car che fu .j. des millors cheualiers qui onques fust al tans le roy vterpandragon ne al tans le roy artu tant comme il pot mener cheualerie. li conte des estoires dient quil fu cousins germains parcheual le galois de par sa meire dont li contes parlera cha auant car li lieus nen est ore mie car il fu fiex hauingues qui fu de la seror iosep qui fu feme espouse bron qui .xvij. fiex ot dont la terre de bertaigne fu puis enluminee & parent prochain celidoine le fils al duc nascien de betique qui la grant merueille del graal vit premierement. & si ert parent al roy pelles de listenois & a ses freres icil ot non nasciens. Icil nasciens ot puis lancelot dou lac le fil au roy ban de benoyc en sa baillie dont li contes vous deuisera toutes les estoires les vns apres les autres si comme eles auendront de iour en iour. Icil nasciens que ie vous di si fu apeles nasciens pour le duc nascien qui tant fu preudomme. & il fu puis de si boine vie que quant il ot laisiet cheualerie quil deuint hermites . . .[88]

---

[88] Sommer, II, p. 221. The number seventeen in this passage is one which a scribe might have gotten from twelve simply by inadvertently adding a v to make xii become xvii. This kind of mistake was very common.

I specifically call attention to the use of »parent« and »parent prochain«, terms which avoid stating a clear relationship (and to the *seventeen*[!] sons of Bron who does have twelve in the *Estoire*, Sommer, I, p. 249). Passages like this one in which a »parenté« of some sort holds a large cast of Grail characters together give the general impression that the Grail Family has been expanded but not completely rearranged. Moments, as in the *Queste* where Perceval is called son of Pellehen or in the *Lancelot*[89] where Perceval was crossed out and replaced by Galaad are dramatic instances that call attention to the lack of coherence about details that abounds. Alain is almost always mentioned in the same sentence with Pelles and Pellinor as a guarantee that he is still a close relative of Perceval's. Bruce has called attention to this practice: »... this trick of leaving scattered in different parts of the text the various elements that are necessary to establish the identity of a character [which] is habitual with the authors of the Grail romances«[90]. Of the *Merlin* continuation, Bruce says: »Besides, the author of this Merlin continuation would be little disposed to drop any member of the Grail family, for it was his policy to crowd into his pages every Arthurian character of any prominence, as is evident from the enormous number of names which this branch of the cycle contains«[91].

Pelles, Pellinor and Pellehen are all fathers in the Vulgate, as well as at some time a Maimed King, Fisher King or a Grail King[92]. Pelles is considered to be the father of Galaad's mother, Pellehen the father of Perceval in the *Queste*, and one of the Pellinors the father of Perceval, clearly only in the *Livre d'Artus*[93]. Only once and incidentally is Alain a father, to Arguistes, in the *Queste*[94]. His displacement in this manner as father of a main Grail hero is thus again attested. Since Pellinor is the father of Perceval in several stories he deserves separate consideration concerning his origin in the Prose *Tristan* and use in the Huth *Merlin* continuation and in the *Livre d'Artus*[95].

---

[89] Sommer, III, p. 29.

[90] Bruce, *Pelles, Pellinor and Pellean*, MPh, XVI (1918–19), 125, note 1.

[91] Ibid., p. 340.

[92] On Pelles as a father of Perceval see Elspeth Kennedy, The Scribe as Editor, in *Mélanges de langue et de littérature du moyen âge et de la Renaissance offerts à Jean Frappier*, 2 vols. (Geneva, 1970), vol. I, p. 527. She cites the passage where one of the three most beautiful women in the world ist »›fille au Roi Mehaignié, ce fu li rois Pelles qui fu peres Perlesvax ...‹ It is quite clear from an examination of the MSS that this is close to the original reading in the archetype of the extant MSS. It is kept in 14 MSS belonging to several different groups, a few of which give Perceval instead of Perlesvaus«.

[93] Bruce, *Pelles, Pellinor and Pellean*, pp. 113–128, 337–350, best summarizes this material.

[94] Sommer, VI, p. 102.

[95] Eilert Löseth, *Le Roman en Prose de Tristan* (Paris, 1890); Renée L. Curtis, *Le Roman en Prose de Tristan* (Munich, 1963); Fanni Bogdanow, *The Romance of the Grail* (Manchester, 1966); Paris and Ulrich, *Huth Merlin*, 1886; Sommer, VII, 1913.

Pellinor appears in the Vulgate *Merlin* continuation first as a brother of Alain and Pelles and later as the father of many sons[96]. In the *Livre d'Artus*, a third *Merlin* continuation, written after the Vulgate Cycle[97], two Pellinors are recognized, the one brother to Pelles and Alain, and the second a cousin, father of Perceval and many sons, who subsequently becomes wounded and behaves like a Fisher King (voyaging in a boat)[98].

Bruce makes the following remarks about Pellinor:

> I will say at once that, in my opinion, Pellinor is the invention of the author of the Vulgate *Merlin* continuation[99].
>
> In compliance with this tendency [to give a definite name to hitherto unnamed characters] the Maimed King is given the name Pellinor, which is formed on the name Pelles... When Pellinor is provided with such an abundance of sons, this is in imitation of Bron, the first Fisher King in de Borron's *Joseph* and in the *Estoire del Saint Graal*. Finally, the author harmonizes the reconstituted Grail family by making Pelles, Pellinor, and Alain, brothers[100].
>
> To come back, however, to the question of Pellinor in the Huth *Merlin*, the character was derived, no doubt, by the author of that romance from the prose *Tristan*... In the prose *Tristan*, too, Pellinor was Perceval's father, and it was no doubt the author of this romance who originally conferred on him that honor[101].
>
> Pellinor appears again in the Merlin continuation of MS 337 [i.e., the text printed by Sommer in Vol. VII under the title *Livre d'Artus*]. Indeed, the peculiarity of this work is that it contains not merely one Pellinor, but two. The one is the original Pellinor (as we may call him) of the Vulgate, the brother of Pelles [and Alain] ... But it is the second Pellinor, the *cousin* of Pelles and Alain, who is here Perceval's father... Perceval's father in these passages is both *roi pescheor* and *roi mahaignie*[102].

The situation seems to be, then, that Pellinor, a name invented for the Maimed King in the Vulgate (formed on the name Pelles, both of which Bruce believed were merely alliterations of Perceval)[103] was taken by the Prose *Tristan* and Huth *Merlin* as a name for Perceval's father and then taken back by the *Livre d'Artus* where all the rôles and associations with the name were used again by two Pellinors. Pellinor, father of Perceval in the *Livre d'Artus,* is maimed partly as a reminiscence of Chrétien's father of Perceval and has many sons partly as a reminiscence of the many sons of Bron (or brothers of Alain). The shifting of rôles was used to displace Perceval and make way for Galaad and at the same time to account for all previous Grail

---

96 Sommer, II, pp. 359, 374, 384.
97 Frederick Whitehead and Roger Sherman Loomis, The *Livre d'Artus*, in *ALMA*, pp. 336–338.
98 Bruce, *Pelles, Pellinor and Pellean*, p. 343.
99 Ibid., p. 337.
100 Ibid., p. 340.
101 Ibid., p. 342.
102 Ibid., p. 343.
103 Ibid., p. 124, notes 1 and 2.

characters while creating new ones. The two main genealogies of the *Estoire* try to account for Galaad's mother and father as direct descendants of Joseph of Arimathea and Celidoine, nephew of the original Maimed King, Mordrain. Mordrain survives nine generations to be healed by Galaad in the *Queste*, but other Maimed Kings are created at various points in the cycle. Two sons are invented for Joseph of Arimathea, Josephe and Galaad who becomes King Galaad of Hocelice, renamed in his honor, Gales. From this line will descend Yvain. There are many such stories in the *Estoire*, accomplishing what Robert's first genealogy set out to do, to relate the heroes of Arthur's time to the conversion of Britain and to the quest of the Holy Grail.

The most recent scholar to discuss the problems of the Vulgate Cycle is Miss Bogdanow. She presents the following suggestions about the deaths of Perceval's father and brothers:

> The *Lancelot* proper, which remodelled Chrétien's account of Perceval's youth, introduces one of Perceval's brothers, Agloval, but does not tell us any more than did Chrétien how the other brothers had been killed. Now the prose *Tristan*, which combines details from both Chrétien and the *Lancelot*, not only identifies Perceval's father as Pellinor, but adds a new theme, the feud between Gauvain and Pellinor's line, to explain how Perceval's father and brothers were killed: Pellinor slew Gauvain's father, King Lot, and Gauvain consequently hated the whole of Pellinor's lineage and killed both Pellinor and two of his sons, Lamorat and Drian[104].

I have quoted Miss Bogdanow here because she has explained the feud in the Prose *Tristan* as a theme invented to »explain how Perceval's father and brothers were killed«. Perceval, since his creation by Chrétien, had been connected with unexplained deaths. If the *Tristan* reuses the detail of the deaths of two brothers of Perceval, it may be that the *Livre d'Artus* reuses the theme of the death of the eleven uncles of Perceval in the death, *en masse*, of the fourteen brothers of Perceval and Agloval. As I previously noted, the *Livre d'Artus* derived Pellinor of the many sons from the *Estoire* (Sommer, II, 359, 374, 384) and Agloval of the many brothers from the *Lancelot* (V, 383ff.) and combined them. What the author has reused is the fact that in the *Lancelot* (Sommer, V, 383) when Agloval returns home he finds his mother lamenting her »autres enfans« who have already died. In two manuscripts of this passage it is six sons who have died. Perceval at this point in the story is fifteen years old and ready to accompany his brother to court. In the *Queste* there is another reference to the death of Perceval's brothers in which his aunt refers to »vostre frere, qui sont mort et ocis par lor outrage«[105].

---

104 Bogdanow, *Romance of the Grail*, pp. 20–21.
105 Pauphilet, *Queste*, p. 73.

That Perceval had brothers whose deaths are unexplained goes back to Chrétien. That there was a family of a great many brothers associated with Perceval has perhaps only three precedents: the eleven brothers of Perceval's father from the *Joseph,* the *Bliocadran* and the *Perlesvaus.* What is important in the *Bliocadran* and the *Perlesvaus* is that the uncles died *en masse,* suffered the same undifferentiated fate, although they themselves are differentiated by name in the *Perlesvaus.* I suggest that the notion of a large number of brothers who die *en masse* has been shifted from the father to the son. In the *Livre d'Artus* the episode concerns the attack by King Agripe, an uncle of Rion, against Perceval's family. Perceval is at this time an infant and the father »encores gisoit en langor des plaies que la lance uencherresse li fist parmi les cuisses ambedeus« (Sommer, VII, p. 236). The rest of the family consists of the anonymous ».xiiij.« brothers, Agloval and the mother. Agloval and his companions defend his land, the Gaste Terre in the Gaste Forest Soutaine, which »Ioseph lor oncles lor laissa danceserie« (Sommer, VII, p. 171). The author is quite careful to list the twenty knights, by name, who come to aid Agloval (p. 240) and his five special companions (p. 239), but the fourteen young brothers live and die as an unidentified group (p. 239). The author then says he is going to explain why Agloval's mother is called the Uueue Dame de la Gaste Forest Soutaine (pp. 243–244). This involved account relates the maiming of Pellinor. After the death of his fourteen sons, he leaves his home to go to the Chastel de la Merueille and his only activity is going off in a boat to visit Corbenic and Alain's castle. Pellinor is condemned to wait for his cousin Pellinor to be healed so that he can be healed and die (p. 243, line 36). In a very few pages, the author has tried to reconcile a great deal of material in the Vulgate, but not very successfully. There are obvious blunders such as calling the Maimed King of Corbenic Agloval's »frere« instead of »uncle« (p. 237, line 5).

I have tried to demonstrate that the fourteen brothers of Perceval is a narrative detail that in part incorporates the notion of the eleven brothers of Bliocadran. It is not only the fact of a great number of brothers, which could be a reminiscence of the twelve sons of Bron (he has seventeen sons in one reference), but the fact of a large number of undifferentiated brothers who die *en masse,* that calls to mind the *Bliocadran.*

4. BLIOCADRAN AND GAHMURET

Students of Wolfram's *Parzival*[106] have long speculated on the question of whether Books I and II of the *Parzival* were influenced by the *Bliocadran Prologue,* or more specifically, whether Wolfram utilized a manuscript of the

---

[106] Editions: Karl Lachmann, *Wolfram von Eschenbach,* 6th ed., rev. by Eduard Hartl (Berlin and Leipzig, 1926. Reprinted 1965); Albert Leitzmann, *Wolfram*

Perceval containing the Prologue. Textual comparisons between the Gahmu-ret prelude and the *Bliocadran* have led, in two studies, to opposite con-clusions. Fourquet maintained that the manuscripts utilized by Wolfram could not have contained the Prologue, whereas Sister M. A. Rachbauer concluded that Wolfram had a manuscript containing the Prologue and that the *Parzival* text utilized its material. Springer, in his résumé of Wolfram studies and problems, states that ». . . opinion is divided whether Wolfram knew and used this particular prologue«[107]. A recent study on Gahmuret[108] states that »we still have no entirely satisfactory theory as to Wolfram's source for this part of the epic«. Another attitude toward the Gahmuret-Bliocadran relationship is expressed by Loomis, among others: common sources for both[109].

Sister M. A. Rachbauer's study of the *Bliocadran* is somewhat compromised by her résumé of the story (p. 6). She claims to have been inspired to make her study by the recent appearance of Hilka's edition, and yet somehow Potvin's old blunder that invented »Camuelles« as a name for Perceval's mother appears in her résumé[110]. Interestingly enough she never refers to Perceval's mother by that name again. The major textual comparisons in her study consist of juxtapositions (pp. 8–12, 17, 18) that are expected to »speak for themselves«. On at least seven occasions[111] Sister Rachbauer states her conclusion that Wolfram knew and used a manuscript of the type of MSS *L* and *P* and that he used the Prologue.

Fourquet is quite severe on all counts with Sister Rachbauer's study. He takes issue with a method that counts the number of similarities between texts as a proof of borrowing[112]. He proposes that one of the manuscripts which Wolfram used was of the type of MS *R* which begins directly with the words of the *Perceval*, having neither dedication nor any prologue[113]. It is

---

von Eschenbach, vol. I, Books I–VI (Tübingen, 1953). Adaptations: Edwin H. Zeydel and Bayard Quincy Morgan, *The Parzival of Wolfram von Eschenbach* (Chapel Hill, 1951); Maurice Wilmotte, *Parzival* (Paris, 1933). Studies: Friedrich Panzer, *Gahmuret, Quellenstudien zu Wolframs Parzival* (Heidelberg, 1940); Fourquet, *Wolfram* (Paris, 1938, 2nd ed. 1966); Sister M. A. Rachbauer, *Wolfram* (Washington, 1934); Birch-Hirschfeld, *Die Sage vom Gral* (Leipzig, 1877); Sprin-ger, Wolfram's *Parzival*, in *ALMA*, pp. 218–250.

[107] Springer, *ALMA*, p. 225.

[108] Lee Stavenhagen, *A Legendary Backdrop for Gahmuret*, Rice University Studies, 53 (1967), p. 43.

[109] Loomis, *Arthurian Tradition and Chrétien de Troyes*, pp. 347–355.

[110] As late as 1962, Louis-Fernand Flutre, in his *Tables des noms propres, avec toutes leurs variantes, figurant dans les Romans du Moyen Age écrits en fran-çais ou en provençal, et actuellement publiés ou analysés* (Poitiers, 1962), lists »Cammuelles« as Perceval's mother. See below notes 186–187 and Textual Note to line 54.

[111] Sister M. A. Rachbauer, *Wolfram*, pp. viii, 8, 13, 87, 253, 255, 257.

[112] Fourquet, *Wolfram*, pp. 102–104.

[113] Ibid., pp. 103, 115, 116, 176.

Fourquet's thesis that Wolfram used one manuscript of Chrétien for Books III–VI (he calls this W_1) and another for Books VII–XII (W_2). The Gahmuret Books I and II he believes are virtually a »free invention«. He is very severe in the matter of MSS L and P, discussing the composite nature of the former and the all-inclusive nature of the latter, as well as the late date of both. He does not, however, seem to consider as probable that Wolfram even used a prototype of these two manuscripts. The *Gahmuret* was composed, he says, after Books III–VI and »dans l'intervalle où il ne possédait plus le premier ms., et n'avait pas encore le second«[114]. Fourquet does not go into any textual comparisons, basing his conclusion that Wolfram did not use the *Bliocadran* on existing manuscript evidence alone.

Fourquet's remarks about Wolfram and his sources are perhaps too rigid. Books III–VI, he says, show a very dependent relationship to Chrétien[115], whereas the rest of the *Parzival* varies in its reliance or dependence upon or in its adaptation of sources. The »roman de Gahmuret« is an »essai de composition libre«[116] and, if W_1 had contained it, »nous en aurions une adaptation, qui en conserverait le détail«[117]. »Si Wolfram avait trouvé le prologue de Bliocadran au début de son premier ms. et l'avait adapté d'aussi près, la quantité de matière reconnaissable, même après de profonds remaniements, serait infiniment plus grande; et nous pourrions peut-être même identifier quelques variantes. Nous concluons donc que le ms. W_1 ne contenait pas le prologue de Bliocadran«[118]. Fourquet propose that Wolfram's attitude toward his sources in this first stage was of »une intensité presque religieuse«[119]. But, »dans la seconde partie, Wolfram, tout en conservant sa piété envers la matière, la domine de plus haut, l'organise plus librement«[120]. Fourquet, then, has discerned three attitudes in Wolfram toward his sources: close adaptation, free adaptation and free invention. What he proposes is very logical and perhaps quite true in many cases: but what would have prevented Wolfram from adapting freely even when he was in possession of W_1 (period of close adaptation) or from adapting closely when in possession of W_2 (period of free adaptation), or from inventing freely at any time? Fourquet may have discovered some principles of Wolfram's method of composition, but he has not at the same time ruled out other possibilities.

It has seemed impossible so far, using textual comparisons of narrative or detailed studies of the manuscript tradition, to determine whether Wolfram

---

[114] Ibid., p. 190.
[115] Ibid., p. 98.
[116] Ibid., p. 190.
[117] Ibid., p. 176.
[118] Ibid., p. 115.
[119] Ibid., p. 99.
[120] Loc. cit.

knew and used the *Bliocadran*. What I shall try to demonstrate is that it is very plausible that Wolfram used the *Bliocadran* to suggest a distribution of narrative details and for his narrative theme in the *Gahmuret*.

One of the results of Hilka's critical edition of the *Perceval* was to settle the question whether all extant manuscripts did in fact contain the mother's speech, vv. 407–488. If even one of the MSS had omitted it, the *Bliocadran Prologue* might have been given more serious consideration as an early addition to the corpus. Miss Weston[121] was one of the first to outline the parallels which struck her among the versions of the Perceval *enfances*. She came to the conclusion that there was an original tale of *enfances* from which Chrétien, Wolfram, the author of the *Bliocadran* and others drew their material – and that it was a written, not an oral tradition[122]. She also felt that the *Bliocadran* was originally not written as a prologue to Chrétien's poem, but inserted later. Although it is true that the prologue was inserted later into the British Museum manuscript, it does not necessarily follow that it was not composed for Chrétien's poem. She drew up a table[123] of twenty-eight items which show elements in common among *Perceval* texts. The *Bliocadran* had elements in common with at least four other texts in addition to the *Parzival*. Her conclusion is that »Much as they resemble each other, our *Perceval* stories all appear to be independent versions of the same original theme«[124]. Miss Newstead also dealt with the notion of common sources for the elements that the *Bliocadran*, Chrétien and *Parzival* have in common. She deduced a common source in oral rather than in written tradition, a great deal of which is derived from traditions concerning the Welsh legends of Bran the Blessed[125]. It has not been my intention to deal at length with studies which trace parallels with Celtic legends, as the material is quite vast and not conclusive enough to suggest what one particular text might owe to another[126].

The two main questions about the *Bliocadran* and the *Gahmuret* are: could the composition of the *Bliocadran* have been early enough for Wolfram to have known and used it; and, if Wolfram did know the *Bliocadran*, in what ways did it influence his composition of Books I and II? In my study of the relationship of the *Bliocadran* to the Didot-*Perceval* and to the *Perlesvaus* I tried to show how the *Bliocadran* used material from the *Joseph* and

---

121 Weston, *Legend of Sir Perceval*, vol. I, pp. 76–101.
122 Ibid., p. 93.
123 Ibid., pp. 88–91.
124 Ibid., p. 100.
125 Helaine Newstead, *Perceval's Father and Welsh Tradition*, RR, XXXVI (1945), pp. 3–31.
126 See the following section, »Bliocadran, the name«, for a discussion of parallels, involving the *Bliocadran Prologue* and other stories, which are exaggerated or false.

Chrétien and then was utilized by the *Perlesvaus*. If these conclusions are valid, then the *Bliocadran* could have been composed early enough (by 1212) to have been known to Wolfram. It is not merely the similarity of the twelve-brothers motif that links the *Bliocadran* and the *Perlesvaus* but the fact that the narrative material suggested in the *Joseph* and then not developed there was taken over by the author of the *Bliocadran*. The manner in which the *Perlesvaus* author used the twelve-brothers motif suggests that he derived the notion as a developed one – and then incorporated it without further elaboration as an illustration of his narrative theme. It is thus just as important to determine the narrative theme for which an author borrowed and used his narrative detail as to list the many sources he might have had for those details.

Fourquet was quite insistent that if Wolfram had known the *Bliocadran* he would have utilized it more closely. As I have already pointed out, the fact that Wolfram had varying attitudes towards his sources and that he even criticized Chrétien means that he felt free to use as little or as much of his source as he wished. The first remarkable alteration that Wolfram made was to eliminate most of the mother's speech from the Chrétien material and to conceive a prologue that would give background about Perceval's father. These are the very conditions that would have eliminated most of the contradictions between the *Bliocadran* and the *Perceval* if they had existed in manuscripts *L* and *P*. What the *Bliocadran* and *Gahmuret* have developed fully, but with different narrative details, is the implication in Chrétien that the practice of chivalry can cause misery when it is not devoted to high purpose. In both works an only son (Gahmuret leaves two wives and two »only« sons) is born after the father departs and the mother (in the second instance in the *Parzival*) flees civilization. Wolfram leaves little doubt that knightly activity was the cause of much mischief in Gahmuret's life. Not only does he leave his first wife, Belakane, in Patelamunt because there was no knightly activity to amuse him, knowing she is expecting their child, but his excuse, the difference of their religions, is untenable. Conversions are a commonplace of medieval love stories in an Eastern setting. Gahmuret had originally grieved his mother when he first set out for knightly adventure. Wolfram has not only found his theme, but he cannot seem to find enough uses for it! Belakane is first seen grieving over her first love, Isenhart, whom she had been testing with knightly activity so long that he was finally killed. Gahmuret wins his second wife, Herzeloide, as the result of a tournament (that does not quite take place) in Waleis, but he is not eager to claim her for his affections are contested by Ampflise, Queen of France, whose devotion he had earned, again as a result of knightly activity. He submits to Herzeloide, but only on the condition that he is allowed to attend a tourney once a month. Shortly after the marriage Gahmuret leaves his wife, pregnant, and goes to aid the Baruch in Baghdad, the ruler whom he had served as a knight before he won Belakane. Six months pass; he dies, and Herzeloide

gives birth to Parzival. The pace of the story at the end is reminiscent of the
Bliocadran: the time from Gahmuret's departure, his death and burial, to the
birth of his son and the mother's flight to the forest is exceedingly swift,
and detail is summary.

Whatever the symbolic interpretation of Gahmuret's chivalric exploits[127], a
decidedly unpleasant effect is produced by his adventures, an unpleasantness
he shares with Bliocadran. These characters are independent of Chrétien, but
are they independent of each other? Both illustrate a critique of worldly
chivalry. For Wolfram to show Gahmuret in such a variety of activities he
had to send him out of the Arthurian world or it would have been *in-
vraisemblant* for him not to have had to confront the Round Table. His
behavior would have been incompatible with the Arthurian code. Bliocadran
is necessarily a sketchy figure. That his brothers all have died in knightly
activity did not dismay him. Gahmuret is from a long line of warriors whose
deaths by the sword have had no effect on his behavior either. These details
must be considered against Chrétien's conception of the father. Not only did
the activity of the father in Chrétien produce crippling and ruin but the
deaths of his sons caused him to die of grief. The narrative details are less
important in this consideration than the narrative theme they illustrate.
It is significant that Wolfram did not choose to portray a sympathetic or
tragic father in the manner of Chrétien, but a compulsive knight in the
manner of Bliocadran. It may be that the Belakane episode was invented in
order to use Feirefiz later in the romance, but to show Gahmuret repeating
his folly would be absurd except as a critique of the compulsive knight, i.e.,
except as illustrative of narrative theme. Both Bliocadran and Gahmuret die
in mid-career and cause great grief. The Eastern war in which Gahmuret
was involved does not elicit the sympathy that death against the Saxon in-
vader would. The important parallel between Bliocadran and Gahmuret is
not the manner of their deaths, the blow to the head so often singled out by
scholars, but the fact that both deaths caused more misery than glory. Wolfram could just as well have shown Gahmuret called to defend a relative in
distress, set upon by villains, bidden to a war through patriotic duty – in
any of a number of tragic or more justifiable situations. My contention is
that Wolfram was not completely free to invent his character. He was at-
tracted to the possibilities suggested by the *Bliocadran,* a portrait of a
compulsive knight as yet unattached to the high purpose of Arthurian
knighthood and unacquainted with the companions of the Grail. Gahmuret,
invented after the model of a Bliocadran, could not be a better contrast to
his son, the loyal one of loving devotion[128].

---

[127] Cf. Springer, *ALMA*, p. 245.
[128] Ibid., pp. 227–228.

5. BLIOCADRAN, THE NAME

The only long, detailed study of the *Bliocadran* was made by Ernst Brugger and it dealt with the name. The following is a summary of his remarks relative to the *Bliocadran*[129]:

> The name was »no doubt« originally a double name, *Blios Cadrans*. *Blios* is also the first component of the name of the Knight *Blihos Bliheris* of the *Elucidation* (v. 162). This name found in the *Elucidation* is an expanded form of the name of a knight *Blioblieris* in the *Erec* of Chrétien (v. 1714). The second component of the name *Blihos Bliheris* is the »well known name *Bleheris* = Welsh *Bledri*« (p. 153). The first part of the name *Blios Cadrans* also occurs by itself. *Blios* is in the *Livre d'Artus* (Sommer, VII, p. 188ff.). In the Vulgate *Suite* (Sommer, II, 103, 148, 453) there is another knight whose name seems to have been *Blios*. It appears as *Drulios de la Case*, *Blois del Casset*, *Blyos de Cassel* or, according to P. Paris, as *Bliois du Chastel*, *Bliois*, *Blios de Casel*. In the *Livre d'Artus* (Sommer, VII) also occur the forms *Bibliors de Casel*, *Blios de la Case*. A third knight in the Vulgate *Suite* is called *Brios del Plastre*, *Bliot du Plessié*, or *Brinos du Plessié* in the *Livre d'Artus*. A fourth knight in the Vulgate *Suite* (Sommer, II, p. 218) is *Blyas li sires de Bleodas un mervelleus chastel* who »is likely to have been originally called *Blios*« (p. 155). This same knight is called *Blios (li sires) de Candaf* in the *Livre d'Artus* (Sommer, VII, pp. 15 and 38) and this name may be a corruption of *Blidoblidas, li fils le roi de Galoee*, a knight in *Meriaduec* (l. 2610).
>
> The name *Bleos* or *Blios* (obl. *Blioc*, *Bliot*) is no doubt of Celtic origin. From Loth: *bleoc* in Old Breton is a gloss to *criniti*. In Cornish the adjective is *bleuak*, in modern Welsh, *bleuog*, hair, and in new Breton, *blio*, hair.
>
> The second part of the name *Blios Cadrans* »was to my mind« the name *Cadroain* with loss of *o* before a stressed syllable and with a not uncommon substitution *-ain* > *-an*. In one form of the name of Bliocadran, *Blocadroon* (MS *P*, 151), a corrupt form however, a »remnant of the *o* we miss« (p. 160) has been preserved. The rhyming vowel is changed, a > o for rhyme with *maison*.
>
> The character *Cadroain* or *Cardroain* appears in two romances, the *Atre Perillous* and *Durmart*. In both romances the character has the surname *le Ro(u)s* (*Durmart*, 2010; *Atre*, 6433). Now *Blios* »was liable to be changed into *Blois* by scribes« (p. 162); thus *Blios Cadroains* as a name for Perceval's father could become *Blois Cadroains* and *Blois* could have been taken as an epithet and become *Cadroains li Blois* [this does not appear anywhere]. Since »*Blois* meant in Old French *blont*, and this colour of hair, after all, was not very different from *ro(u)s*,« then, »li *Ro(u)s* which was an extremely common epithet, may have supplanted *li Blois*« (pp. 162–163). The characters, however, in *Durmart* and *Atre*, are enemies of Arthur and not at all like Perceval's father. This shows that Bliocadran was not originally the name of Perceval's father. Originally Perceval's father was Alain de Gomeret (p. 163).

---

[129] Ernst Brugger, Bliocadran, the Father of Perceval, in *Medieval Studies in Memory of Gertrude Schoepperle Loomis* (Paris and New York, 1927), pp. 147–174. Brugger refers to »*Suite Merlin* B.N. 337« where I use *Livre d'Artus* or Sommer, VII, to refer to this part of the Vulgate Cycle. For »Wauchier's *Grail*« I say Second Continuation.

In the Italian *I cantari di Carduino* the hero of the romance »is certainly identical with *Cardroain*« (p. 163). *Carduino* does not have the epithet. The *Carduino enfances* are similar to the *Perceval enfances* and are more closely related to the *Bliocadran* version than any other. The father's name here is *Dondinello* (Fr. Dodinel). »If Carduino corresponds to Bliocadran, the name ought to be not that of the hero, but that of the hero's father« (p. 165). The epithet associated with *Dodinel, li Sauvages,* is also not used in *Carduino,* as it is inappropriate in this romance. What may have occurred is that father and son roles are reversed: Dodinello would be more appropriate as the son and Carduino the father. The hero of the Italian romance grew up in a *selva grande* (I, 6), hunting beasts and *a vedere parea un uon selvagio* (I, 16). This is the Dodinel character.

Another *Biaus Desconeüs* version involves Gauvain's son in the *First Continuation* [Lioniaus, or Lieoniax] who is described thus, »En la cambre com hom sauvages Se porficot, si ert trop biaus« (Potvin, 20604–05) (p. 167)[130]. Dodins occurs in *Erec* (v. 1700) and in the *Second Continuation* (v. 29058). *Dodins* is the oldest form of the name. It can be traced to the meaning »foolish«. This theme of the *nice, sot* or fool underlies Perceval, a *Biaus Desconeüs* type of hero. From the behavior of Lionel, called Dodinel in the German translation of the *Second Continuation,* and from the description of the character, comes a basis for the confusion of names for a character who is a »*dodinel,* i.e., a young fool« (p. 170). The source of the Italian poem may have been a lost Dodinel romance [just as the source of the *Bliocadran* is a lost *Perceval* romance (p. 152)]. The confusion of names may be in part due to the fact the hero learns his name late in the poems of the *Desconeüs* type. Moreover, the father, Dodinello, is mentioned only twice. If Cardroain was originally Dodinel's father, his role was like Bliocadran's, Perceval's father, but his character is not like that of *Cardroain le Ros* in the *Durmart* (from which the *Atre* derived its personage).

»An important and primitive element in the Perceval story is that the hero's duty was vengeance« (p. 171). This »primitive« element is in the *Perlesvaus* where Perceval's father Alain does have an enemy and usurper, *li sire des Mores* (More[i]f – Moravia [Moray], Scotland). This is the same wilderness where Tristan and Iseut sought refuge and is the home of the abductor of Guenievre. In the *Durmart, Cardroain le Ros* is brother of Brun de Morois who is nephew of the *roi des Mores.* If, then, Cardroain came from *Morois* he could have been *li sire des Mores* of the *Perlesvaus,* the enemy of Perceval's father and then »by confusion« the name could have been transferred to Perceval's father »since they were owners of the same dominions, the one as rightful proprietor, the other as usurper« (p. 173). This process may be one way of explaining how Perceval's father came to be called Bliocadran (p. 173).

The second component of the name is also of Celtic origin. *Ca(r)d(r)oain* could be the same as *Cadoain* in the Prose *Lancelot* and in the *Lai du Cor* or even as Geoffrey's *Cadvanus.* There are two components: *cat, cad* = combat and *win, wen* = white, happy (from Loth). Another first component could be *cadr* = strong, handsome in Old Welsh and handsome in Breton. This component occurs in the name of one Breton saint *Cadroc* (from Loth). The suffix, Breton *oc, uec, uc, ec,* Welsh *awc,* was used to abridge names composed of two terms of which

---

130 These lines are quoted from Roach, *Continuations,* vol. III, MS *L,* 8018–19; cf. vol. III, MSS *ASP,* 8028–30; vol. I, MSS *TVD,* 1350–51; vol. II, MSS *MQU,* 18082–83.

the second was omitted: *Cadroc* could equal *Cadr-win* »postulated by *Cadroain*« (p. 173). The three adjectives, *cadr*, *win* and *bleoc* [handsome or strong and fair-haired] are appropriate to a hero (p. 174).

Several scholars have referred to this analysis by Brugger in a passing fashion. Loomis, for example, merely refers to it in a footnote: »For surmises (mistaken in my opinion) as to this name [Bliocadran]«[131]. He accepts Miss Newstead's theories that the name must have originated in Bran. She also mentions Brugger's article in a footnote, but she refers the reader to Bruce for an opinion about the origin of the name: »*Bliocadrans* has probably suffered corruption at the hands of the scribes until the true form is no longer recognizable«[132]. Thompson also refers to Brugger's article in a footnote as an »elaborate« theory[133] and he would add the name Blancand(r)in to the list of names proposed by Brugger.

Brugger is probably correct in his identification of the Celtic components of the name Bliocadran. The most recent dictionary of the Welsh language indexes *blewog* [*blew* + *og*] as hairy, shaggy, bushy; *cadarn* as strong, powerful, steadfast; and *cadr* as handsome, comely, fine, powerful, mighty, puissant[134]. The second component of the name may thus be *cadr* + *win*, as Brugger suggested, or *cadarn*, with metathesis of r. Rachel Bromwich discusses many names in the triads that contain the component *cat-* or *cad-*, »battle«[135].

According to Brugger there are three components, *Blios*, *Cadrans*, and *Bleheris*, that can be shown to have been combined with each other in ways that suggest a relationship among various characters in the romances. The object of such a demonstration is to remove Bliocadran from uniqueness and to prove that the name was not merely the spontaneous invention of an author. The many examples of *Blios* (and variant spellings) that Brugger finds in the Vulgate demonstrate only the association of this first component with the name of a knight. The second part of the name involves the following identifications: *Cadrans* is the counterpart of Cadroain or Cardroain of the *Atre périlleux* and the *Durmart* (*Atre* character derived from *Dur-*

---

131 Loomis, *Arthurian Tradition and Chrétien de Troyes*, p. 355, note 59.
132 Newstead, *Perceval's Father and Welsh Tradition*, p. 4, note 7. Cf. Bruce, *Evolution*, II, 90, note 10.
133 Thompson, Additions to Chrétien's *Perceval*, in *ALMA*, pp. 210–211, note 3.
134 *Geiriadur Prifysgol Cymru*, a Dictionary of the Welsh Language (Caerdydd: Gwasg Prifysgol Cymru, 1950, to Fasc. xxiii, *gorsaf*, 1970), entries under *blewog*, *cadarn* and *cadr*. As a noun *cadarn* can mean mighty one, strong one, warrior, giant. See also Robert Williams, *Lexicon Cornu-Britannicum* (London, 1865) for entries after *gorsaf*: *wyn*, adj., white, blessed, var. of *gwyn*, white, fair, pleasant, glorious, blessed. Lewis Morris, *Celtic Remains* (London, 1878), p. 55, lists *Cadarn* as a surname.
135 Rachel Bromwich, *Trioedd Ynys Prydein, The Welsh Triads* (Cardiff, 1961), pp. 289–297; cxiv, note 1.

mart character); *Cardroain* has the epithet *le Rous* which could have supplanted *le Blois* (a scribal error for *Blios*); Cardroain le Rous is the brother of Brun de Morois who is the nephew of the Roi des Mores; if, then, Cardroain also came from Morois he could be the unnamed *sire des Mores* in the *Perlesvaus*, enemy of Perceval's father, and then, »by confusion«, the name was transferred to Perceval's father because they both disputed the same lands, one as rightful owner, the other as usurper. The leap made by Brugger here seems unfounded. Why could not the usurper have been Brun, Cardroain's brother? In the *Durmart*, Brun, the abductor of Guenievre, is defeated by the hero and reconciled to Arthur; Cardroain is killed by Durmart. Either brother could have fulfilled the usurper's role in the earlier *Perlesvaus*.

The second romance that Brugger discusses is the *Carduino*[136]. In order to establish a relationship between *Bliocadran* and *Carduino* he posits a lost common source in a Dodinel romance and a confusion of names resulting in a reversal such that the father's name was originally and appropriately Carduino and the son's was Dodinello. If one could establish a relationship between these two works it could only be that of influence by the *Bliocadran* upon the *Carduino*. Such discussion could not, without identifying the lost common source, shed light on the source of the name for the *Bliocadran* author.

At the beginning of his chapter Brugger mentions incidentally that »Blios Cadrans« shared its first component with the name of the knight *Blihos Bliheris* of the *Elucidation*. The Blihos Bliheris of this work is very likely taken from the name in a list of knights in the *Erec*. The name, spelled Bliobleheris by Foerster in his text (v. 1714), is spelled in the seven manuscripts as Bleoberis (MSS *PV*), Blios Blieris (MS *H*), Bleobleheris (MS *B*), Bleosblieris (MS *A*), Blioberis (MS *C*) and Bliobeheri (MS *E*). As Thompson pointed out[137], Miss Weston made an association of names that would identify the maistre Blihis of verse 12 of the *Elucidation*, Blihos Bliheris of verse 162, the Bleheris, Bleobleheris of the First Continuation and the Bleheris of the Second Continuation as variations of the same name and as having one source, the *Breri* mentioned in Thomas' *Tristan* and the *Bledhericus* of Giraldus Cambrensis. Thompson's conclusion is probably the most likely: »A compromise is possible: the author of the *Elucidation* may have chosen the name Blihos Bliheris as being that of a knight, but noticing that the second component of the name is the same as the name of the famous storyteller, familiar to him from Pseudo-Wauchier or Wauchier, he emphasized

---

[136] Pio Rajna, ed., *I Cantari di Carduino* (Bologna, 1873. Reprinted in *Scelta di Curiosità litterarie*, vol. XXXVII, Dispensa 135 [Bologna, 1968]); Antonio Viscardi, Arthurian Influences on Italian Literature from 1200 to 1500, in *ALMA*, pp. 419–429.

[137] Thompson, *The Elucidation*, p. 79.

the storytelling abilities of the knight to a greater extent than was usual in the case of a defeated fighter who reported at Arthur's court«[138].

In the many arguments involving Bliobleheris and its variants the first element of the name was not an issue. Chrétien created his name in the *Erec* from two components, the second of which may have reflected the famous storyteller or, as Rachel Bromwich pointed out[139], the historical figure *Bledericus dux Cornubiae*. The second component of the name Bliocadran has not furnished such rich possibilities for sources. Brugger proposed Cardroain, a figure in two late romances, whose connection to the Perceval corpus is highly questionable.

Rather than seek the possible origin of Cadrans in late romances, I propose that two earlier works may have been known to the *Bliocadran* author, the

---

[138] Ibid., p. 81. There is much discussion on this subject. See: G. Paris, *Breri*, Romania, VIII (1879), 425–428; E. Löseth, *Prose Tristan* (1890), Table Analytique, »Bliob(l)eris«; J. Bédier, ed., *Roman de Tristan*, vol. II (1905, SATF 1902), pp. 95–99; J. Weston, *Wauchier de Denain*, Romania, XXXIII (1904), 333–334; Weston, *Wauchier de Denain and Bleheris (Bledhericus)*, Romania, XXXIV (1905), 100–105; Weston, *Legend of Sir Perceval*, 2 vols. (1906–09), passim; W. Gruffydd, *Bledhericus, Bleddri, Breri*, Revue Celtique, XXXIII (1912), 180–183; J. Loth, *Romans de la Table Ronde* (1912), pp. 33–37; J. Loth, *Les Mabinogion*, vol. I (1913), pp. 72–75; J. Weston, *From Ritual to Romance*, 1920 (Reprinted, Anchor Books, 1957), pp. 192–194; Bruce, *Evolution* (1923, 2nd ed. 1928), vol. I, pp. 156–157 note, pp. 285–286 and note, vol. II, p. 89 and note 9; E. Brugger, *Der Dichter Bledri – Bleheri – Breri*, ZFSL, XLVII (1924), 162–185; R. S. Loomis, *Bleheris and the Tristram Story*, Modern Language Notes, XXXIX (1924), 319–329; F. Lot, *Encore Bleheri – Breri*, Romania, LI (1925), 397–408; R. S. Loomis, *Problems of the Tristan Legend: Bleheris…*, Romania, LIII (1927), 82–102; A. W. Thompson, *Elucidation* (1931), pp. 52–54, 78–81, 83 n. 94; J. Frappier, *Etude Mort Artu* (1936), p. 200; Mary Williams, *More about Bleddri*, Etudes Celtiques, II (1937), 219–245; R. S. Loomis, *Arthurian Tradition* (1949), pp. 18–21, 39; J. Marx, *La Légende arthurienne* (1952), pp. 4, 28, 163, 217, 306, 338–339, 371; H. Wrede, *Die Fortsetzer des Gralsromans Chrestiens von Troyes* (Diss. Göttingen, 1952); W. Kellermann, Le Problème de Breri, in *Romans du Graal* (1956), pp. 137–148; R. S. Loomis, *Wales and the Arthurian Legend* (Cardiff: University of Wales Press, 1956), pp. 193–195; H. Newstead, *The Tryst beneath the Tree: An Episode in the Tristan Legend*, Romance Philology, IX (1955–1956), 284; R. S. Loomis, *Some Objections to the Celtic Origin of the Matière de Bretagne*, Romania, LXXIX (1958), 47–77 (esp. p. 75); Loomis, Newstead, Micha, Thompson, chapters in *ALMA* (1961), passim; P. Gallais, *Formules de Conteur…*, Romania, LXXXV (1964), 203, 205–206; P. Gallais, Bleheri, la Cour de Poitiers et la diffusion des récits arthuriens sur le continent, in *Moyen Age et Littérature Comparée* (Paris: Didier, 1967), pp. 47–49 (Actes du VIIème Congrès national de littérature comparée, Poitiers, 1965); D. D. R. Owen, *The Evolution of the Grail Legend* (1968), pp. 53–55, 62; G. D. West, *Index*, entries under: »Bleheris«, »Bleheri«, »Bliobleheris«, »Breri«; Roach, *Continuations*, vol. IV, *Second Continuation* (1971), pp. 539–540, note to lines 29351–57.

[139] Bromwich, *The Welsh Triads*, p. cxv.

Lai du Cor, from which he could have known the name Cadains, and *Meraugis*[140], from which he could have known the name Gorvains Cadruz (both mentioned briefly by Brugger). This example from the *Meraugis* has more similarity to the name Blios Cadrans and does not posit a lost common source for the two works. »Cadrut«, Micha pointed out[141], »may well represent the Welsh adjective *cadrauc*, meaning ›strong, mighty‹.« Gorvains Cadruz(s) as a prototype for Cadrans has in its favor the facts that Cadruz has a similar Celtic derivation, that it is used as the second component of a name and that it appears in an early romance.

The author of the *Bliocadran* could have known such early romances as *Erec, le Bel Inconnu,* the First and Second Continuations, the *Elucidation* or *Vengeance Raguidel* in all of which appears a version of the name Bliobleheris, often in two-part form. He may have known that Blios was an epithet but he knew at least that it was used as one part of a double name. Chrétien, working with a second element that had richer connotations, Bleheris, created the name of a knight in which the first element was not disguised. The *Bliocadran* author used the same first element which he could have known from any number of romances, beginning with the *Erec,* and a second element existing at least in the double name Gorvains Cadruz. Further research might reveal another prototype for the name Cadrans, but the use of Cadrus in Gorvain Cadrus attests to an early name that used the second component in the same manner as the name in the *Bliocadran.* The fact that Cadrus is sometimes omitted in the *Meraugis* may indicate that Cadrus was recognized as an epithet and as an appropriate one for a major figure in a romance. If the *Bliocadran* author saw in this component the meaning of »cat« or »cad«, warrior, war-like or battle, then his choice of a name was completely appropriate for the war-loving character he portrayed.

Of the many parallels drawn between the Perceval *enfances* and those of Cuchulainn, Finn, Peredur and Pryderi, perhaps the most striking is the mystery or misfortune concerning the father of each of them. Of the two Peredurs one is called son of Eliffer Gosgorddvawr[142]. This name suggests a possible source of the name of Perceval's uncle in *Perlesvaus,* Gosgallians, and of the other forms in the First Continuation, Guellans Guenelaus (MS *L* 7671), Gulle Genelax (*A* 7633), Greloguevaus (*M* 17741), Galozgrenax (*Q* 17741), Grelogrenaus (*U* 17741). Nitze had said of the name in the *Perles-*

---

[140] Mathias Friedwagner, ed. Raoul von Houdenc. Sämtliche Werke. *Meraugis von Portlesguez* (Halle, 1897).

[141] Alexandre Micha, Miscellaneous French Romances in Verse, in *ALMA* (pp. 358–392), p. 374.

[142] Bromwich, *The Welsh Triads,* pp. 488–498. See also J. Loth, *Les Mabinogion,* 2 vols. (Paris, 1913), II, 47–120. Mrs. Bromwich says the name Gosgorduavr > Cascord maur, p. 491.

vaus that it was apparently »coined«[143]. Loomis[144] tried to draw a parallel between the epithet le Gros of Alain and the name of this uncle. The authenticity of the passage in the First Continuation is in question and Perceval, in this unique reference, is called the son of this personage only in two manuscripts, but it does seem significant that some scribes recalled or approximated a name for Perceval's father that may be associated with Gosgorddvawr and Gosgallians. The name in the First Continuation is unique and spontaneous in the manner of the appearance of the name Bleheris in the Second Continuation (MS *L* 29351) in one manuscript against all the others. There is no development of these names in the stories that contain them. Rather there is testimony to the knowledge by some scribes and to the knowledge of the author of the *Perlesvaus* of a name approximated by them and that was attached if not to Perceval at least to one of his prototypes in a Celtic source[145].

Nitze had said that Gosgallians was apparently »coined«. Such names, however, like Guellans Guenelaus, etc., do not look like attractive inventions by a French author, but rather like an effort to reproduce a name known about and thought to be attached to Perceval or to one of his prototypes. If such a name as son of Eliffer Gosdorddvawr for Peredur was known to Chrétien, it is understandable that he might avoid approximating it. In addition to the confusion of the two Peredurs, the assimilation of the stories of Peredur and Pryderi may also be a reason for Chrétien to avoid the issue of what the father's name was in these stories. The form of the name in the First Continuation suggests knowledge of a name like Gosgorddvawr, but such evidence does not constitute the basis of any »tradition« of Perceval's father since the names are not developed. In a like situation, if the *Bliocadran* author knew it, he was not bound to use it any more than was Chrétien.

Loomis and Miss Newstead have drawn attention to various parallels between the *Bliocadran Prologue* and the stories of Bran the Blessed. Of the name Loomis said, »Bliocadran ... should be a grotesque deformation of Bran, and we should be prepared to find correspondences between Bliocadran, Bran de Gomeret and Gahmuret. That is precisely what we do find«[146]. It is because of parallels he draws between the stories that he feels the name derives from Bran.

Loomis adopts the view of Miss Newstead[147] that »one of the most persistent traditions regarding the other descendants of Bran is the sanctity of their

---

143 Nitze, *Perlesvaus*, II, 198.
144 Loomis, *Arthurian Tradition and Chrétien de Troyes*, p. 352, note 43.
145 C. f. Bromwich, *The Welsh Triads*, p. 490. For Mrs. Bromwich, Perceval is a »loose approximation« of Peredur »and not vice-versa«. Moreover, she points out that Peredur and Pryderi each have two suggested fathers.
146 Loomis, *Arthurian Tradition*, p. 348.
147 Ibid., p. 243.

sepulchres; Ban de Benoic, Bliocadran, Gahmuret, and the Fisher King in *Sone de Nansai* – all of whom she successfully derives from Bran – were interred in holy places«. The following are Miss Newstead's assertions on this point: »Gahmuret's sumptuous burial in a distant land and the entombment of his relics in a minster correspond to the burial of Bliocadran in a minster far away from his home...[148] Like Bliocadran, Gahmuret, and the Fisher King in *Sone*, Ban is buried in a center of religious worship, the Royal Minster...[149] Finally, the powerful tradition in the *Bliocadran Prologue, Parzival,* and *Perlesvaus* that Perceval's father was buried in a splendid tomb in a place of religious worship finds a counterpart in the burial of Bran's head in the White Hill in London«[150]. The relevant text of the *Bliocadran* is as follows (verses 236–244):

> Ne vesqui que deus jors aprés,
> Que il fu mors sans demorer.
> En un mostier l'ont fait porter;
> Si compaignon grant duel en firent,
> Lor dras et lor ceviax descirent.
> Et quant il fu dedens l'eglise,
> Si li firent molt bel service,
> Puis le porterent enterrer.
> De lui ne voel ci plus conter...

There is nothing in this text to indicate any more than an ordinary burial. The burial was not *in* a minster, nor was it far from his home. Bliocadran travelled only one day to reach the tournament.

Another parallel Miss Newstead draws is between the great grief of the father in Chrétien and Bliocadran's »grief at the untimely death of close relatives«[151]. There was, in the *Bliocadran,* a certain amount of irony on the part of the author who described Bliocadran's grief. Bliocadran was impatient and eager to return to the activity that took eleven brothers from him. Chrétien depicted the father as so afflicted by grief that he died of it. Bliocadran's grief was so insincere that he got it over with as soon as possible. And even if grief had been equally sincere on the part of each of them, what would it prove? Grief is a natural concomitant of the death of a relative. The rôle of grief in the two works calls attention to the differences between them in depicting the father, and not to a parallel.

Loomis draws a parallel between the *Bliocadran* and the *Parzival* in that they are both supposedly strongly associated with North Wales. Gahmuret became King of North Wales through marriage and »Bliocadran is a knight of Wales, he participates in a tournament held by the King of Wales, and

---

[148] Newstead, *Perceval's Father and Welsh Tradition,* p. 6.
[149] Ibid., p. 25.
[150] Ibid., p. 29.
[151] Ibid., p. 5.

his widow retires to a castle on the sea of Wales«[152]. As with the remarks
about a splendid burial even a casual glance at the text would correct such
ideas (verses 656–669):

> Tant ont entendu a l'esrer
> Q'a un castel vienent tot droit
> Qui sor la mer de Gale estoit,
> Et molt estoit biax et plaisans;
> Calfle l'apelent païsant
> Et trestout cil de la contree.
> Iluec a sa gent assamblee
> Que ele avoit o lui mené.
> Mais n'i a gaires demoré,
> Ançois mut atout son harnois,
> Plus rice n'ot ne quens ne rois,
> Et ses gens avoec lui alerent.
> Onques un jor ne sojornerent
> Tant qu'en la forest sont esré,

The widow merely stopped at Calfle on the sea of Wales for scarcely a day
in her haste to reach the forest. Nor can one say positively where Calfle is
located. There remains of these parallels among Gahmuret, Bliocadran and
Bran perhaps only prowess as a warrior (a commonplace).

6. GEOGRAPHICAL INDICATIONS

The home of Bliocadran is one day's journey from the site of the tournament
announced by the *rois de Gales* for his own people and for those of *Cornwall* against the *Gaste Fontaine*. When he dies after the first day's battle
he is buried nearby. A messenger sent out by the lady to Bliocadran arrives
the same day. He is told by Bliocadran's men to report to her that they will
return after a visit to the King of Wales, but no indication is given about the
distance to be travelled.
Seven months after the death of Bliocadran and the birth of her son the lady
decides to go to the *gaste forest* to hide her son from the dangers of chivalric
pursuits. She tells the plan to her steward who advises her to pretend that
she is going on a pilgrimage to *Saint Brandain d'Escoce* (line 554), *A Saint
Brandain qui est d'Escoce* (line 587), to disguise her flight. With more than
one hundred loaded carts and wagons secretly assembled and sent ahead
(lines 637–644; presumably she would catch up with them), she travels by
way of *Calfle* (MS P *Cafle*), *sor la mer de Gale*. It is a total journey of more

---

[152] Loomis, *Arthurian Tradition*, p. 348 and The Origin of the Grail Legends, in
ALMA, p. 292.

46

than fifteen days with brief stops (*Onques un jor ne sojornerent,* line 668)[153]. They travel into the forest until the lady chooses a clear area in the middle of the *gaste forest* which is *sans fin* or *cent liues* wide.

According to the index of G. D. West, the *Gaste Fontaine* and *Calfle* are unique with the *Bliocadran*[154]. *Saint Brandain* is where the Chevalier Vermeil was buried in the Gerbert Continuation (line 12221), but *Saint Brandain d'Escoce* does not appear in any other verse romance. The pretended journey was toward Saint Brandain d'Escoce, but ended in the *gaste forest*.

It is not within the scope of this study to reconsider the many arguments and speculations about Perceval's birth and dwelling place, but the fact that these two areas may be widely separated has been largely ignored. Now it has been suggested that the *Valdone* of the *Perceval* may be Snowdon[155]. Loomis remarks that this locality »harmonizes perfectly with Prof. Newstead's evidence that Perceval's father was king of North Wales«[156]. However, Snowdon would be where the family fled to, not from, so that Valdone = Snowdon is not to be associated with Perceval's father unless the original home and the waste forest were not far from one another. This was not the interpretation of the *Bliocadran* author.

In the *Perlesvaus* Kamaalot, the home of Perceval, seemed to Nitze like modern Camelford on the west coast of Cornwall, south of Tintagel. Another castle of Perceval's mother, however, is near Oswestry, in northern Wales. Could this be an attempt to account for two locations, a southern birthplace and a northern association with the youth of the hero[157]?

---

[153] Miss Weston, *Legend of Sir Perceval,* I, 63, says, »The lady sets out, and comes to a castle, Caflé, *sur la mer de Gales,* and from thence enters the forest. After twelve days' wandering they find a glade suitable for their purpose, build a house, and remain there fourteen years before the opening of the Story.« The amount of time it took to reach the *gaste forest* is not indicated. The twelve days is based on MS *P.*

[154] G. D. West, *An Index of Proper Names in French Arthurian Verse Romances,* entries under: »Gaste Fontaine«, »Gaste For(i)est«, »Calfle«, »Gales«, »Morrois«, »Mores«, »Brandain, Saint«, »Cornoaille«.

[155] William A. Nitze and Harry F. Williams, *Arthurian Names in the Perceval of Chrétien de Troyes,* Analysis and Commentary (Vol. 38, no. 3, University of California Publications in Modern Philology, 1955, pp. 265–298), pp. 291–292; Roger Sherman Loomis, *From Segontium to Sinadon – the Legends of a Cité Gaste,* Speculum, XXII (1947), 520–533.

[156] Loomis, *Arthurian Tradition,* p. 490.

[157] Nitze, *Perlesvaus,* II, 197–198. Carmen has reexamined these place names in two articles: *The Perlesvaus and Bristol Channel,* Research Studies, XXXII (1964), 85–105; *South Welsh Geography and British History in the Perlesvaus,* pp. 37–59, in *A Medieval Miscellany,* ed. Norris J. Lacy (Lawrence: University of Kansas Publications, 1972). In the first article he locates Perceval's home Camaalos in Pembrokeshire at Camros (pp. 92–94), and in the second article he locates Perceval's other home, the Clef de Gales, at Abergavenny (pp. 42–43).

For Graeme Ritchie, Perceval's home is yet further north, »on the border of Galloway and within reasonable distance of Carlisle«[158], and Valdone is the »narrow gorges of the Done (now Doon) on the northern boundary of Galloway«[159]. Ritchie determines this location partly from the fact that the five knights whom Perceval met in the forest had come from Carlisle in five days. The text of the Perceval reads *Carduel* (lines 336 and 839). This name is often interpreted as meaning Carlisle, but the evidence is not very strong.

For the author of the *Bliocadran* a journey of more than fifteen days separates the original home of Perceval from the waste forest home. The indication that the lady and her people were travelling toward a *Saint Brandain d'Escoce* sounds like a northerly journey. The fact that they stopped on the way at a place on the »sea of Wales« could mean a southern Wales origin for Perceval's home. Or, could the original home have been near Snowdon and the journey have ended in Doon in Galloway?

Carman gives some clues about journeying in the romances[160]. He discusses a reasonable amount of time from near London to the north Welsh border as nine days (to Tanebourc). From Snowdon to Doon in Galloway across the Irish Sea is about the same distance. As a land journey for a large party however, it is unreasonable to consider these latter points as a fifteen-day journey except, perhaps, by horsemen unencumbered. The *Bliocadran* author, in proposing a swift (as possible) journey of more than fifteen days, assumes that Perceval's birthplace and the *gaste forest* are different locations. The author of the *Perlesvaus,* who does not discuss a flight to the forest, does, however, consider two separate locations for Perceval's home. In the *Perceval* the distance fled does not seem great (lines 450–454), but the passage is vague. The *Bliocadran* makes a better case for an isolated location but its reference points do not help to determine precise locations. From a point in South Wales to Snowdon is a reasonable fifteen-day journey. The size of the forest, however, in which the lady wandered may rule out Snowdon as the end of the journey she undertook in the *Bliocadran.*

In summary: Snowdonia is the likely home of Perceval in Chrétien and is perhaps not far removed from his birthplace. The *Perlesvaus* suggests two geographical locations, without discussing a flight to the woods. For Graeme Ritchie the whole *Perceval* story has a northern setting, in Galloway, but without a distinction between Perceval's birthplace and subsequent home. The *Bliocadran* does make a distinction between the birthplace of Perceval and the waste forest dwelling; and, because of the location of the tournament

---

[158] R. L. Graeme Ritchie, *Chrétien de Troyes and Scotland,* the Zaharoff Lecture for 1952 (Oxford, 1952), p. 18.
[159] Ibid., p. 20.
[160] Carman, *Pseudo-Map Cycle,* p. 73.

and the beginning of the journey, Perceval's birthplace does sound at least
like Wales.

The name of Calfle, Cafle, »sor la mer de Gale«, is unique to the *Bliocadran*.
A candidate for identification, phonologically possible but geographically
disconcerting, is Kaleph, a castle in the Vulgate *Estoire* (Sommer, I, 228) to
which Josephe retired before the battle of Galefort between Nascien and
Ganor, Lord of Galefort, and the king of Northumberland. The castle of
Kaleph is designated as a half day from Galefort which is on the Humber
(Sommer, I, 225). The second mention of Kaleph is of a »chastel qui estoit
apeles caleph. si fu pres del roialme de norgales« (Sommer, I, 236) where
Mordrain and his party alighted in Britain to join Nascien and his group.
Lot despaired of identifying Caleph: »Caleph, château situé sur la mer près
de la cité de ›Norgales‹ et, en même temps à une demi-heure de Galafort,
lequel est sur le Humber(!)«[161]. There are, indeed, many problems but the
castle is a *half day*, not a *half hour* from Galefort and Norgales here is a
kingdom, not a city. There is more territory involved in these designations
than implied by Lot.

But are Kaleph and Caleph the same castle? If two were meant, one could
be inland and near the eastern extremity of Norgales and the other could
be near the sea. There are perhaps insurmountable problems with these locations but what is significant for the present purpose is the fact that Caleph
is associated with the sea. The Calfle-Cafle of the *Bliocadran* is most likely
on the west coast, on the *mer de Gale*, and an east coast association with
Perceval's home does not seem likely. Kaleph-Caleph, however, may be
modeled on a component of many British place names which are associated
with a sea coast.

Loomis identified »Calflé« in the following manner in a textual note to the
Lanzelet[162], where he discusses the place name Dyoflê: »... it is not irrelevant
to recall that there was an earthwork called Dinlleu ... which lies on the
coast at the base of Snowdon about five miles south of Carnarvon... One
has only to change the letter *o* in Dyoflê to *n* to get Dynflê, and the result
would sound very much like Welsh Dinlle... The origin of Dyoflê seems
settled by the fact that a variant name of Dinlleu was Caer Leu..., and
according to the Bliocadran Prologue to Chrétien's *Conte del Graal* ...
Perceval's mother, queen of North Wales, after the death of her husband
visited a castle on the sea of Wales called Calflé or Caflé. This seems to be
as clearly a scribal corruption of Carflé as Dyoflê is a corruption of Dynflê;
and Carflé and Dynflê would represent respectively Caer Leu and Dinlleu,
two names of the same coastal fort«. Loomis' logic is rather questionable in
these deductions and decidedly undermined by his using for proof the asser-

---

161 Lot, *Etude Lancelot*, p. 147.
162 Trans. K. G. T. Webster, rev. R. S. Loomis (Columbia University Press, 1951),
    pp. 186–187.

tion that Perceval's mother was Queen of North Wales. I have elsewhere shown that this oft-repeated assertion is not supported by the text of the Prologue.

A Scottish gazetteer[163] lists four places in the north: *Calf*, a small island northeast of Orkney ($1^{1}/_{2} \times {}^{3}/_{4}$ miles); *Calf* or *Calve*, an island in Tobermory harbor, Argyllshire, and another little island called *Calfa*, also in Argyll. Another *Calva* is an islet off Sutherland. *The Concise Oxford Dictionary of English Place-Names*[164] discusses Old English *calf*, *cealf* (pl. *calfra*) as a common first element in many place names. Calfle-Cafle in the *Bliocadran*, then, may be associated with real place names associated with the sea and with the north. The author of the name could have been aware that his creation, without designating an actual place, gave the effect of a proper name for a castle situated on the sea and in the north.

The location of St. Brendan is not more specific than that of Calfle. Associations are with the west coast of Britain. In the *Dictionnaire d'histoire et de géographie ecclésiastiques* are the following geographical indications associated with this Saint: »Il y a des raisons de croire que Brendan [de Clonfert, † ca. 577 ou 583] fit un voyage par mer à une des îles de la côte occidentale de l'Ecosse: Adamnan mentionne dans sa *Vita sancti Columbae* une visite de Brendan à saint Columcille à Iona ... Le voyage de Brendan en Ecosse fournit probablement le noyeau aux récits de navigation dont il devint le héros et qui forment une littérature aussi fictive que volumineuse... Le culte de saint Brendan jouissait d'une grande popularité dans toute l'Europe; des églises et des lieux portent son nom en Ecosse, en Angleterre, en Bretagne, en Normandie, en Flandres ... en Hollande, et même dans les pays des bords de la Baltique«[165]. There is perhaps nothing to be made of the fact that Iona in Argyll is not far from the island of Calf or Calve in Tobermory harbor, both off the island of Mull. Any itinerary for Perceval's mother involving these real locations seems unlikely, but the association with a northern coastal setting recalls Ritchie's speculations. For him the setting for *Perceval* is the Scottish border but unfortunately, although he mentions the *Bliocadran*[166] and the references to *Saint Brandain d'Escoce* in it, he says not a word about Calfle, Cafle. St. Brendan of Scotland was most likely to have been in Scotland. Baring-Gould and Fisher report[167] that there are no churches in Wales dedicated to St. Brendan despite some testimony that

---

[163] Francis H. Groome, *Ordnance Gazetteer of Scotland*, 3 vols. (London, 1903), I, 221, 223.

[164] Eilert Ekwall, ed., *The Concise Oxford Dictionary of English Place-Names*, 4th ed. (Oxford, 1960).

[165] *Dictionnaire d'histoire et de géographie ecclésiastiques*, X (1938), 531–534.

[166] Ritchie, *Chrétien de Troyes and Scotland*, pp. 19–20. He dates the *Bliocadran* as ca. 1230.

[167] S. Baring-Gould and John Fisher, *Lives of the British Saints*, 4 vols. (London, 1907), I, 260.

he once lived at Llancarvan with St. Finan and at one time it was supposed his body lay at Branscombe, Devon, under the Welsh form of the name Branwalader[168].

If Arthur was supposed to have held sway from Cornwall to Carlisle, where but to southwest Scotland would Perceval's mother have fled for the isolation she sought away from all chivalry[169]? Perceval's original home in the *Bliocadran* is associated with the *terre de Gale, rois de Gales,* the *Gaste Fontaine* and *Cornuaille*. A South Wales or at least a Welsh territory seems suggested by these locations. It seems unlikely that a tourney involving »those of Cornwall« would be held farther north than in North Wales. North Wales, however, presents problems of definition. Brugger would extend it as far north as the Firth of Clyde, which would include Galloway in North Wales[170]. Thus a northward journey toward St. Brendan of Scotland with a stop at Calfle, on the *mer de Gale,* is all that is definite. The key to a reconsideration of the area would lie in the identification of Calfle or of Saint Brandain d'Escoce. A Scottish identification for Calfle would help to relocate the whole story northward. The *Bliocadran* author may have ignored, as he did with other narrative details, the Valdone of Chrétien in an effort to suggest a refuge far outside Arthur's realm and may have used Calfle to suggest an association with Scotland as an indication of such isolation.

In summary, we may say that although Calfle cannot be definitely located, its associations with the sea and the north suggest a more northerly *gaste forest* than one in Snowdonia. Caleph from the Vulgate Cycle, although on the east coast, was nevertheless associated with the sea and located as far north as the Humber. Saint Brendan is also associated with northern west-coast locations. If one considers there were no churches in Wales dedicated to St. Brendan, the definition by Ritchie of the Valdone as located in Galloway and Brugger's definition of North Wales as reaching as far as the Firth of Clyde, there emerges a strong indication that the *Bliocadran* author was sending Perceval outside Wales to the wilds of Scotland. The *Perlesvaus* does not use this setting, yet it retains the notion of two widely separated areas associated with Perceval's home. In the *Perceval,* the hero's birthplace and dwelling place may not be so widely separated. The *Bliocadran* author, starting with the indications of the *Perceval,* may have wanted to portray more vividly an isolated dwelling place for the hero. Snowdonia may even have

---

[168] Ibid., p. 261.

[169] For a summary of medieval conceptions of Scotland see Peter Rickard, *Britain in Medieval French Literature, 1100–1500* (Cambridge, England, 1956), pp. 206–220. See also Rachel Bromwich, *Scotland and the Earliest Arthurian Tradition,* BBSIA, XV (1963), 85–95.

[170] See G. D. West, *An Index of Proper Names in French Arthurian Verse Romances,* entry under »Gales¹«.

been the starting place, rather than the end, of the journey for the *Blio-cadran* author[171].

---

[171] Was the journey's end in Ireland? Hilka (note to line 587 of the *Bliocadran*) brings up the notion of *Escoce* as the primitive name for Ireland. The verse romances, however, refer to these locations as distinct. There seems no reason to assume that the *Bliocadran* author confused the two places, that he resorted to the primitive name for Ireland, or that he was unaware of the origin of the very famous Irish saint. Tatlock (*Legendary History of Britain* [Berkeley and Los Angeles, 1950], pp. 8, 9, 78) reports that Geoffrey of Monmouth »shows no awareness that in early centuries Scoti meant the Irish«. Also, »Scotia came definitely to be applied to Scotland and not Ireland about the ninth century... Scots, this word for the Irish ... became archaic about the eleventh century...« That the poem refers to drowning in the sea (lines 738–740) does not necessarily mean that the lady's people thought she was going to Ireland. To look »par mer et par terre« (line 736) is a common expression. What her people thought, upon finding no trace of her, was, logically, that she must have been swallowed up by the sea.

The poem says that the lady secretly assembled her riches in *cars et caretes plus de cent* (line 639) and sent them out in advance of her departure (634–647). To the people, then, only a small party departed with the lady, quite capable of making a sea crossing if necessary, whereas the real party, including the baggage, seems prepared to travel only by land. It could be that the announced designation of the journey to Saint Brandain d'Escoce was also meant to mislead the people. Could she have meant to be ambiguous so that either Ireland or Scotland could have been implied by the name: a small party seems to set out on a pilgrimage to a St. Brendan in Ireland, whereas a heavily encumbered party actually plods its way toward Scotland where there is also a St. Brendan?

MANUSCRIPTS AND EDITIONS

1. THE MANUSCRIPTS

The poetic text of the *Bliocadran Prologue* is preserved in two Old French manuscripts and, in shortened form, in a prose version printed in 1530, of which five known copies are extant. The manuscripts have been described many times. It is from these printed descriptions, from examination of photographs of the manuscripts and from a brief personal examination of *Additional 36614* in the British Museum that the following descriptions have been compiled.

L. London, British Museum, *Additional 36614* (formerly Ashburnham Library, Barrois 1), second half of the thirteenth century, 279 folios, vellum, 310 × 220 mm., two columns to the page, 30 to 32 lines per column, Picard dialect[172].

The manuscript contains Chrétien's *Prologue*, on folio 1 to 1c, line 15 (verses 23–24 Hilka ed., are omitted and verse 64 was omitted and inserted at the bottom of 1c); the *Bliocadran Prologue*, from folio 1c to 7d, line 28; Chrétien's *Perceval*, 7d to 84a, line 10; First Continuation, 84a to 163b,

---

[172] Modern Language Association Rotograph No. 64. The Library of the University of Pennsylvania owns a microfilm of the complete manuscript. Descriptions can be found in Jessie L. Weston, *Wauchier de Denain as a continuator of Perceval and the Prologue of the Mons MS.*, Romania, XXX (1904), p. 343 and in the same author's *The Legend of Sir Perceval, Studies upon its Origin, Development, and Position in the Arthurian Cycle*, 2 vols. (London, 1906–09), I, 39–41; *Catalogue of Additions to the Manuscripts in the British Museum in the years MDCCCC–MDCCCCV* (London, 1907 [Cat. no. 29]), pp. 156–157 (The *Catalogue* says a fuller description will be given in vol. III of the *Catalogue of Romances*. Such a description was not included in J. A. Herbert, *Catalogue of Romances in the Department of Manuscripts in the British Museum*, vol. III [London, 1910]); Alfons Hilka, *Der Percevalroman . . .* (Halle, 1932) pp. IV–V; Alexandre Micha, *La Tradition manuscrite des romans de Chrétien de Troyes* (Paris, 1939, Geneva, 1966 [Publications Romanes et Françaises, XC]), pp. 61–62; William Roach, *The Continuations of the Old French Perceval of Chrétien de Troyes*, 4 vols. (Philadelphia, 1949–71), I, xx–xxii; Pierre Gallais, *Formules de conteur et interventions d'auteur dans les manuscrits de la Continuation-Gauvain*, Romania, LXXXV (1964), 181–229.

line 10; Second Continuation, 163*b* to 268*a*, line 22; *Vita Mariae Aegyptiacae*, 268–279[173]. From folio 1 to folio 268, the end of the Second Continuation, the manuscript continues without a break. It is immediately visible, however, at line 11, folio 84*a*, the beginning of the First Continuation, that a new hand has taken over; also, the first large initial of the First Continuation, at 84*b*, line 2, is visibly different from the last large initial of the *Perceval*, 83*c*, line 19. This second hand continues into the Second Continuation and ends in the middle of line 21 of folio 169*d*. The change of hand here is quite visible and it looks as if an erasure had been made from this point to the end of the column. The third hand continues to the end of the Second Continuation.

The insertion of the *Bliocadran Prologue*, first described by Miss Weston[174] shortly after the purchase of the manuscript by the British Museum (1901), is summarized by Professor Roach: »This MS seems to have contained at first only Chrétien's *Perceval*, ending at exactly the same point as MS *A* (Hilka 9234). It had originally 78 folios, made up of nine gatherings of eight folios each, plus a tenth gathering of six folios, with Chrétien's poem ending in the first column of the fifth folio of this last gathering. This folio was originally number 77, but is now 84, because of seven extra folios intercalated in the first gathering to contain the *Bliocadran*«[175]. The folios are numbered in a modern hand in the upper right-hand corner of each recto. The first numbering was later crossed out to include three inserted flyleaves. It is the earlier, crossed-out numbering that is here referred to, so that folio 1 contains the beginning text of the manuscript. The *Bliocadran* contains 800 octosyllabic verses.

The *Bliocadran* was inserted into the first gathering of the MS after folio 1 had been filled with Chrétien's *Prologue* and the beginning of the *Perceval* (Hilka 69–112). The scribe removed these 44 verses of the *Perceval* from folio 1 verso with acid[176] and began to copy the *Bliocadran* directly after the last line of Chrétien's *Prologue* (Hilka 68). The *Bliocadran* fills six of the seven inserted folios and ends in 7*d*, line 28. The scribe then began copying the *Perceval* immediately, copying the first four lines to finish 7*d*. Folio 8 (the seventh inserted leaf) therefore had to contain only 40 verses of the poem in order to make it match with folio 9 (originally folio 2) that also had already been copied. The scribe therefore filled in 8*a* and 8*d*, leaving 8*b* and 8*c* blank. Many of the lines on folio 8 were split in half in order to try to fill at least two columns, but these two columns fall short by four lines each. The blank column 8*b* has been filled in with a dreadful drawing of a

---

[173] This *Vita* is not in the Modern Language Association Rotograph No. 64. See Roach, *Continuations*, I, p. xx, note 3.

[174] Weston, *Legend of Sir Perceval*, I, pp. 39–41.

[175] Roach, *Continuations*, I, p. xx.

[176] Weston, *op. cit.*, p. 40, note 1; Roach, *op. cit.*, p. xxi, note 3.

plumed devil and, at the top, letters (four lines high) of open tracing, the first two (of five) being *or*.

The decorating of the *Bliocadran* was never finished. Only the first large initial is filled in, and space was left for large initials at lines 53, 119, 161, 305, 401, 457, 541, 567, 623 and 731, with a guide letter visible in the margins at lines 161, 305, 457, 541, 567. The ruling is clearly visible on all seven of the inserted leaves. The third inserted leaf (folio 4) had clearly been mended before it was used, as the writing (lines 356–359 on 4*b* and 388–390 on 4*c*) has been made to fit before and after the vertical mending. The damage to the fourth inserted leaf (folio 5) and to the sixth (folio 7) occurred after they were copied. The ink is decidedly browner on these inserted leaves than that of 1 recto and 9 recto, the folios enclosing the insertion. The columns containing the *Bliocadran* are not of uniform length, having 30, 31 or 32 lines. Folio 5, for example, has 31 lines in *a* (one verse occupying two lines) and 32 lines in *b*. The hand of the copyist, according to Weston, Hilka and Roach, has some resemblance to the first hand that copied the Continuations and »there is no great interval of time between any of the scribes«[177].

P. Mons, Bibliothèque publique, 331/206 (formerly 4568), thirteenth century, 244 folios, vellum, 289 × 205 mm., two columns to the page, 45 lines per column, northeastern dialect[178].

---

[177] Weston, *loc. cit.*

[178] Modern Language Association Rotograph No. 5, which contains fifteen sheets only. Descriptions can be found in Wilhelm Ludwig Holland, *Über eine Handschrift von Crestiens Gedichte li Contes del Graal*, Germania, II (1857), 426–427 (Holland mentions a reference to the Mons manuscript by Bethmann in the Archiv der Gesellschaft für ältere deutsche Geschichtskunde, VIII [1843], 474); Charles Potvin, *Bibliographie de Chrestien de Troyes, comparaison des manuscrits de Perceval le Gallois, un manuscrit inconnu* (Brussels, Leipzig, Ghent, Paris, 1863), pp. 13, 17–21, 61–66; and the same author's *Le Perceval de Chrestien de Troyes. Un manuscrit inconnu. Fragment unique de ce manuscrit*, Jahrbuch für romanische und englische Literatur, V (1864), 26–50, and *Chrestien de Troyes. Perceval le Gallois, publié d'après le manuscrit de Mons*, 6 vols. (Mons, 1865–71), I, i–iv; VI, pp. LXIX–LXXXVI (these latter pages also incorporate the introductory pages that appear in vol. I); Weston, *The Legend of Sir Perceval*, I, 38–39, 62–63; Paul Faider and Mme Faider-Feytmans, *Catalogue des manuscrits de la Bibliothèque Publique de la ville de Mons* (Ghent, Paris, 1931 [Universiteit te Gent, Werken uitgegeven door de Faculteit der Wijsbegeerte en Letteren, 65]), pp. 352–353 (the manuscript is no. 778 in the catalogue, bearing the number 331/206. Potvin gives the manuscript number as 4568 [vol. VI, p. LXIX] of the »Bibliothèque Communale« of Mons); Albert Wilder Thompson, *The Elucidation, a Prologue to the Conte del Graal* (New York, 1931), pp. 7–8; Hilka, *Percevalroman*, pp. V, XXI, XXIII; Micha, *Tradition manuscrite*, pp. 57–58 (Micha erroneously refers to folios where he should say pages); Roach, *Continuations*, I, xxiii–xxiv.

The MS has modern pagination from page 1 (first page of the text) to page 487. The MS contains the *Elucidation*, pages 1 to 6b, line 5; a rubric of two lines; the *Bliocadran*, pages 6b, line 8 to 15a, line 45, end of column; a rubric of one line; Chrétien's *Perceval*, 15b, line 2 to 119b, line 14; the First Continuation, 119b, line 15 to 229b, line 20; a two-line rubric; the Second Continuation, 229b, line 23 to 375a, line 35; Manessier's Continuation, 375a, line 36, to 487a. The MS was copied by a single scribe.

The *Bliocadran* begins on page 6b, line 8, with an illuminated capital, one of forty in the MS, showing a figure on horseback conversing with a figure at a window. There are 798 verses: verses 599–600 are omitted (numbering according to MS *L*), verse 17 is omitted and a verse between 66 and 67 is supernumerary. It is written in a small, neat hand with few abbreviations.

G. French prose version, *1530 Prose*. Tresplaisante et Re= // creatiue Hystoire // du Trespreulx et Vaillant Cheuallier // Perceual le galloys Jadis cheuallier // de la Table ronde. Leq̄l acheua // les aduētures du saīct Gra // al. Auec aulchuns faictz // belliqueulx du noble // cheuallier Gauuaī // Et aultres Che // ualliers estās // au temps // du noble // Roy // Arthus / non au parauant Imprime. // Auec priuilege, // On les vend au Pallais a Paris / En la bou= // tique de Jehan lōgis. Jehan sainct denis / et Gal // liot du pre / Marchants libraires demourant au= // dict lieu. The colophon reads, in part, »... Le tout nouuellement Imprime // a Paris / pour hōnestes personnes Jehan // sainct denys. et Jehan longis / ... Et fut // acheue de Imprimer le premier iour de Se // ptembre. Lan mil cinq cens trente«. 220 numbered leaves (from »feuillet .i.« to »feuillet .ccxx.« in upper right-hand corners), four added leaves preceding »feuillet .i.«, 25 × 38¹/₂ cm., five plates and two illustrations, two columns of generally 44 lines to each page[179].

There are five copies mentioned by various scholars, in Berlin, British Museum, Nantes, Bibliothèque Nationale and Library of Congress[180]. The British Museum copy contains four added leaves that precede *feuillet 1*[181].

---

[179] Modern Language Association microfilm No. 8 of British Museum copy. Very complete descriptions can be found in Thompson, *Elucidation*, pp. 9–13; Hilka, *Percevalroman*, pp. VII–VIII, 483–614. Hilka prints the entire text from the Berlin copy to the end of Chrétien's *Perceval*. See also Roach, *Continuations*, I, xvi, note 3, xxxii. It is Roach who first uses the siglum *G* to designate the 1530 Prose; Potvin, *Bibliographie*, p. 16; Weston, *Legend of Sir Perceval*, I, 43; Jean Frappier, Sur le *Perceval en Prose* de 1530, in *Fin du Moyen Age et Renaissance, mélanges de philologie française offerts à Robert Guiette* (Antwerp, 1961), pp. 233–247.

[180] Thompson, *Elucidation*, p. 13, note 11, mentions all but the Berlin copy; for this see Hilka, *Percevalroman*, pp. VII and 483–614.

[181] The British Museum copy (Modern Language Association microfilm No. 8) lacks the table of contents. For these see Thompson, *loc.cit.* and Hilka, pp. 485–

These seven pages (folio 1 recto to folio 4 recto) have page headings »Elucidation de Hlystoire [sic] du Graal«. The eighth page (folio 4 verso) is occupied by a woodcut of a mounted knight brandishing a sword.

The *Elucidation* proper occupies folio 1 recto to the first column of folio 3 recto, line 29. The *Bliocadran* begins immediately with the chapter title and the indication that it is chapter four of the »Elucidation de Hlystoire [sic] du Graal«. The chapter heading reads: »Comment Bliocadras pere de Perceual le Galloys fust occis a ung tournoy publicque par le Roy de galles pres la gaste fontaine / ou il fist des vaillances infinies au tournoy deuãt que le Roy de Galles & luy se combatissent. // Chappitre quatriesme.«. The text of the *Bliocadran* then begins at the top of column 2, folio 3 recto (page 5) and ends in column 2, folio 4 recto, line 25 (page 7). This page ends with the words »Cy apres vient le Prologue de cil // qui redigea le cõpte en ancienne Ri // me Francoyse qui puis a este mis en // tel escript comme vous le poues veoir // a present.«. The text of the *Bliocadran* occupies a total of 191 printed lines.

The signatures indicated on these four inserted leaves are *AA* on folio 1 recto (page 1), *AA.ii.* on page 3 and *AA.iii.* on page 5, all in the lower right-hand corner. There is no signature on page 7. Page 8 is occupied by the woodcut indicated above. Folio 5 is the original first page of the book. It is headed »Cy commence le Prologue de lacteur.«. In the upper right-hand corner is the numbering »feuillet .i.« and in the lower corresponding corner, the gathering number »a.i.«. This numbering proceeds consecutively to »feuillet .ccxx.«. The title »Perceual le Gallois« appears for the first time at the top of folio 6 recto (page 11 or »feuillet .ii.«). The *Perceval*, First Continuation, Second Continuation and Manessier's Continuation occupy from »feuillet .ii.« to »feuillet .ccxx.« recto[182].

Of the *Elucidation* proper in this version (chapters 1 to 3) Thompson says it is »a free prose paraphrase of the prologue we have been calling the *Elucidation*, together with a truncated version of the *Bliocadran*«[183].

The prosification of the *Bliocadran* uses lines 1–237 of the poetic text, ending with the death of Bliocadran. The name appears eighteen times in the text as *Bliocadras* and once as *Blyocadras* (as compared to ten appearances of the name in the poetic text. For forms of the name, see Textual Notes, note to line 26).

---

492. The chapters in the table of contents do not contain the four chapters of the »Elucidation de Lhystoire du Graal«. The page headings use *Hlystoire* four times, *Lhystoire* twice and *Hlistoire* once, and *Elucidacion* twice, *Elucidation* five times.

182 See Roach, *Continuations*, I, xxxii, for a description of the *Perceval* and Continuations in the 1530 Prose.

183 Thompson, *Elucidation*, p. 10.

2. THE EDITIONS

The *Bliocadran* was first printed in 1863 by Charles Potvin in his *Bibliographie de Chrestien de Troyes*[184]. He refers to the Mons manuscript on the title page as »Un Manuscrit Inconnu« and reproduces as the frontispiece a facsimile of the beginning of the *Bliocadran,* showing its illuminated large initial. As headings to his chapter (p. 89) containing the *Bliocadran,* Potvin inserts the chapter title from the 1530 Prose and a »summary« in seven lines of Books I and II of the *Parzival.* The line numbers of the *Bliocadran* are 485–1284 (the text is misnumbered: line 1100 = 1098 and so on to the end where 1284 = 1282), line 1 being the first line of the *Elucidation,* and line 1283 the first line of the *Perceval.* It is not clear how this »manuscrit inconnu« came to his attention. However, it was already known to other scholars. In 1857 in Germania, Wilhelm Ludwig Holland gives his thanks to Bethmann who, in 1843, published a notice of the manuscript. Holland then gives a brief summary that includes the first twenty-two verses of the *Bliocadran*[185].

Potvin, having called attention to his »manuscrit inconnu«, printed the *Bliocadran* again in 1864, in the Jahrbuch für romanische und englische Literatur. In this article Potvin called attention to the Mons manuscript which, he believed, owed part of its importance to the facts that »l'œuvre entière y est attribuée à Chrestien de Troyes – et l'on y trouve une introduction et un premier chapitre qu'aucun autre manuscrit ne contient«. Potvin refers to the *Bliocadran* as »le premier chapitre«, and to the *Elucidation* as an »introduction«. The numerous critical notes, many of which Potvin ignored, were prepared for him by Auguste Scheler[186].

In 1865 Potvin published, as Tome I of a printing of the entire Mons manuscript, the *Elucidation,* the *Bliocadran* and Chrétien's *Perceval* to verse 9190 (= Hilka 7816)[187]. His transcription of the *Bliocadran* in 1865 is fairly

---

184 Potvin, *Bibliographie de Chrestien de Troyes,* pp. 89–118.

185 Holland, *Über eine Handschrift,* Germania, II (1857), pp. 426–427. See note 178 above for full reference.

186 Potvin, *Le Perceval de Chrestien de Troyes,* Jahrbuch für romanische und englische Literatur, V (1864), 26–50. The text is misnumbered: 400 = 395 and so on to the end where 803 = 798.
Potvin would have done well to heed Scheler's critical notes more attentively. Scheler did not, however, look at the manuscript in order to catch the blunder of line 54 (the creation of »Kammuëlles«).

187 There are six volumes in this edition. In the set in the University of Pennsylvania Library (all of one set, no. 12 of a printing of 200 and destined for M. Charles de Bettignies, avocat, à Mons, member of the Société des Bibliophiles belges, séant à Mons), volume I (1865) contains the two prologues and the *Perceval* to line 9190 (= Hilka 7816). Volume II (1866) interrupts the poem with the *Roman en Prose (Perlesvaus),* and volumes III–VI resume the rest of the poetic text to the end of the Mons manuscript. The *Roman en Prose* was afterwards

accurate with very few regularizations of spelling or printing errors. Potvin made most of his emendations, however, without recording them or the manuscript reading in his Notes. It is for this reason that Hilka's edition of the text, using Potvin's printed edition and not the manuscript itself, does not give an accurate picture of manuscript *P*, but rather of Potvin's 1865 edition.

In 1932, Hilka, in an appendix to the *Percevalroman*, published a composite edition of manuscripts *L* and *P* of the *Bliocadran*. Hilka did not have a photograph of the Mons manuscript, but rather worked from Potvin's printed edition of 1865. Also, he was faithful to Foerster's principles of editing that seek to reconstitute a text[188].

The following analysis of Hilka's edition of the *Bliocadran* summarizes the state of Hilka's text of the *Bliocadran*. It reveals in category 1 that Hilka's unnecessary changes of MS *L* using MS *P* followed principles of regularized spelling and grammatical uniformity, with a certain number of choices due to caprice. In category 2a, erroneous readings of MS *L* in text, only the reading of line 695 is completely puzzling. In category 2b, erroneous read-

---

baptized »Première Partie« and the poetic texts »Deuxième Partie«, so that later arrangements of the six volumes place the *Roman en Prose* first, as volume I, and the poetic text becomes »Deuxième Partie, tomes I–V« (or volumes II–VI of the set). In the University of Pennsylvania set the »Introduction« is at the end of volume VI, I–LXXXVI and incorporates the short introduction of volume I on pp. LXXXII–LXXXV. Line 54 of the *Bliocadran* is one clue to the various stages of publication of volume I. In 1863, 1864 and in some printings of 1865 (not the specially designated ones for members of the *Société*) the error that created a name for Perceval's mother appears. »Kammuëlles« was in the copy reviewed by Paul Meyer (Revue Critique d'Histoire et de Littérature, No. 35 [1er Septembre, 1866], pp. 129–137) who pointed out the error rather disdainfully (p. 136). The error was corrected by Potvin and does not appear in the printings on »large paper«, also dated 1865. Thus volume I occurs both with and without this »name« for Perceval's mother. As late as 1962 Flutre indexed this name. His source was the Jahrbuch and volume I, undoubtedly a copy on »papier ordinaire«. Since the *Roman en Prose* later became volume I in the series of six, the dates for volumes I–VI are often erroneously given as »1866–71«.

188 Hilka, *Perceval*, pp. V, IX, XXIII. In his »Vorrede« Hilka acknowledges the use of Modern Language Association rotographs of MSS *E* and *L* (Nos. 54 and 64), but not of Modern Language Association Rotograph No. 5 (first fifteen sheets of MS *P*). In his review of Hilka's edition, Maurice Wilmotte (Romania, LIX [1933], 453–461) mentions that he was asked by Foerster to collate the Mons manuscript for him, but »Puis ce fut la guerre . . .« (p. 454) and Foerster's death. The state of the text of the *Bliocadran* is analyzed by Albert W. Thompson, *The Text of the Bliocadran*, RPh, IX (1955–56), 205–209. He says, »Although Hilka's text is presented as if it were a composite of *L* and *P*, it is clear that he did not consult MS *P*, but used only Potvin's *Perceval*« (p. 206). Thompson gives a sample of Hilka's inaccuracies which the present analysis attempts to give in full.

ings in variants from MS *L,* it is possible to consider the omission of a variant from *L* as an error of Hilka's reading of the text of *L,* and thus to place these examples under 2a. This is a more serious charge, however, and difficult to prove. Category 3 reveals that Hilka's dependence on Potvin's printed text of MS *P* does not reflect the state of that manuscript, but rather of the printed text. In most cases Potvin's emendations or errors are the source of the errors in Hilka's readings of MS *P.* I have recorded the places where Potvin did give a note about his emendation in 1865. Hilka, it seems, ignored most of Potvin's critical notes, some of which contained the correct manuscript reading. In category 4, unnecessary changes of MS *L* not based on *P,* almost all are due to a concern for regularized spelling. In category 5 are several cases where a correct reading of the manuscripts or an interpretation of the text is in question. The reading of Hilka's text or variant is placed before the >, and the reading of the MS or a suggested correction after it. An asterisk (*) after an example indicates a discussion in the Textual Notes.

1. *Unnecessary changes of L using P in Hilka's text (P > L)*

1 le > la – 6 n'i > ne – 25 larges > sages* – 26 Bliocadrans > Bilocadran* – 29 fenis > feni* – 33 liés > lié – 34 tous iriés > tout irié – 42 merci > merchi – 43 ci > si* – 44, 68, 395, 457 çou > ce – 44 grans > grant – 47 et > no et* – 50 tout > tous* – 71 Ceus ki > Cex qui – 79 viegnes > vegnes; 499, 327 viegne > vegne; 127 viengnent > vegnent – 93, 100 encore > encor – 97 cest > cel – 129 samedi > semedi – 137 Qui > Si – 138, 688 jusqu'al > dusq(u)'al – 145, 161 Bliocadrans > Bliocadron – 147 a fait tost > ot fais tos* – 149 li > si – 154 repria mout doucement > reproie molt dolcement – 176 Comme > Come – 178 Chevaucierent > Cevaucierent – 180 Bliocadran[s] > Bliocadron – 186, 194, 205, 214 Bliocadrans > Bliocadras – 192 mautalent (*MS* mautelent) > maltalent – 195, 518 la > le – 200 jusqu'au > dusqu'au – 204 Cel j. ni perdirent noient > Ainc le jor n'i perdi nïent* – 205 l'a > l'ot – 207 Que > Car – 210 andui > andoi – 217 vole en esclices > li vole en clices* – 222 derriere > deriere; 762, 770 arriere > ariere – 223 Parut > Paru* – 223 fiers > fers – 234, 786 loing > loig – 243 l'en porterent > le porterent – 256, 756 issi > isi – 258 nonciés > només – 270, 520, 756 sont > sunt – 275 tors > tort* – 300 trestout > trestot – 302 movoir > muevre – 305, 401 La > Li – 313 del > de – 351, 486, 619, 638, 721 serjant > sergant; 573 serjans > sergans – 353 cevaucié > cevalcié – 353 erré > esré; 656 errer > esrer – 362 salit > sailli* – 364 enseigniés > enseigniés – 382 crucefiiés > crucefiés – 387, 493 bone > boine – 389 savés > verrés* – 420 je > jou – 428 cris > cri – 441 tos (*MS* tot) > tous – 444 Que > Qui* – 444 coreciés > corecié – 446, 505 Ensi > Isi – 469 fu tous tans > estoit tous ses – 492 cointes > gentes – 495, 637 envoiié > envoié – 500, 614 noient > nïent* – 526 Preudom > Prodom – 530 ocis > ochis – 537, 697, 744 fame > feme –

541 proiié > proié – 542 otroiié (*MS* ottroiié) > otroié – 549 nos > l'a. –
550 nos > vos – 551 feïssiés > faisïés* – 552 deïssiés > deïsiés* – 555, 565
bonement > boinement – 560 sire > sires – 574 tenans > tenant* –
575 vinrent > murent* – 576 murent > vinrent* – 591 voel > vuel –
613, 754 chose > cose – 621 Et de çou qu'ele > De çou que ele – 630 afiier
(*MS* affiier) > afïer – 634 durant > devant* – 635 tresor > tressor –
646 s'aperçut > s'aperciut – 651 tote > toute – 652 la > sa – 652 estoit >
fu – 657 C'a > Q'a –657 vinrent > vienent – 659 i fist bel et plaisant >
estoit biax et plaisans – 663, 667 li > lui – 668 sejornerent > sojornerent –
669 entré (*MS* entret) > esré* – 670 jours > jors – 676 et dru > foillu* –
690 si > se – 727 cevaucier > cevalcier – 733 nel > ne* – 738 quidoient >
cuidoient – 746 enfes > emfes – 749 m. et c. f. > mere c. f.* – 755 unes gens
> une gent* – 758 Ce sont li diable (*MS* dyable) en a. > C'est dïables tout
en a.* – 759 > empené > enpené – 761 o eus (*MS* od eus) n'i a. > o els vos
n'arestés* – 766 lo > lou – 769, 771 jou > je – 775 qu'il > que –
775 Jusqu'au > Dusq'al – 783 c'ains > ainc* – 789 encontre > contre –
798 ont > a

2. *Erroneous readings of L* (Hilka > MS *L*)

a. *In text*

695 .V. > .C. – 739 Qu'ele (–1) > Que ele – 745 come > com

b. *In variants*

It is possible to consider the omission of a variant from *L* as an error of
Hilka's reading of the text of *L* and thus to place such examples under
category 2a. This is a more serious charge, however, and difficult to prove.
1 no variant > la – 14, 596 gerres > guerres* – 26 Bliocadran > Bilocadran* – 29 no variant > feni* – 44 no variant > grant – 71 no variant >
Cex qui – 137 no variant > Si sen – 186, 194 Bliocadron > Bliocadras –
223 no variant > fers – 243 no variant > le porterent – 254 baptiser >
baptisier – 258 nomciés > només – 373 no variant > deboinairement –
387 boene > boine – 389 verrés *P* > verrés *L* – 389 no variant > qe –
390 porront > poront* – 394 no variant > nen v.* – 444 no variant >
Qui* – 457 no variant > ce – 464 no variant > porensee (*MS* p̄ensee) –
477 no variant > Vodra – 499 no variant > vegne – 526 no variant >
Prodom – 544 no variant > leu – 621 no variant > De çou que ele –
646 s'apercuit > s'aperciut – 647 Qu'il > Qu'el (*MS* Q'l) – 657 no variant
> Q'a – 668 un jor > no variant (text reads *un jor*) – 670 no variant >
jors – 687 no variant > sot (no stroke over *o*) – 688, 775 Dusq'al >
Dusq'al – 706 no variant > tant tost – 733 no variant > ne (*MS* difficult
to read)* – 738 no variant > cuidoient – 746 no variant > emfes

3. *Erroneous readings of P* (Hilka > MS *P*)

a. *In text*

95 com > con. Potvin had changed MS *con* to *com* – 192 mautalent > mautelent. Potvin had emended and has a note – 441 tos > tot. Potvin's text – 739 Qu'ele (-l) > Que ele – 695 .V. > .C. – 745 come > com. Potvin's text reads *comme*

b. *In variants*

7–8 *in L umgestellt* > also in *P*. Potvin emended, with note – 37 viut > vaut. Potvin emended, with note – 47 no variant > seul. Potvin emended – 53 femme > feme. Potvin emended – 54 K'am mervelles > K'a mervelles – 66 *P* adds a line not recorded by Hilka. Potvin has a note – 81–82 *in P umgestellt* > not so. Potvin reversed these lines, with note – 124 en liu remaingne > en lui remaingne. Potvin emended – 141 tournoiement > tornoiement. Potvin's text – 243 l'emporterent > l'enporterent. Potvin's text – 247 no variant > ki. Potvin emended – 313 no variant > ke. Potvin emended – 320 De coi que nous dit [n. avom] > De coi ke nous dit n. avon. Potvin's variant – 371 no variant > monne. Potvin emended – 375 no variant > Si a dit par b. r. Potvin emended (no variant) – 389 verrés *P* > verrés *L* – 390 porront > poront. Potvin used *poront* in text but *porront* in note – 421 signor > ami. Potvin emended (no variant) – 454 no variant > Vous – 483 quide > quident. Potvin emended (no variant) – 499 no variant > hastiument. Potvin emended, with variant – 514 no variant > p. tot v. Potvin emended – 535 Et moi > Od moi. Potvin used *Od moi* in text (correctly) but said in note the MS reads *Et moi*. This note erroneously written for 535 but meant for 538 – 537 feme *P* > feme *L* – 538 Od vous > Et vous. Potvin emended (see 535 above) – 585 no variant > çou que j'avoie pieça. Potvin emended (no variant) – 627 ki illuec > ki iluec. Potvin's text – 655 no variant > elle. Potvin's text – 661 no variant > conree *or* contee. Potvin emended – 668 no variant > nul jor – 676 foillu *P* > foillu *L* – 737 no variant > riens. Potvin emended – 748 s'assit > s'assist. Potvin's text – 751 no variant > vous – 753 Cevriex *L* > Cevrieus *P* – 761 no variant > arrestes – 784 no variant > bieste. Potvin's text

4. *Unnecessary changes of L in text not based on P* (Hilka > *L*)

39 ferrer > ferer – 187 loi[n]g > loig – 260 seignor > segnor – 141 Qu'aler > Q'aler; 267 qu'a > q'a; 296 Qu'avés > Q'avés – 341 av[r]oit > avoit (see note to this line) – 373 deboineirement > deboinairement – 477 Voldra > Vodra – 544 lieu > leu – 584 jo > je – 650 O li > Od li*

142–143 See note to these lines – 193–194 froisse > frosse. See note to these lines – 183 Hilka gives variant from *P* as *ancomencier* – or is it *aucomencier*? Difficult to read manuscript here – 211 Hilka's text reads *come*. Is this a reading of *P (con)* or of *L (9)*? No variant is given – 389–390 See note to these lines – 419–420 Direct quotation in Hilka begins at 420. See note to these lines – 432 Hilka gives no variant from *P*. It could be *loece*, but the manuscript is difficult to read here – 606 peüissent (Hilka) > peuissent (Text). Diaeresis not necessary; cf. Hilka, p. 789.

3. PLAN OF THE PRESENT EDITION

The present edition uses MS *L* as base manuscript and gives all the variants from MS *P*. Potvin's line numbers are given in the left-hand margin at intervals of every ten lines. My line numbers, which correspond with Hilka's, are in the right-hand margin. Folio and column indications for MS *L* are also given in the left-hand margin.

In general, the attitude toward the base manuscript has been conservative. Recommendations concerning the solution of abbreviations, treatment of hiatus, etc., have been followed particularly according to suggestions of the Société des Anciens Textes (Romania LII [1926], 243–249) and of William Roach in his edition of the Continuations (*Continuations*, I, pp. xlii–xliii), among others (see Abbreviations preceding Textual Notes).

Comments on syntax, rime, morphology, semantics and scribal practices are to be found in the Textual Notes. The text is too short to draw generalized conclusions about the language of the author. For further comments on MS *L*, see pp. 53–55 above.

The two-line capitals of the Text indicate episodes or logical divisions of the story. These correspond to the divisions of the manuscript at lines 53, 161 and 457. Other episodes begin at lines 244, 656 and 725.

The edition is completed by a Summary of Episodes, Textual Notes, Index of Proper Names and a Glossary. The Glossary gives a summary of all forms of irregular verbs and of many regular verbs. Inclusion of words has generally been based on peculiarities of orthography, meaning or usage.

4. A COMPARISON OF THE *BLIOCADRAN PROLOGUE* AND THE 1530 PROSE *PERCEVAL*

In his edition of the *Conte du Graal* in 1932 Hilka prints, from the Berlin copy, the text of the 1530 Prose to the end of the *Perceval* proper. A comparison of his transcription of the *Bliocadran* chapter with the British

Museum copy shows that his transcription is accurate. He indicates the beginning of »fol. AA.III^v« (p. 499, line 20) and of »fol. AA.IV^r« (p. 500, line 32) neither of which appears in the BM copy. Hilka also prints the »Table of Contents« which does not exist in the British Museum copy[189].

Frappier, in his comparison of various passages of the 1530 Prose and the *Perceval* judges Hilka's printing of the text by saying that: »[il] a quelque peu modernisé la présentation du texte en distinguant *u* et *v*, en ajoutant accents, apostrophes, trémas, cédilles. Il a signalé (p. 792) quelques-unes des bévues les plus graves commises par le traducteur et des fautes d'impression qui pullulent dans l'édition de 1530. Toutefois, un peu découragé par leur nombre et leur fréquente grossièreté, il n'a pas poussé jusqu'au bout la toilette du texte (dont la ponctuation, notamment, laisse fort à désirer) et il s'en est remis, pour une amélioration moins incomplète, à la compétence du ›lecteur averti‹«[190].

The following analysis presents some of the more radical departures by the 1530 Prose from the verse versions. As Frappier showed, there is an unevenness in the »translation«; some passages are beautifully handled and others rather mutilated. The *Bliocadran* section, »Chappitre quatriesme« (and final chapter) of the »Elucidation de Hlystoire du Graal«, corresponds to the verse as far as line 237. The »translator« was thus not interested in the poem but in the information about the death of the father of Perceval. There emerges from a comparison of the prose and verse a curious alteration in the portrait of Bliocadran and the circumstances of his death.

The chapter heading contains misinformation: »Comment Bliocadras pere de Perceual le Galloys fust occis a ung tournoy publicque par le Roy de galles pres la gaste fontaine ou il fist des vaillances infinies au tournoy devant que le Roy de Galles & luy se combatissent.« The chapter heading contradicts the prosification itself, however, which says that »ung damoisel« jousted with Bliocadran and killed him[191].

The prose asserts that the eleven brothers of Bliocadran died »en peu de temps« (Hilka 499, 4), but no indication of time is given in the poem (*Bl.* 19–21). The prose says that Bliocadran was »le plus courtoys et le plus saige de tous les aultres« (Hilka 499, 5–6), whereas the poem does not exalt Bliocadran above his brothers (*Bl.* 1–26). The prose indicates that Bliocadran

---

[189] See notes 179, 180, and 181 above.

[190] Frappier, Sur le *Perceval en Prose* de 1530, in *Mélanges Guiette*, p. 235, note 1. Thompson (*Text of the Bliocadran*, RPh, IX [1955–56], 207–209) is rather harsh on Hilka, saying his printing of the 1530 Prose can »serve pretty well« (p. 207, note 10). He points out, however, only two errors. In the *Bliocadran* section there are no serious errors. The text, as Frappier says, needs at most only some punctuation.

[191] I refer to Hilka's page and line numbers in his 1932 edition. Thus here Hilka 500, 47–501, 12 is to be compared to the *Bliocadran (Bl.)* 208–225.

grieved »long temps apres leur mort« and that »il demeura si morne et si fort pensif que tous ceulx qui le veissent cuidassent bien qu'il ne survesquist pas longuement apres eulx« (Hilka 499, 10–12). This is a very significant rationalization on the part of the prosifier (*Bl.* 28–36). In the discussion of the personality of this hero, whom we have called a compulsive knight errant, it seemed significant that Bliocadran is presented in the poem as all but disregarding the deaths of no less than eleven brothers in order to pursue his sport. The prose »corrects« these negative suggestions of the poem, rationalizing the text to present what should have been the reasonable attitude of the hero under the circumstances.

The prose persists in the softening of the portrait of Bliocadran. It gives as a reason for his wanting to return to jousting that he goes »pour son dueil alleger« (Hilka 499, 16) of which there is nothing in the poem (*Bl.* 37–40). Bliocadran consented not to go, but no allusion is made in the prose at this point to the absence of an heir that in part seems responsible for his not leaving at first (compare Hilka 499, 25–28 and *Bl.* 53–71). In fact the wife's pregnancy, mentioned in the poem in verse 59, is not mentioned in the prose until after the arrival of the messenger (Hilka 500, 3–6). The effect of the prose version is to mitigate the negative impression given by the poetic text in which Bliocadran's desertion of his wife at a critical moment is quite clear. The prose asserts that Bliocadran did not stay home »gramment« (Hilka 499, 29–30), whereas the poem underlines that it was two years (*Bl.* 55), during which time there was great desire for a child. The prose text, by giving news of the tournament first and mentioning the impending birth afterwards (the reverse of the poem) also reverses the importance of the two events. Perhaps it was a desire to harmonize the prologue with Chrétien that caused the prosifier to eliminate the fact that it was a first child who was awaited (Hilka 500, 3–4). The effect, however, is to mitigate the negative impression given by the poem.

Bliocadran's words to his wife as he takes leave of her are, in the poem: »Dame, taisiés, De vostre duel vos apaisiés« (*Bl.* 155–156), whereas the prose reports that, although refusing not to go, he had concern for her: »si luy fist creancer que le tournoyment feru il ne sejourneroit en nul lieu tant qu'il fust revenu au chastel« (Hilka 500, 6–7).

When Bliocadran and his knights arrive at where the tournament is to take place they lodge not in the castle (as in MS *L*) but »moult furent bien receuz d'ung bon preudhomme qui leur feist tout l'honneur dont il se peult adviser« (Hilka, 500, 13–14). This place of lodging follows MS *P* (there are other contradictions; see textual note to lines 164–167).

A small detail, not in the poem, is that »Le lendemain apres avoir ouy la messe« Bliocadran and his men went to the tournament (Hilka 500, 16). I see in this detail yet another effort on the part of the prosifier to soften the portrait of Bliocadran by showing him following normal procedures. The prosifier, as Frappier pointed out, rationalized the poetic texts so that he presented often an interpretation of what reasonably should be, rather than what actually was, in the poems.

The first joust, won by Bliocadran, is recounted with no explanation for its violence in the poem (*Bl.* 184–207). The prose version gives the following rationalization for the violence: »De celle jouste fust moult loué Bliocadras et non mye a tort car le Chevallier qu'il avoit ainsy durement encontré n'estoit mye aise a abbatre ains estoit preudhomme et fort Chevallier« (Hilka 500, 32–35). In the poem, in only two lines (202–203), there is a mere suggestion that a full mêlée ensued, but the prosifier decided to spell out this general violence (Hilka 500, 35–47) in order to justify the second and mortal encounter of Bliocadran with the jouster who kills him. The unexplained violence of this second encounter in the poem (*Bl.* 208–226) led the prosifier to rationalize that »cil vient pour venger le dommage que Bliocadras leur faict« (Hilka 501, 3–4). It is to be remembered that I considered the unjustified violence of this encounter as an indication of the *Bliocadran* poet's negative attitude toward the tournament in general. Signs of this attitude have been, at every point, removed from the prose text.

The poetic text does not attempt to elicit sympathy for Bliocadran upon his death (lines 235–237). The prose text, however, shows an entirely different attitude. His knights reassured him »qu'il n'au[r]oit[192] garde de mourir pour le coup. Non faict il seigneurs je n'ay garde d'en reschaper car je ne cuide pas vivre deux jours entiers si vous prie que me faciez venir le chappelain qui me vienne aprester et ilz le firent comme il avoit demandé: et puis ne demeura pas gram(e)ment qu'il ne fust mort car au deuxiesme jour apres comme il avoit asseuré rendit il l'esprit a dieu« (Hilka 501, 18–24).

By increasing the time and extent of Bliocadran's grief over his brothers, explaining his desire to joust as a way of assuaging that grief, mitigating the importance of the impending birth, softening his words to his wife as he departs, having him hear mass before the tournament, saying that his first adversary is difficult to defeat, inventing a scene of general violence not in the poem, giving a reason to the second adversary for the violence of the encounter and, finally, by showing Bliocadran asking for a priest after which »rendit il l'esprit a dieu«, the author of the prose version has created an idealized Bliocadran who does not correspond very greatly to the figure of the poem.

Thompson pointed out that »The 1530 paraphrase appears not to be based on either of the extant manuscripts«[193]. A comparison of the *Bliocadran* portion of the 1530 Prose with the verse version reveals, however, that the prosifier worked from a poem that must have been substantially the same as

---

[192] See note to line 341 of the poem where the text also used *avoit* instead of *avroit* (as emended by Hilka) and where this use of the imperfect instead of the expected conditional conveys the effect of certainty on the part of the speaker.
[193] Thompson, *Text of the Bliocadran*, p. 208.

the one we have in manuscripts *L* and *P*. The narrative used by the prosifier is the same in both versions, but the redactor of the prose version imposed his own interpretation upon the text by rearranging the narrative details and by distorting the theme in accord with his own notions of Bliocadran as an appropriate father for Perceval.

BIBLIOGRAPHY

ALMA. See Roger Sherman Loomis. *Arthurian Literature in the Middle Ages*.

Arnold, Ivor ed. *Le Roman de Brut de Wace*. 2 vols. Paris, 1938–40. (Société des anciens textes français)

Atre périlleux. See Brian Woledge.

Auberee. See Georg Ebeling.

Aucassin et Nicolette. See Hermann Suchier.

Baist, Gottfried ed. *Crestien's von Troyes Contes del Graal (Percevaus li galois)*, Abdruck der Handschrift Paris, français 794. Nicht im Buchhandel, [1909]. (Reprinted 1912, »In Kommission: G. Ragoczy [K. Nick], Freiburg i. B.«)

Baring-Gould, S. *The Lives of the Saints*. Vol. V. rev. ed. Edinburgh: John Grant, 1914.

– and John Fisher. *The Lives of the British Saints*, the Saints of Wales and Cornwall and such Irish Saints as have Dedications in Britain. 4 vols. London: Charles J. Clark, 1907.(For the Honourable Society of Cymmrodorion)

Bédier, Joseph ed. *Le Roman de Tristan par Thomas, poème du XIIᵉ siècle*. 2 vols. Paris: Didot, 1902–05. (Société des anciens textes français)

–. *La Tradition manuscrite du Lai de l'Ombre, réflexions sur l'art d'éditer les anciens textes*. Paris: Champion, 1929. (Offprint from Romania, LIV [1928], 161–196, 321–356)

Bel Inconnu. See G. Perrie Williams.

Bell, Penelope. The Relationship of Manessier's Continuation to the Prose Romances of the Vulgate Cycle. Bryn Mawr, Pennsylvania, 1956. (Unpublished Master of Arts thesis, Bryn Mawr, Pennsylvania, 1956)

Béroul, *Tristan*. See Alfred Ewert.

Birch-Hirschfeld, Adolf. *Die Sage vom Gral, ihre Entwicklung und dichterische Ausbildung in Frankreich und Deutschland im 12. und 13. Jahrhundert*. Leipzig, 1877.

Blaess, Madeleine. *Arthur's Sisters*, Bulletin Bibliographique de la Société Internationale Arthurienne, VIII (1956), 69–77.

Blancandin. See Sweetser.

Bogdanow, Fanni. *Morgain's Role in the Thirteenth-Century French Prose Romances of the Arthurian Cycle*, Medium Aevum, XXXVIII (1969), 123–133.

–. *The Rebellion of the Kings in the Cambridge MS. of the Suite du Merlin*, University of Texas Studies in English, XXXIV (1955), 6–17.

–. *The Romance of the Grail*, a Study of the Structure and Genesis of a Thirteenth-Century Arthurian Prose Romance. Manchester: Manchester University Press, 1966.

Bromwich, Rachel. *Trioedd Ynys Prydein, The Welsh Triads*, edited with Introduction, Translation and Commentary. Cardiff: University of Wales Press, 1961.

–. *Scotland and the Earliest Arthurian Tradition*, Bulletin Bibliographique de la Société Internationale Arthurienne, XV (1963), 85–95.

Bruce, James Douglas. *The Evolution of Arthurian Romance from the Beginnings down to the Year 1300*. 2 vols. 2nd ed., with a supplement by Alfons Hilka. Göttingen and Baltimore, 1928. (Reprinted, Peter Smith, 1958)

– ed. *Mort Artu*, an Old French prose romance of the XIIIth century, being the last division of the ›Lancelot du Lac‹, now first edited, from MS. 342 (fonds français) of the Bibliothèque Nationale, with collations from some other MSS. Halle: Niemeyer, 1910.

–. *Pelles, Pellinor and Pellean in the Old French Arthurian Romances*, Modern Philology, XVI (1918–19), 113–128, 337–350.

Brugger, Ernst. *Alain de Gomeret, ein Beitrag zur arthurischen Namenforschung.* Halle: Niemeyer, 1905. (Offprint from *Aus romanischen Sprachen und Literaturen: Festschrift für Heinrich Morf von seinen Schülern dargebracht.* Halle, 1905, pp. 53–96)

–. Bliocadran, the Father of Perceval, in *Medieval Studies in Memory of Gertrude Schoepperle Loomis*, ed. Roger Sherman Loomis. Paris: Champion, New York: Columbia, 1927, pp. 147–174.

Brunot, Ferdinand. *Histoire de la Langue française des origines à 1900*. Vol. I. *De l'époque latine à la Renaissance.* 3rd ed. Paris: Colin, 1924.

Brut. See Ivor Arnold.

Buffum, Douglas Labaree. *Le Roman de la Violette, ou de Gerart de Nevers* par Gerbert de Montreuil. Paris: Champion, 1928. (Société des anciens textes français)

Carduino. See Pio Rajna.

Carman, J. Neale. *The Perlesvaus and Bristol Channel.* Research Studies, a quarterly publication of Washington State University, XXXII (1964), 85–105.

–. *Prose Lancelot, III, 29.* Romance Philology, VI (1952–53), 179–186.

–. *The Relationship of the Perlesvaus and the Queste del Saint Graal.* Lawrence, Kansas: University of Kansas, 1936. (Bulletin of the University of Kansas, XXXVII [1935–36], no. 13, Humanistic Studies, vol. V, no. 4, July, 1936)

–. South Welsh Geography and British History in the *Perlesvaus*, in *A Medieval French Miscellany*, Papers of the 1970 Kansas Conference on Medieval French Literature. ed. Norris J. Lacey. Lawrence, Kansas: University of Kansas Publications, 1972, pp. 37–59. (Humanistic Studies, 42)

–. *A Study of the Pseudo-Map Cycle of Arthurian Romance* to investigate its historico-geographic background and to provide a hypothesis as to its fabrication. Lawrence, Kansas: The University Press of Kansas, 1973.

Carmody, Francis J. *Perceval le Gallois, roman du douzième siècle.* Berkeley, California, 1970. (Privately printed)

Catalogue of Additions to the Manuscripts in the British Museum in the years MDCCCC–MDCCCCV. London, 1907. (Catalogue no. 29)

Chambers, E. K. *Arthur of Britain.* London, 1927. (Reprinted 1964)

Chevalier au Lion (Yvain). See Mario Roques.

Chevalier de la Charrete (Lancelot). See Mario Roques.

Chevaliers as deus espees. See Wendelin Foerster.

Cligés. See Alexandre Micha.

Constans, Léopold. *Le Roman de Troie par Benoit de Sainte-Maure,* publié d'après tous les manuscrits connus. Vol. V. Paris: Didot, 1909. (Société des anciens textes français 1904)

Conte du Graal. See Gottfried Baist, Alfons Hilka, Charles Potvin and William Roach.

Cosman, Madeleine Pelner. *The Education of the Hero in Arthurian Romance.* Chapel Hill: University of North Carolina Press, 1965, 1966.

Cross, Tom Peete. *Motif Index of Irish Myths.* Bloomington, Indiana, 1952. (Indiana University Publications, Folklore Series, no. 7, 1952)

– and Clark Harris Slover eds. *Ancient Irish Tales.* New York: Henry Holt, 1936.

Curtis, Renée L. *Le Roman de Tristan en Prose.* Vol. I. Munich: Hueber, 1963.

–. *Tristan Studies.* Munich: Fink, 1969.

Dictionnaire d'histoire et de géographie ecclésiastiques. 16 vols. Paris, 1912–. (to »Falloux«)

Durmart le Galois. See Joseph Gildea.

Ebeling, Georg ed. *Auberee, altfranzösische Fablel,* mit Einleitung und Anmerkungen. Halle: Niemeyer, 1895.

Ekwall, Eilert ed. *The Concise Oxford Dictionary of English Place-Names.* 4th ed. Oxford: At the Clarendon Press, 1960.

Elwert, W. Theodor. *Traité de Versification française des origines à nos jours.* Paris: Klincksieck, 1965. (Bibliothèque Française et Romane, Série A: Manuels et Etudes linguistiques, 8)

Erec et Enide. See Wendelin Foerster and Mario Roques.

Evans, Dafydd. *Lanier, histoire d'un mot.* Geneva: Droz, 1967. (Publications Romanes et Françaises, 93)

Ewert, Alfred ed. *The Romance of Tristran by Béroul,* a Poem of the Twelfth Century. 2 vols. Oxford: Blackwell, 1939–70. (Volume I reprinted 1971)

Faider, Paul and Mme Faider-Feytmans. *Catalogue des manuscrits de la Bibliothèque Publique de la ville de Mons.* Ghent and Paris, 1931. (Universiteit te Gent, Werken uitgegeven door de Faculteit der Wijsbegeerte en Letteren, 65)

Farnsworth, William Oliver. *Uncle and Nephew in the Old French Chansons de Geste,* a study in the survival of Matriarchy. New York: Columbia University Press, 1913. (Columbia University Studies in Romance Philology and Literature, 14)

Flutre, Louis-Fernand. *Table des noms propres, avec toutes leurs variantes figurant dans les Romans du Moyen Age écrits en français ou en provençal et actuellement publiés ou analysés.* Poitiers, 1962. (Publication du Centre d'Etudes Supérieures de Civilisation Médiévale, 2)

Foerster, Wendelin ed. *Li Chevaliers as deus espees,* altfranzösische Abenteurroman. Halle: Niemeyer, 1877.

–. Chrétien de Troyes. *Erec und Enide.* Halle: Niemeyer, 1890. (Kristian von Troyes Sämtliche Werke, III); 2nd ed. 1909. (Romanische Bibliothek, XIII)

– and Hermann Breuer eds. *Les mervelles de Rigomer von Jehan,* altfranzösischer Artusroman des XIII. Jahrhunderts. 2 vols. Dresden, 1908–15. (Gesellschaft für romanische Literatur, 19, 39)

–. *Wörterbuch zu Kristian von Troyes' sämtlichen Werken.* Zweite veränderte Auflage von Hermann Breuer. Halle: Niemeyer, 1933. (Romanische Bibliothek, 21)

70

Fouché, Pierre. *Le Verbe français, étude morphologique.* 2nd ed. Paris: Klincksieck, 1967. (Tradition de l'humanisme, IV)

Foulet, Lucien. *Petite Syntaxe de l'ancien français.* 3rd ed. Paris: Champion, 1930. (Classiques français du moyen âge, 21. 2e série: Manuels. Reprinted 1966)

–. *Sire, Messire,* Romania, LXXI (1950), 1–48, 180–221; LXXI (1951), 31–77, 324–367, 479–528.

Fourquet, J. *Wolfram d'Eschenbach et le Conte del Graal,* les divergences de la tradition du *Conte del Graal* de Chrétien et leur importance pour l'explication du *Parzival.* Paris, 1938. (Publications de la Faculté des Lettres de l'Université de Strasbourg, 87. 2nd ed. Paris: Presses Universitaires de France, 1966, Publications de la Faculté des Lettres et Sciences Humaines de Paris-Sorbonne, Série ›Etudes et Méthodes‹, 17)

Frappier, Jean. *Chrétien de Troyes.* Paris: Hatier, 1957. (Connaissance des Lettres, no. 50. 3rd ed. 1968)

–. *Chrétien de Troyes et le mythe du Graal,* étude sur *Perceval* ou le *Conte du Graal.* Paris: Société d'édition d'enseignement supérieur, 1972.

–. *Etude sur la Mort le Roi Artu, roman du XIIIe siècle, dernière partie du Lancelot en Prose.* Paris: Droz, 1936. (2nd ed. Geneva: Droz, Paris: Minard, 1961, Publications Romanes et Françaises, 70)

– ed. *La Mort le Roi Artu,* roman du XIIIe siècle. Paris: Droz, 1936. (3rd ed. Geneva: Droz, Paris: Minard, 1964, Textes littéraires français, 58)

–. Sur le *Perceval en Prose* de 1530, in *Fin du Moyen Age et Renaissance, Mélanges de philologie française offerts à Robert Guiette.* Antwerp: De Nederlandsche Boekhandel, 1961, pp. 233–247.

–. *Le Roman Breton. Introduction des origines à Chrétien de Troyes. (Les origines de la légende arthurienne: Chrétien de Troyes.)* Paris: Centre de Documentation Universitaire, n.d. (»Les Cours de Sorbonne«)

–. *Le Roman Breton. Perceval ou le Conte du Graal.* Paris: Centre de Documentation Universitaire, 1953, 1966. (»Les Cours de Sorbonne«)

Friedwagner, Mathias. Raoul von Houdenc. *Meraugis von Portlesguez.* Halle: Niemeyer, 1897. (*Sämtliche Werke,* I)

Gallais, Pierre. *Formules de conteur et interventions d'auteur dans les manuscrits de la Continuation-Gauvain,* Romania, LXXXV (1964), 181–229.

Gautier, Léon. *La Chevalerie.* 3rd ed. Paris: Welter, 1895.

Geiriadur Prifysgol Cymru, a Dictionary of the Welsh Language. Caerdydd: Gwasg Prifysgol Cymru, 1950–. (To Fasc. xxiii, *gorsaf,* 1970).

Gerbert de Montreuil. See Mary Williams (*Perceval* Continuation) and Douglas Labaree Buffum (*Roman de la Violette*).

Giffin, Mary E. *A Reading of Robert de Boron,* Publications of the Modern Language Association of America, LXXX (1965), 499–507.

Gildea, Joseph, O.S.A. ed. *Durmart le Galois,* roman arthurien du treizième siècle. 2 vols. Pennsylvania: The Villanova Press, 1965–66.

– ed. *Partonopeu de Blois,* a French Romance of the Twelfth Century. 2 vols. Pennsylvania: The Villanova Press, 1967–70.

Gliglois. See Charles H. Livingston.

Golther, Wolfgang. *Parzival und der Gral in der Dichtung des Mittelalters und der Neuzeit.* Stuttgart, 1925.

Gossen, Charles Théodore. *Grammaire de l'ancien picard.* 2nd ed. Paris: Klincksieck, 1970. (Bibliothèque Française et Romane, Série A: Manuels et Etudes linguistiques, 19)

Griffith, R. H. *Sir Perceval of Galles: A Study of the Sources of the Legend.* Chicago, 1911.

Groome, Francis H. *Ordnance Gazetteer of Scotland.* 3 vols. London: Caxton, 1903.

Haidu, Peter. *Aesthetic Distance in Chrétien de Troyes: Irony and Comedy in Cligés and Perceval.* Geneva: Droz, 1968. (Histoire des Idées et Critique littéraire, 87)

Hatcher, Anna Granville. *From »ce suis je« to »c'est moi« (The ego as Subject and as Predicative in Old French),* Publications of the Modern Language Association of America, LXIII (1948), 1053–1100.

Heinzel, Richard. *Über die französischen Gralromane.* Vienna, 1891. (Denkschriften der kaiserlichen Akademie der Wissenschaften in Wien, philosophisch-historische Classe, XL, Abhandlung 3)

Henry, Albert. *Etudes de Syntaxe expressive, ancien français et français moderne.* Paris, 1960. (Université Libre de Bruxelles, Travaux de la Faculté de Philosophie et Lettres, 19)

– ed. *Le Jeu de Saint Nicolas de Jehan Bodel.* Brussels, Paris, 1962. (Université Libre de Bruxelles, Travaux de la Faculté de Philosophie et Lettres, 21)

– ed. *Les Œuvres d'Adenet le Roi.* Tome I, *Biographie d'Adenet, la Tradition manuscrite.* Bruges: De Tempel, 1951; tome II, *Beuvon de Conmarchis.* Bruges: De Tempel, 1953; tome III, *Les Enfances Ogier.* Bruges: De Tempel, 1956. (Rijksuniversiteit te Gent, Werken uitgegeven door de Faculteit van de Wijsbegeerte en Letteren, nos. 109, 115, 121); tome IV, *Berte aus grans piés.* Brussels and Paris, 1963; tome V, vol. I, *Cleomadés. Texte.* Brussels, 1971; tome V, vol. II, *Cleomadés. Introduction, Notes, Tables.* Brussels, 1971. (Université Libre de Bruxelles, Travaux de la Faculté de Philosophie et Lettres, 23 and 46)

Hilka, Alfons. *Die Jugendgeschichte Percevals im Prosa-Lancelot und im Prosa-Tristan,* Zeitschrift für romanische Philologie, LII (1932), 513–536.

– ed. *Der Percevalroman (Li Contes del Graal) von Christian von Troyes,* unter Benutzung des von Gottfried Baist nachgelassenen handschriftlichen Materials. Halle: Niemeyer, 1932. (Christian von Troyes sämtliche erhaltene Werke, herausgegeben von Wendelin Foerster, V)

Hippeau, C. *Messire Gauvain, ou La Vengeance de Raguidel,* poème de la Table Ronde par le trouvère Raoul. Paris, 1862. (Collection des poètes français du moyen âge)

Histoire littéraire de la France, ouvrage commencé par des religieux bénédictins de la Congrégation de Saint-Maur et continué par des Membres de l'Institut (Académie des inscriptions et belles-lettres). 39 vols. Paris, 1865–1952.

Hoepffner, Ernest. *La Folie Tristan de Berne.* 2nd ed. Paris, 1949. (Publications de la Faculté des Lettres de l'Université de Strasbourg, Textes d'Etude, 3)

–. *La Folie Tristan d'Oxford.* 2nd ed. Paris, 1943. (Publications de la Faculté des Lettres de l'Université de Strasbourg, Textes d'Etude, 8. Reprinted 1963)

Holland, Wilhelm Ludwig. *Crestien von Troies, eine literaturgeschichtliche Untersuchung.* Tübingen, 1854.

–. *Über eine Handschrift von Crestiens Gedichte li Contes del Graal,* Germania, II (1857), 426–427.

Hopkins, Annette Brown. *The Influence of Wace on the Arthurian Romances of Chrestien de Troies.* Menasha, Wisconsin: Banta, 1913.

Hunt, Tony. *The Prologue to Chrestien's »Li Contes del Graal«,* Romania, XCII (1971), 359–379.

Hutchings, Gweneth ed. *Le Roman en prose de Lancelot du Lac, le Conte de la charrette.* Paris: Droz, 1938.

Ivy, Robert H. *The Manuscript Relations of Manessier's Continuation of the Old French Perceval.* Philadelphia: University of Pennsylvania, 1951. (Romance Languages and Literatures, Extra series, no. 11)

Kennedy, Elspeth. The Scribe as Editor, in *Mélanges de langue et de littérature du moyen âge et de la Renaissance offerts à Jean Frappier (q.v.).* Vol. I, 523–531.

Lachmann, Karl ed. *Wolfram von Eschenbach.* 6th ed., rev. Eduard Hartl. Berlin and Leipzig: de Gruyter, 1926. (Reprinted 1965)

Långfors, Arthur. *Les Incipit des poèmes français antérieurs au XVIe siècle,* répertoire bibliographique, établi à l'aide de notes de M. Paul Meyer. Paris: Champion, 1917. (Reprinted 1970)

Langlois, Ernest. *Table des noms propres de toute nature compris dans les chansons de geste imprimés.* Paris: Bouillon, 1904.

Lanzelet. See K. G. T. Webster.

Lecoy, Félix ed. *Les Romans de Chrétien de Troyes,* édités d'après la copie de Guiot (Bibl. nat. fr. 794), vol. V, tome I, (to vs. 6008), *Le Conte du Graal (Perceval).* Paris: Champion, 1973. (Classiques français du moyen âge, 100)

Leitzmann, Albert ed. *Wolfram von Eschenbach.* 6th ed. Vol. I. Tübingen: Niemeyer, 1953. (Altdeutsche Textbibliothek, 12)

Lerch, Eugen. *Historische französische Syntax.* Vol. I. Leipzig: Reisland, 1925.

Levy, Raphael. *Chronologie approximative de la littérature française du moyen âge.* Tübingen: Niemeyer, 1957. (Beihefte zur Zeitschrift für romanische Philologie, 98)

Lister, John Thomas ed. *Perlesvaus, Hatton Manuscript 82, Branch I.* Menasha, Wisconsin: The Collegiate Press (George Banta), 1921. (University of Chicago Dissertation)

Livingston, Charles H. ed. *Gliglois,* a French Arthurian Romance of the Thirteenth Century. Cambridge: Harvard University Press, 1932. (Harvard Studies in Romance Languages, VIII)

Löfgren, Gunnel. *Etude sur les prépositions françaises OD, ATOUT, AVEC,* depuis les origines jusqu'au XVIe siècle. Uppsala, 1944.

Loomis, Roger Sherman ed. *Arthurian Literature in the Middle Ages: A Collaborative History.* Oxford, 1959, 1961. (Abbreviated *ALMA*)

–. *Arthurian Tradition and Chrétien de Troyes.* New York: Columbia University Press, 1949.

–. *Arthurian Tradition and Folklore,* Folklore, LXIX (1958), 1–25.

–. *Celtic Myth and Arthurian Romance.* New York: Columbia University Press, 1927. (Reprinted 1967 from revised edition of 1935)

–. *From Segontium to Sinadon – the Legends of a Cité Gaste,* Speculum, XXII (1947), 520–533.

–. *The Grail: from Celtic Myth to Christian Symbol.* Cardiff: University of Wales Press and New York: Columbia University Press, 1963.

–. The Origin of the Grail Legends, in *ALMA (q.v.),* pp. 274–294.

73

–. *Some Additional Sources of Perlesvaus*, Romania, LXXXI (1960), 492–499.

–. *Studies in Medieval Literature, a Memorial Collection of Essays*, ed. by Dorothy Bethurum Loomis, foreword by Albert C. Baugh and bibliography by Ruth Roberts. New York: Burt Franklin, 1970.

Löseth, Eilert. *Le Roman en Prose de Tristan, le Roman de Palamède, et la Compilation de Rusticien de Pise*, analyse critique, d'après les manuscrits de Paris. Paris: Bouillon, 1890.

Lot, Ferdinand. *Les Auteurs du Conte du Graal*, Romania, LVII (1931), 117–136.

–. *Etude sur le Lancelot en Prose*. Paris: Champion, 1918. (Bibliothèque de l'Ecole des Hautes Etudes, no. 226. Reprinted 1954 with additions by M. Lot-Borodine.)

Loth, J. *Contributions à l'étude des Romans de la Table Ronde*. Paris: Champion, 1912.

–. *Les Mabinogion, du Livre Rouge de Hergest*, avec les variantes du *Livre Blanc de Rhydderch*, traduits du gallois avec une introduction, un commentaire explicatif et des notes critiques. 2 vols. Paris: Fontemoing, 1913.

Lybeaus Desconus. See M. Mills.

Mandel, Jerome and Bruce A. Rosenberg eds. *Medieval Literature and Folklore Studies, Essays in Honor of Francis Lee Utley*. New Brunswick, N.J.: Rutgers University Press, 1970.

Manessier's Continuation. See Robert H. Ivy and Charles Potvin.

The Manly Anniversary Studies in Language and Literature. Chicago: University of Chicago Press, 1923.

Marx, Jean. *La Légende arthurienne et le Graal*. Paris, 1952. (Bibliothèque de l'Ecole des Hautes Etudes, Section des Sciences religieuses, LXIV)

–. *Nouvelles Recherches sur la littérature arthurienne*. Paris: Klincksieck, 1965. (Bibliothèque Française et Romane, Série C: Etudes littéraires, IX)

Mélanges de langue et de littérature du moyen âge et de la Renaissance offerts à Jean Frappier, Professeur à la Sorbonne, par ses collègues, ses élèves et ses amis. 2 vols. Geneva: Droz, 1970. (Publications Romanes et Françaises, CXII)

Meraugis de Portlesguez. See Mathias Friedwagner.

Meyer, Paul. Review of Charles Potvin, *Perceval le Gallois*, vol. I *(q.v.)*, in Revue Critique d'Histoire et de Littérature, I, no. 35 (September 1866), 129–137.

Micha, Alexandre. Miscellaneous French Romances in Verse, in *ALMA (q.v.)*, pp. 358–392.

– ed. *Les Romans de Chrétien de Troyes*, édités d'après la copie de Guiot (Bibl. nat. fr. 794), vol. II, *Cligés*. Paris: Champion, 1957. (Classiques français du moyen âge, no. 84. Reprinted 1965)

–. *La Tradition manuscrite des romans de Chrétien de Troyes*. Geneva: Droz, 1966. (Publications Romanes et Françaises, XC. Reprinting of 1939 edition)

Michelant, Henri and Paul Meyer eds. *L'Escoufle, roman d'aventure*, publié pour la première fois d'après le manuscrit unique de l'Arsenal. Paris: Didot, 1894. (Société des anciens textes français)

Mills, M. ed. *Lybeaus Desconus*. Oxford University Press, 1969. (Early English Text Society, 261)

Morawski, Joseph ed. *Proverbes français* antérieurs au XVe siècle. Paris: Champion, 1925. (Classiques français du moyen âge, 47)

Morcovescu, Nicolas. La Légende de Gauvain dans les romans du Graal avant 1200. Philadelphia, 1963. (Unpublished Doctoral Dissertation, University of Pennsylvania, 1963)

Morris, Lewis. Celtic Remains. London: J. Parker, 1878.

Mort Artu. See James Douglas Bruce, Jean Frappier and H. Oskar Sommer.

Newell, William Wells. The Legend of the Holy Grail, Part VII, Journal of American Folklore, XV (1902), 54–55.

Newstead, Helaine. Bran the Blessed in Arthurian Romance. New York: Columbia University Press, 1939. (Columbia University Studies in English and Comparative Literature, 141)

–. The »Enfances« of Tristan and English Tradition, in Studies in Medieval Literature in Honor of Professor Albert Croll Baugh, ed. MacEdward Leach. Philadelphia: University of Pennsylvania Press, 1961, pp. 169–185.

–. Perceval's Father and Welsh Tradition, The Romanic Review, XXXVI (1945), 3–31.

Nitze, William A. and Harry F. Williams. Arthurian Names in the Perceval of Chrétien de Troyes, Analysis and Commentary. Berkeley and Los Angeles: University of California Press, 1955. (University of California Publications in Modern Philology, vol. 38, no. 3, pp. 265–298, 1 map)

–. The Fisher King and the Grail in Retrospect, Romance Philology, VI (1952–53), 14–22.

–. The Fisher King in the Grail Romances, Publications of the Modern Language Association of America, XXIV (1909), 365–418.

– and T. Atkinson Jenkins eds. Le Haut Livre du Graal, Perlesvaus. 2 vols. Chicago: University of Chicago Press, 1932–37. (The Modern Philology Monographs of the University of Chicago)

–. On the Chronology of the Grail Romances. II: The Date of Robert de Boron's Metrical Joseph, in The Manly Anniversary Studies in Language and Literature. Chicago: University of Chicago Press, 1923, pp. 300–314.

–. Perceval and the Holy Grail: An Essay on the Romance of Chrétien de Troyes. Berkeley and Los Angeles: University of California Press, 1949. (University of California Publications in Modern Philology, vol. 28, no. 5, pp. 281–331)

– ed. Robert de Boron. Le Roman de l'Estoire dou Graal. Paris: Champion, 1927. (Classiques français du moyen âge, 57)

–. The Sister's Son and the Conte del Graal, Modern Philology, IX (1911–12), 291–322.

Nutt, Alfred T. Studies on the legend of the Holy Grail with especial reference to the hypothesis of its Celtic origin. London, 1888.

Nyrop, Kr. Grammaire historique de la langue française. 6 vols. Copenhagen, Leipzig, New York, Paris: vol. I, 5th ed., 1935; vol. II, 5th ed., printed 1968; vol. III, 2nd ed., 1936; vol. V, 1925.

O'Gorman, Richard F. An Edition of the Prose Version of Robert de Boron's Joseph d'Arimathie. Philadelphia, 1962. (Unpublished Doctoral Dissertation, University of Pennsylvania, 1962)

–. The Prose Version of Robert de Boron's Joseph d'Arimathie, Romance Philology, XXIII (1969–70), 449–461.

– La Tradition manuscrite du Joseph d'Arimathie en prose de Robert de Boron, Revue de l'Histoire des textes, I (1971), pp. 145–181.

Oman, Charles. *A History of the Art of War*, the Middle Ages from the Fourth to the Fourteenth Century. London: Methuen, 1905.

Orlandi, Ioannes ed. *Navigatio Sancti Brendani*. Vol. I. Milan, Varese: Cisalpino, 1968.

Owen, D. D. R. *The Evolution of the Grail Legend*. Edinburgh and London, 1968. (St. Andrews University Publications, LVIII)

Painter, Sidney, *French Chivalry*, Chivalric Ideas and Practices in Mediaeval France. Baltimore: Johns Hopkins Press, 1940. (Reprinted 1957, Cornell University Press, Great Seal Books)

Panzer, Friedrich. *Gahmuret, Quellenstudien zu Wolframs Parzival*. Heidelberg: Winter, 1940. (Sitzungsberichte der Heidelberger Akademie der Wissenschaften, philosophisch-historische Klasse, Jahrgang 1939–40, 1. Abhandlung)

Paris, Gaston. Meraugis de Portlesguez, in *Histoire littéraire de la France (q.v.)*, XXX (1888), 220–237.

– and Jacob Ulrich eds. *Merlin, roman en prose du XIIIe siècle*, publié avec la mise en prose du poème de Merlin de Robert de Boron, d'après le manuscrit appartenant a M. Alfred H. Huth. 2 vols. Paris, 1886. (Société des anciens textes français)

–. Rigomer, par Jehan, in *Histoire littéraire de la France (q.v.)*, XXX (1888), 86–96.

Pauphilet, Albert. *Chrestien de Troyes, le Manuscrit d'Annonay*. Paris: Droz, 1934.

–. *Etudes sur la Queste del Saint Graal, attribuée à Gautier Map*. Paris: Champion, 1921.

–. *Le Legs du Moyen Age, études de littérature médiévale*. Melun: d'Argences, 1950.

– ed. *La Queste del Saint Graal, roman du XIIIe siècle*. Paris: Champion, 1923, 1949. (Classiques français du moyen âge, 33. Reprinted 1967)

Pickford, Cedric E. Miscellaneous French Prose Romances, in *ALMA (q.v.)*, 348–357.

Plummer, Charles. *Bethada Náem nÉrenn, Lives of Irish Saints*, Edited from the Original MSS. with Introduction, Translations, Notes, Glossary and Indexes. Vol. I. Oxford: At the Clarendon Press, 1922.

Pope, Mildred K. *From Latin to Modern French with Especial Consideration of Anglo-Norman*. Rev. ed. Manchester University Press, 1952. (Publications of the University of Manchester, 229, French Series no. VI. Reprinted 1966)

Potvin, Charles. *Bibliographie de Chrestien de Troyes*, Comparaison des manuscrits de Perceval le Gallois. Un manuscrit inconnu. Chapitres uniques du manuscrit de Mons. Autres fragments inédits. Brussels, Leipzig, Ghent, Paris, 1863.

– ed. *Chrestien de Troyes. Perceval le Gallois, publié d'après le manuscrit de Mons*. 6 vols. Mons, 1865–1871. (Société des Bibliophiles Belges séant à Mons, 21): vol. I, *Chrestien de Troyes. Perceval le Gallois*, verses 1–9190 (1865); vol. II, *Perceval le Gallois ou le Conte du Graal*, Première Partie: le Roman en Prose [Perlesvaus] (1866); vol. III, *Perceval le Gallois ou le Conte du Graal*, Deuxième Partie: le Poème, verses 9191–10601, First Continuation, verses 10602–20148 (1866); vol. IV, *Idem*, verses 20149–21916, Second Continuation, verses 21917–30498 (1868); vol. V, *Idem*, verses 30499–34934, Manessier, verses 34935–40472 (1870); vol. VI, *Idem*, verses 40473–45379 (1871).

–. *Le Perceval de Chrestien de Troyes. Un manuscrit inconnu. Fragment unique de ce manuscrit*, Jahrbuch für romanische und englische Literatur, V (1864), 26–50.

Rachbauer, Sister Mary Aloysia. *Wolfram von Eschenbach,* a study of the relation of the content of Books III–VI and IX of the *Parzival* to the Crestien manuscripts. Washington: The Catholic University of America, 1934. (The Catholic University of America Studies in German, vol. IV)

Rajna, Pio ed. *I Cantari di Carduino,* giuntovi quello di *Tristano* e *Lancielotto* quando combattettero al petrone di Merlino. Bologna, 1873. (Poemetti Cavallereschi) (Reprinted in *Scelta di Curiosità Letterarie,* inedite o rare, dal secolo XIII al XIX, in appendice alla Collezione di Opere inedite o rare. Vol. XXXVII, Dispensa 135. Bologna: Commissione per i testi di lingua, 1968)

Rickard, Peter. *Britain in Medieval French Literature, 1100–1500.* Cambridge, England: At the University Press, 1956.

Ritchie, R. L. Graeme. *Chrétien de Troyes and Scotland.* The Zaharoff Lecture for 1952. Oxford: At the Clarendon Press, 1952.

Roach, William. The Conclusion of the *Perceval* Continuation in Bern MS. 113, in *Studies in Medieval Literature in Honor of Professor Albert Croll Baugh,* ed. MacEdward Leach. Philadelphia: University of Pennsylvania Press, 1961, pp. 245–254.

– ed. *The Continuations of the Old French Perceval of Chrétien de Troyes.* 4 vols. Philadelphia: The American Philosophical Society, 1949–71. (Vols. I and II reprinted 1965)

– ed. *The Didot-Perceval According to the Manuscripts of Modena and Paris.* Philadelphia: University of Pennsylvania Press, 1941.

– ed. *The Modena Text of the Prose Joseph d'Arimathie,* Romance Philology, IX (1955–56), 313–342.

– ed. *Le Roman de Perceval ou Le Conte du Graal,* publié d'après le MS fr. 12576 de la Bibliothèque Nationale. 2nd ed. Geneva: Droz, Paris: Minard, 1959. (Textes littéraires français, 71)

–. *Transformations of the Grail Theme in the First Two Continuations of the Old French Perceval,* Proceedings of the American Philosophical Society, CX (1966), 160–164.

Romans du Graal aux XIIe et XIIIe siècles, Les. Paris, 1956. (Colloques internationaux du Centre National de la Recherche Scientifique, III)

Roques, Mario ed. *Les Romans de Chrétien de Troyes édités d'après la copie de Guiot* (Bibl. nat. fr. 794): vol. I, *Erec et Enide,* 1952; vol. III, *Le Chevalier de la Charrete,* 1958; vol. IV, *Le Chevalier au Lion (Yvain),* 1960. Paris: Champion, 1952–60. (Classiques français du moyen âge, 80, 86, 89. Reprinted 1963–65)

Rupp, Theodore H. The Influence of Chrétien de Troyes on Jehan's *Les Mervelles de Rigomer.* Philadelphia, 1954. (Unpublished Doctoral Dissertation, University of Pennsylvania, 1954)

Sandkühler, Konrad tr. *Gauwain sucht den Gral, erste Fortsetzung des »Perceval« von Chrestien de Troyes.* Stuttgart, 1959.

Schlauch, Margaret. Review of Albert W. Thompson. *The Elucidation, a Prologue to the Conte del Graal (q.v.),* in The Romanic Review, XXIII (1932), 148–150.

Schofield, William Henry. *Studies on the Libeaus Desconus.* Boston: Ginn and Co., 1895. (Harvard Studies and Notes in Philology and Literature, 4)

Schultz, Alwin. *Das höfische Leben zur Zeit der Minnesinger.* 2nd ed. 2 vols. Leipzig: Hirzel, 1889.

Schultz-Gora, Oskar. *Zwei altfranzösische Dichtungen, La Chastelaine de Saint Gille, Du Chevalier au Barisel.* 4th ed. Halle: Niemeyer, 1919.

Schwan, Eduard and Dietrich Behrens. *Grammaire de l'ancien français,* tr. Oscar Bloch. 4th ed. Leipzig: Reisland, 1932.

Selmer, Carl ed. *»Navigatio Sancti Brendani Abbatis« from Early Latin Manuscripts.* Notre Dame, Indiana: University of Notre Dame Press, 1959. (Publications in Mediaeval Studies, The University of Notre Dame, XVI)

Sommer, Heinrich Oskar. *Galahad and Perceval,* Modern Philology, V (1907–08), 291–341.

–. *The Vulgate Version of the Arthurian Romances Edited from Manuscripts in the British Museum.* 7 vols. and Index. Washington, 1908–16. (Reprinted 1969)

Springer, Otto. Wolfram's *Parzival,* in *ALMA (q.v.),* pp. 218–250.

Stanton, Amida. Gerbert de Montreuil as a Writer of Grail Romance: An Investigation of the Date and the more Immediate Sources of the Continuation of *Perceval.* Chicago, 1939. (Unpublished Doctoral Dissertation, University of Chicago, 1939)

Stavenhagen, Lee. *A Legendary Backdrop for Gahmuret,* Rice University Studies, LIII (1967), 43–56.

Strucks, Carsten. *Der junge Parzival in Wolframs von Eschenbach »Parzival«, Crestiens von Troyes »conte del gral«, im englischen »Syr Percyvelle« und italienischen »Carduino«.* Borna–Leipzig, 1910. (Inaugural Dissertation)

Suchier, Hermann ed. *Aucassin et Nicolette,* texte critique, tr. Albert Counson. 7th ed. Paderborn, 1909.

Sweetser, Franklin P. *Blancandin et l'Orgueilleuse d'Amour,* roman d'aventures du XIIIᵉ siècle. Geneva: Droz, Paris: Minard, 1964. (Textes littéraires français, 112)

Tatlock, J. S. P. *Greater Irish Saints in Lawman and in England,* Modern Philology, XLIII (1945–46), 72–76.

–. *The Legendary History of Britain.* Geoffrey of Monmouth's *Historia Regum Britanniae* and its Early Vernacular Versions. Berkeley and Los Angeles: University of California Press, 1950.

Thompson, Albert Wilder. Additions to Chrétien's *Perceval* – Prologues and Continuations, in *ALMA (q.v.),* pp. 206–217.

–. *The Elucidation, a Prologue to the Conte del Graal.* New York: Publications of the Institute of French Studies, Inc., 1931.

–. Review of Alfons Hilka. *Der Percevalroman (q.v.),* in Modern Philology, XXX (1932–33), 438–441.

–. *The Text of the Bliocadran,* Romance Philology, IX (1955–56), 205–209.

Thompson, Stith. *Motif-Index of Folk-Literature.* 2nd ed. 6 vols. Bloomington, Indiana: Indiana University Press, 1955–58.

Tobler, Adolf. *Mélanges de Grammaire française,* traduction française de la deuxième édition par Max Kuttner avec la collaboration de Léopold Sudre. Paris, 1905.

–. *Le Vers français, ancien et moderne,* traduit sur la deuxième édition allemande par Karl Breul et Léopold Sudre, avec une préface par M. Gaston Paris. Paris, 1885. (Reprinted 1972)

–. *Vom französischen Versbau alter und neuer Zeit.* Leipzig: Hirzel, 1894.

Tyssens, Madeleine. Les Sources de Renaut de Beaujeu, in *Mélanges de langue et de littérature du moyen âge et de la Renaissance offerts à Jean Frappier (q.v.).* Vol. II, 1043–55.

Utley, Francis Lee. *Arthurian Romance and International Folktale Method*, Romance Philology, XVII (1963–64), 596–607.

Vengeance Raguidel. See C. Hippeau.

Vinaver, Eugène. *King Arthur's Sword, or the Making of a Medieval Romance*, Bulletin of the John Rylands Library, Manchester, XL (1957–58), 513–526.

–. *La Mort de Roland*, Cahiers de Civilisation médiévale, VII (1964), 133–143. (Reprinted in *A la Recherche d'une poétique médiévale*. Paris: Nizet, 1970)

–. *The Rise of Romance*. Oxford: At the Clarendon Press, 1971.

Viollet-le-Duc, Eugène Emmanuel. *Dictionnaire du mobilier français du moyen-âge de l'époque carolvingienne à la Renaissance*. 6 vols. Paris, 1858–75.

Viscardi, Antonio. Arthurian Influences on Italian Literature from 1200 to 1500, in *ALMA (q.v.)*, pp. 419–429.

Voyage of St. Brendan. See Ioannes Orlandi, Carl Selmer and E. G. R. Waters.

Wagner, Robert-Léon. *Les Phrases hypothétiques commençant par »si« dans la langue française, des origines à la fin du XVIe siècle*. Paris: Droz, 1939.

Waitz, Hugo. *Die Fortsetzungen von Chrestien's Perceval le Gallois nach den Pariser Handschriften*. Strasbourg: Trübner, 1890.

Waters, E. G. R. ed. *The Anglo-Norman Voyage of St. Brendan by Benedeit*, a poem of the early twelfth century. Oxford: At the Clarendon Press, 1928.

Webster, Kenneth G. T. trans. Ulrich von Zatzikhoven. *Lanzelet*, A Romance of Lancelot translated from the Middle High German. Revised and Provided with Additional Notes and an Introduction by Roger Sherman Loomis. New York: Columbia University Press, 1951.

–. The Twelfth-Century Tourney, in *Anniversary Papers by Colleagues and Pupils of George Lyman Kittredge*, presented on the completion of his twenty-fifth year of teaching in Harvard University, June, MCMXIII. New York: Russell and Russell, 1913, pp. 227–234. (Reissued 1967)

Weidner, Georg ed. Robert de Boron. *Der Prosaroman von Joseph von Arimathia*, *mit einer Einleitung ueber die handschriftliche Ueberlieferung*. Oppeln, 1881.

Weinberg, Bernard. *The Magic Chessboard in the Perlesvaus: an Example of Medieval Literary Borrowing*, Publications of the Modern Language Association of America, L (1935), 25–35.

West, G. D. *Grail Problems, I: Silimac the Stranger*, Romance Philology, XXIV (1970–71), 599–611; *Grail Problems, II: The Grail Family in the Old French Verse Romances*, Romance Philology, XXV (1971–72), 53–73.

–. *An Index of Proper Names in French Arthurian Verse Romances, 1150–1300*. Toronto: University of Toronto Press, 1969. (University of Toronto Romance Series, 15)

Weston, Jessie L. *The Legend of Sir Perceval*, Studies upon its Origin, Development, and Position in the Arthurian Cycle. 2 vols. London, 1906–09. (Grimm Library, 17 and 19)

–. *Wauchier de Denain as a continuator of Perceval and the Prologue of the Mons MS.*, Romania, XXXIII (1904), 333–343.

Wheatley, Henry B. ed. *Merlin or the Early History of King Arthur: a Prose Romance* (about 1450–1460 A.D.), edited from the unique ms. in the University Library, Cambridge, with an Introduction containing Outlines of the History of the Legend of Merlin by William Edward Mead. Vol. I. London, 1899. (Early English Text Society, 10. Reprinted 1969)

Whitehead, Frederick and Roger Sherman Loomis. The *Livre d'Artus*, in *ALMA* (q.v.), pp. 336–338.

Williams, G. Perrie. Renaut de Beaujeu. *Le Bel Inconnu*, roman d'aventures. Paris: Champion, 1929. (Classiques français du moyen âge, 38)

Williams, Mary ed. Gerbert de Montreuil. *La Continuation de Perceval*. 2 vols. Paris: Champion, 1922–25. (Classiques français du moyen âge, 28, 50)

–. *Essai sur la composition du roman gallois de Peredur*. Paris, 1909.

Williams, Robert. *Lexicon Cornu-Britannicum:* A Dictionary of the ancient Celtic language of Cornwall, in which words are elucidated by copious examples from the Cornish works now remaining; with translations into English. The synonyms are also given in the cognate dialects of Welsh, Armoric, Irish, Gaelic, and Manx; shewing at one view the connection between them. Llandovery: Roderic, London: Trubner, 1865.

Wilmotte, Maurice. *L'Etat actuel des études sur la légende du Gral*, Bulletin de l'Académie royale de Belgique, XV (1929), 100–122.

–. *Le Poème du Gral et ses auteurs*. Paris: Droz, 1930.

–. Review of Alfons Hilka. *Der Percevalroman (q.v.)*, in Romania, LIX (1933), 453–461.

–. *Le Roman du Gral* d'après les versions les plus anciennes, traduit et adapté avec introduction. Paris: La Renaissance du livre, 1930.

Woledge, Brian. *L'Atre périlleux*, études sur les manuscrits, la langue et l'importance littéraire du poème, avec un spécimen du texte. Paris: Droz, 1930.

– ed. *L'Atre périlleux*, roman de la table ronde. Paris: Champion, 1936. (Classiques français du moyen âge, 76)

Yvain. See Mario Roques.

Zeydel, Edwin H. and Bayard Quincy Morgan trans. *The Parzival of Wolfram von Eschenbach*. Chapel Hill: University of North Carolina, 1951. (University of North Carolina Studies in the Germanic Languages and Literatures, 5)

SUMMARY OF EPISODES

Episode I: 1–52
There were in Wales twelve brothers considered to be the richest and most powerful in the country. They were all held in high esteem and were brilliant knights who often gained fame in tournaments and battles. But, as often happens, even to a powerful man, misfortune befell them, and eleven had been killed. Only one of them remained, and this was Bliocadran. He was greatly grieved about his dead brothers, but one cannot mourn forever, and so he prepared to return to the tournaments. His wife and all his friends begged him to remain, for his country would be without its lord, sad and afflicted by his absence. He acceded to their pleas.

Episode II: 53–160
Two years have passed and his wife is about to give birth to their first child. All are joyful about this event for the people love their lord greatly. One day, close to the time of the birth of the child, a messenger comes riding hard to the castle. Bliocadran bids him welcome and offers him hospitality. The messenger, however, had not eaten that day and so asks for bread and wine immediately. After he has eaten, the lord asks him to tell his news. He announces that there is to be a tournament that week held by the King of Wales for his own people and those of Cornwall against those of the Gaste Fontaine. It promises to be a great tournament, worthy of being seen. Bliocadran replies immediately that he will come. The messenger goes on his way. The next morning Bliocadran orders preparations and summons his knights. This time he is not to be stopped by the pleas of his wife and his people. He departs, leaving everyone surprised and troubled.

Episode III: 161–243
Bliocadran and his knights arrive at the site of the tournament and lodge the night in a castle. The next day he and his men ride quickly to the tournament as they wish to be in the front ranks. In the first joust, Bliocadran unhorses his adversary and captures the mount as booty. A general mêlée follows. In the second joust with an excellent young warrior, a violent encounter ensues. Bliocadran is mortally wounded and falls to the ground in a swoon. His knights carry him back to the castle where they had lodged. In two days he is dead. His knights hold a fine service for him and, with much grief, they bury him.

Episode IV: 244–456

Three days after Bliocadran had left for the tournament his wife gave birth to a son. She immediately sent word to him. When her messenger arrived with the news, Bliocadran was already dead and there remained only his knights to rejoice about the son, which they could hardly do because of their grief. They warned the messenger that, when he returned, he was not to say a word to the lady about the death of her lord. Rather he was to say to her that they had all gone to the King who had held the tournament. The valet did as they said, telling the lady that the knights would not return before eight days. Eight days later the knights assembled to devise a plan. A spokesman proposed that they enlist the aid of an abbot to break the news to her. The abbot agreed and immediately set out to speak with the lady, asking the knights to remain behind until he had done so. He arranges a careful speech. He reminds her first about the love she should have for God »who was crucified for our sins. She should serve and honor Him. Whatever He gives her, she should receive with a good will. And so she will see that everyone dies and no one escapes«. Finally, he tells her that her lord is dead. She must consider her soul; may God make her strong! The abbot consoled and comforted her, but it was a bitter comfort. The knights then arrive and there is general mourning. Her grief is bitter and she laments her loss and the fact that she was ever born to suffer so greatly. The lady has masses sung, having called all the people together. And so she grieved for a long time, turning to her son for comfort.

Episode V: 457–655

Seven months passed and it was April. Many times the lady had pondered how she could keep her son from being a knight, from using arms or from even hearing about knighthood. If he were to die, as did his father and uncles, she would kill herself soon after. And so she decided to go to the waste forest. None of her people will know about this before her son is grown; he would see no one except those who would be around him. She summoned her steward, a fine man and the head of a large family. She tells him of her desire to leave and to live in the waste forest so that her son may not be killed. She wishes him to accompany her with his family. She cannot leave him behind, and he cannot stay behind. He, in turn, proposes a plan whereby she should call her people together and tell them she is going on a pilgrimage to St. Brendan of Scotland. They are to pledge themselves to her on behalf of her son and to acclaim him lord, holding the land in his name. She accepts his plan and immediately summons a parliament. She announces her pilgrimage and asks for their allegiance to her son. They protest that she stay longer or at least that she leave their young lord behind, but that is one thing she will not do. Many call out wishing to accompany her. She has her barons swear allegiance to a nephew whom they will obey until she and her son return. She had, however, a month before, already assembled

82

her belongings and sent them ahead. The day after the parliament she departed without delay.

Episode VI: 656–724

Travelling quickly, the lady arrived at Calfle, a castle on the sea of Wales. There she assembled all those who were to accompany her. Now with all her belongings, they travelled, scarcely stopping a day, until they entered the forest. And there they wandered fifteen days until they reached an isolated clearing, watered by a large stream. Isolated, beautiful and well provided with water, the spot is chosen for their dwelling. Her steward agrees with her choice and sets his eight sons to overseeing the work of building their refuge. The house is built and the land planted.

Episode VII: 725–800

Fourteen years have passed. The son now knows how to ride well and to handle the javelin. Her people had searched by land and sea but had never found her. They believed that she and her household must have perished in the sea, and so left off the search. The son came to believe there were no other people in the world but those around him since he had »de sens petit«. The mother sat him down and, embracing him, told him that, when hunting in the forest, if he should see men »dressed as though they were covered with iron«, they would be devils, and they would devour him. He is to retreat quickly, cross himself, not losing a moment, and to say his credo. He promises to follow her instructions. The next day he arose to hunt. When he returned at the end of the day his mother went to greet him, asking him to tell her what he found. »Diversion and pleasure« was his answer. The mother did not inquire further and the young man said no more.

BLIOCADRAN

1c

En la terre de Gale estoient
Dose frere qui molt valoient;
Cerquier peüst on la contree,
Tant come estoit et longe et lee, 4
Et le païs tout environ,

490 Mien essïent ne trovast on
Nul chevalier de si haut pris,
Si riche d'avoir ne d'amis, 8
De castiax ne de fermetés,
De bois, de rivieres, de pres.
Si estoient bon chevalier,
Hardi et combatant et fier, 12
Et sovent aloient par terres
As tornoiemens et as guerres

1d Por los et por pris conquester.
500 Mais d'els ne vos voel plus conter, 16
Mais bien vos puis dire [e]n la some
Que sovent mesciet a preudome
Et molt i ot de desconfort:
Li onse frere furent mort, 20
Que il n'en i remest c'uns seus
Qui les terres et les aleus
Aprés eus toutes maintenoit,
Car sages et preudom estoit, 24
Cortois, sages et emparlés:

510 Bilocadran ert apelés

P *rubric* Ci endroit comence li contes
del saint greail
1 L *large initial,* P *illuminated initial*
En le tiere
3 P Cerkier
5 P tot
6 P ensiant ni t.
7–8 *LP inv.*
8 P rice
9 P castiaus et de fremetes

10 P bos
12 P Hardit
16 P M. jou ne vos v. pas c.
17 P om.
19 P Car m.
22 P le tiere ot et les honeurs
23 P De tous eskeu li estoit
24 P Et s. et courtois e.
25 P Larges et molt bien e.
26 P Bliocadrans

El païs de toutes les gens.
Molt durement estoit dolens   28
De ses freres qui sont feni,
Molt en ert mornes et pensis.
Mais tout adés ne doit on mie
Duel demener, car c'est folie;   32
Ains doit on faindre c'on soit lié
Tele ore c'on est tout irié . . .
Home qui ne se velt retraire
520 De bien quant il le velt parfaire.   36
Mais cil ne volt plus delaier,
Ses armes fist aparellier
Et ses cevax tre[s] bien ferer;
As tornoiemens velt aler.   40
Mais sa feme et tout si ami
Li dïent: »Biax sire, merchi!
Remanés, si n'i alés mie,
Car ce sero[it] molt grant folie;   44
2a   Se vos i alés, çou saciés,
530 Que vostre terre lairïés
Toute seule, desconsellie,
Vostre gent dolante et irie.«   48
Tant li ont dit et tant proié
Que il lor a tous otroié
Que il n'ira n'ensi n'ensi.
Lié en sont quant il l'ont oï.   52

[L]i sire remest o sa feme,
      Qui mervelles ert prodefame,
Bien largement encor deus ans
540 Que ne porent avoir enfans,   56
Ne nul n'e[n] avoient eü,
Tant que Dex les a porveü

---

29 P fenis
31 P adies
32 P car cert f.
33 P on faire con s. lies
34 P eure con e. tous iries
35 P ki ne se viut
36 P viut
37 P vaut
39 P son ceval t. b. fierer
40 P tournoiemens viut
41 P femme
42 P biaus s. merci

43 P R. ci ni
44 P C. cou s. m. grans f.
45 P vous
46 P tiere laississies
47 P seul et desconsillie
50 P tout otroiie
51 P Quil nen ira ensi nensi
52 P Liet
53 LP large initial, P sires r. od sa
54 P Ka mervelles ert bone dame
56 P peurent
58 P ke

Si que la dame ençainte fu.
Grant joie en ont tout cil eü,   60
Qui lor seignor aiment de rien;
Et li sires, çou saciés bien,
En ot si grant joie a son cuer
Qu'il ne pot greignor a nul fuer   64
Avoir, ce saciés de verté.

550
La dame a tant l'enfant porté
Qu'ele fu pres de l'acoucier.
Ce fu un jor aprés mangier   68
Que li sire apoiés estoit
As fenestres, si esgardoit
Cex qui venoient le cemin.
Atant es vos sor un roncin   72
Un escuier errant tout droit,
Qui grant aleüre venoit.
Dedens la cort s'en est entrés,
Si descent devant les degrés.   76
Quant li sire le vit venir,
Son ceval comande a tenir
Si dist: »Amis, bien vegnes tu!«
Et cil li a tost respondu: 80
»Et vos soiés li bien trovés
Come chevaliers esprovés,
Fait li vallés, biax sire ciers«,
Qui n'estoit mie si laniers   84
De respondre, ançois fu senés.

570
Li sire dist: »Se m'en creés,
Vos remanrés anuit mais ci;
Bon ostel arés, je vos di,   88
Et si ferons de vos grant feste.«
– »Sire, fait il, ce puet bien estre,
Mais itant me faites doner
Pain et vin, si irai disner,   92

2b

550

570

61 *P* signor
63 *P* ot mout g.
64 *P* Que ne p. gregnor
65 *P* vrete
66 *P adds* Et tant venu et tant ale
67 *P* pries
68 *P* Cou
69 *P* apoiies
71 *P* Ceus ki

72 *P* vous
75 *P* le court en e.
77 *P* sires
79 *P* viegnes
81 *P* vous
83 *P* biaus
86 *P* sires d. se me c.
87 *P* Vous r. a. mes ci
88 *P* vous

86

Car je ne manjai encor hui.«
Et li sire respont celui:
»Mais assés«, tant con lui plaira.
580 Un chevalier apelé a,   96
Si dist: »Prendés cel escuier,
Faites li tost aparellier
A disner et pensés de lui,
Que il ne manja encor hui.«   100
Et cil maintenant l'en mena,
De çou qu'il pot honoré l'a;
Si li done assés a mangier,
En la sale les un vergier,   104
A bele ciere. Et quant il ot
590 As[s]és mangié, tant con lui plot,
2c La nape comande a oster,
Qu'il ne voloit plus demorer.   108
Fors de la cambre en est issus.
Li sire est contre lui venus
Si li a dit cortoisement:
»Biax amis, se Dex vos ament,   112
De vos noveles nos contés,
Des plus voires que vos savés.«
– »Certes, sire, jo vos dira[i],
600 Ja mençoignieres n'en serai,   116
Fait li vallés, se Dex m'ament,
Ja n'en mentirai de noient.
[L]i rois de Gales a empris
Por trestos cex de son païs   120
Et por tos cex de Cornuaille
Tornoiement qui ert sans faille
Vers cex de la Gaste Fontaine;
Ne velt pas que en lui remaigne,   124
Ains envoie par ceste terre
610 Por chevaliers cerquier et querrer,

93 *P* jou ne mangai encore h.		112 *P* Biaus
94 *P* sires		114 *P* vous
96 *P* apielet		115 *P* jel
97 *P* p. cest e.		116 *P* mencognieres
100 *P* Car il ne manga encore h.		119 *L* large initial
102 *P* De quanquil p.		120 *P* trestous ceus
103 *P* Et si li dona a m.		121 *P* tous ceus de cornualle
105 *P* Et biele c. q.		122 *P* Tornoiement q. e. s. falle
106 *P* com il pot		123 *P* ceus de le g.
108 *P* Que ne v.		124 *P* viut p. q. enlui remaingne
111 *P* courtoisement		126 *P* cierkier

Qu'il i vegnent a lor pooir;
Et le jour vos dirai por voir,   128
Que il i soient semedi.
Biax sire, por Deu, venés i,
Si verrés le tornoiement,
Les chevaliers et la grant gent   132
Quant il i seront tuit venu.«
Li sire li a respondu
Que il ira, se Dex le gart.

620   Li vallés atant se depart   136
Si s'en vait trestout son cemin.
Li sire lait dusqu'al matin
2d   Que il mande ses chevaliers,
Et si dist a ses escuiers   140
Q'aler velt au tornoiement,
Si s'atornent isnelement;
Et cil sont trestuit assamblé.
Quant il sont ensamble aüné,   144
Bliocadron en fist grant feste.

630   Li sire mais plus n'i areste;
Ses somiers ot fais tos cargier
Et son harnois aparellier.   148
Atant si chevalier s'en vont.
Cil de la vile proié ont
A mon seignor Bliocadron
Qu'il remansist en sa maison,   152
Et sa feme de cuer dolent
Li reproie molt dolcement.
Et il li dist: »Dame, taisiés,

640   De vostre duel vos apaisiés.«   156
Atant s'en est d'aus departis,
Laissiés les a tos esbahis;

127 P viengnent
128 P jour
129 P samedi
130 P Biaus s. p. dieu
132 P et le g.
133 P tout
134 P sires
137 P Qui sen
138 P sires l. jusqual
140 P Et comande s.
141 P Kaler viut
142 P Cil
143 L Et il s., P Et si s. trestout

144 P Et q. il s. tout a.
145 P Bliocadrans
146 P sires m. p. ni arreste
147 P a fait tost c.
149 P A. li c.
151 P monsignor blocadroon
153 P femme
154 P repria mout doucement (mout
       written in full)
156 P vos abaissies
157 P diaus
158 P tous

Et cil proient au Creator
Que il conduie lor seignor.   160

B liocadron est tant alés,
  Et cil qu'il a od lui menés,
Que il sont ensamble venu
Pres del camp ou li tornois fu;   164
Mais a destre main l'ont laissié,
En un castel sont herbergié;
Bel ostel orent a talent
Li sire et trestoute sa gent.   168
A l'endemain plus n'i estont,
Au tornoiement venu sont.
Et quant il furent tuit ensamble,
Armé se sont, si con moi samble,   172
Et desor les cevax monterent.
Et cil dela molt se hasterent
Si vinrent ausi radement
Come quarriax quant il destent;   176
Et li nostre trestot serré
Cevaucierent vers la cité
Tout le passet la u s'en vont.
Bliocadron el premier front   180
Avoec lui ot ses chevaliers,
Qu'il voloit estre tous premiers
Por le tornoi acomencier.
Atant es vos el cief premier   184
Un chevalier qui tost randone,
Et Bliocadras esperone,
Qui molt l'avoit de loig visé.
Et cil le ra bien avisé,   188
Si se rest adreciés vers lui
Et s'entrefierent ambedui.

650

3a

660

670

159 P creatour
160 P signor
161 LP *large initial*, P Bliocadrans
     a t. ale
162 P mene
164 P Au castiel ou li tournois
165 P a diestre sont herbegie
166 P un ostel mout aaisie
167 P Et il lorent bon a t.
173 P cevaus
176 P quariaus q. il descent

177 P trestout siere
178 P Chevaucierent
179 P la il sen
180 P Bliocadran
182 P iestre
183 P aucomencier
184 P vous
185 P ki
186 P bliocadrans esporonne
187 P lonc
190 P Si

Mais cil le fiert premierement
Sor son escu par maltalent   192
Si que sa lance brise et frosse,
Et Bliocadras par angoisse
Le fiert el pis sos le mamele
680   Que parmi l'arçon de la sele   196
Le mist a terre contreval
Parmi la crupe del ceval.
Lors l'a a un vallet doné
Qui dusqu'au harnois l'a mené;   200
La sele et le frain ont osté.
Et tout li autre [i] ont josté
3b   A cele fois molt fierement.
Ainc le jor n'i perdi nïent   204
Bliocadras, si bien l'ot fait
690   Que tout le loënt de son fait,
Car molt l'ot fait et bien et bel.
Atant voit venir un dansel   208
Grant et fort et bien a ceval;
Molt estoient andoi vassal.
De tant com il porent viser
Ne finerent d'esperoner,   212
Si se vinrent entreferir.
Bliocadras fiert par aïr
Que li escus peçoie et fent;
700   Mais li haubers pas ne desment   216
Et sa lance li vole en clices,
Si que cil le voient des lices.
Cil ra Bliocadran feru
Par desus l'orle de l'escu   220
Enmi le vis, parmi la ciere,
Que par le haterel deriere

192 *P* Sour s. e. p. mautelent   206 *P* de cel f.
193 *P* Si ke sa l. b. et froisçe   207 *P* Que m. lot fet
194 *P* bliocadrans p. angoisce   210 *P* andui
195 *P* s. la m.   211 *P* con
197 *P* a tiere del ceval   212 *P* desporonner
198 *P* la c. contreval   213 *P* vienent
199 *P* dounet   214 *P* Bliocadrans
200 *P* Que jusquau h. la menet   216 *P* haubiers
201 *P* siele   217 *P* lance v. en esclices
202 *P* jouste   219 *P* bliocadrans
203 *P* m. durement   220 *P* deseur
204 *P* Cel j. ni perdirent noient   221 *P* Emmi le v. p. le c.
205 *P* Bliocadrans si b. la f.   222 *P* hateriel derriere

Paru tos li fers de la lance.
Il n'en puet mais se il balance, 224
Que il estoit a mort navrés;
710 A terre caï tos pasmés,
Mais li suen l'ont tost relevé,
Qui por lui ont grant duel mené. 228
Lors li fisent faire une biere,
Si l'en porterent en litiere
El castel u il ont esté;
Molt l'ont iluec reconforté, 232
Sel coucierent molt dolcement
En une cambre loig de gent,
3c Et si le firent bien confés.
720 Ne vesqui que deus jors aprés, 236
Que il fu mors sans demorer.
En un mostier l'ont fait porter;
Si compaignon grant duel en firent,
Lor dras et lor ceviax descirent. 240
Et quant il fu dedens l'eglise,
Si li firent molt bel service,
Puis le porterent enterrer.

De lui ne voel ci plus conter, 244
De lui ne del tornoiement,
730 Ançois vos voel dire coment
La dame, qui remese estoit
A son ostel, se maintenoit 248
Aprés çou que il s'en ala;
Que trois jors plus ne demora
Que la dame ot un damoisel;
Onques nus hom ne vit tant bel. 252
Au mostier le fisent porter
Sel font baptisier et lever.

223 *P* Parut tous li fiers
224 *P* Cil ne pot m.
226 *P* A tiere kai jus p.
227 *P* sien
228 *P* pour
230 *P* lemporterent
231 *P* castiel u il ot e.
233 *P* docement
234 *P* loing
235 *P* fisent b. confies
236 *P* apries
237 *P* il moru s.
238 *P* fet
239 *P* compagnon g. d. en fisent
240 *P* caveus detirent
242 *P* fisent
243 *P* lenporterent entierer
244 *P* ne vos voel plus nomer
245 *P* tournoiement
246 *P* Ains vos vorrai d.
247 *P* ki
250 *P* Que .iiii. jours ne d.
252 *P* v. plus b.

	Et quant il fu crestïenés,	
740	Ses nons fu isi apelés	256
	Con s'il onques ne fust seüs	
	Ne només ne amenteüs.	
	Par un vallet que ele avoit	
	A son segnor envoia droit	260
	La dame, car savoir voloit	
	Confaitement se maintenoit	
	Et qu'ele avoit un fil eü	
	Que onques mais si biax ne fu.	264
	Et cil qui dire li ala,	
750	Mort et enfoï le trova.	
3d	Les noveles q'a aportees	
	A a ses compaignons contees,	268
	Et il en furent tout molt lié,	
	Mais de lor seignor sunt irié	
	Si qu'il ne puent joie faire.	
	Atant li vallés s'en repaire	272
	Tout le cemin qu'il ot venu;	
	Et cil li ont bien deffendu	
	Qu'il ne desist n'a droit n'a tort	
760	Que lor sire fust ensi mors,	276
	Ains desist qu'il estoit alés	
	Au roi qui les avoit mandés,	
	Et si fist il de verité.	
	Et tant a le cemin erré	280
	Qu'en la vile entre a esperon,	
	Si descent dalés le dognon	
	U la dame gisoit amont.	
	Del vallet molt grant joie font	284
	Tout cil que il a encontrés.	
770	En la cambre s'en est entrés,	
	La dame et trestote sa gent	
	A salüé premierement	288

255 *P* crestiennes   268 *P* compagnons
256 *P* issi apieles   270 *P* signor sont
257 *P* f. veus   271 *P* porent
258 *P* Ne noncies ne apierceus 275 *P* tors
259 *P* elle   278 *P* ki
260 *P* signor   281 *P* Ken la v. e. a esporon
261 *L* d. por faire savoit   282 *P* dongnon
263 *P* kele   285 *P* ke
264 *P* m. plus biaus   286 *P* cambre en est (-l)
266 *P* enfoui   287 *P* trestoute
267 *P* ka

Et il fu molt bien respondus.
»Mes sire vos mande salus,
Fait li vallés, dame; et saciés
Qu'il ne fu onques mais si liés   292
De nul enfant con de cestui;
Molt en cremoit avoir anui,
Grant joie a de vostre peril
780   Q'avés passé et de son fil.   296
Et si vos di que s'il peüst
Que molt volentiers vos eüst
4a   Veüe; li rois l'a mandé
U il en sont trestot alé,   300
En Gales, le jor que g'i fui,
Que a lor muevre por voir fui,
Et tout si compaignon aprés:
Devant huit jors ne venront mes.«   304
Li dame qui el lit gisoit
790   De son seignor tres bien cuidoit
Que cil li desist verité
De çou qu'il l'avoit la trové,   308
Por çou qu'il l'afiçoit si bien;
Mais il ne li desist por rien,
C'on li avoit bien deffendu.
La dame a son termine fu   312
Tant que tans fu de relever.
Huit jors aprés sans demorer
Sont li chevalier assamblé,
800   Qui al tornoi erent alé   316
U li sire ot esté ocis.
»Seignor, molt somes entrepris,
Fait uns chevaliers, rices hom,
De çou que nos dit n'en avon   320

290 *P* Mesire
291 *P* v. et bien sacies
292 *P* Que ne
293 *P* e. que de
296 *P* Kaves
297 *P* vous
299 *P* Veu mais li
300 *P* trestout
302 *P* movoir
303 *P* compagnon
304 *L* D. .vii. j.
305 *LP* large initial, *P* La d. ki

306 *P* signor mout b. quidoit
308 *P* De son signor quot la t.
309 *P* Por ce quil
311 *P* desfendu
313 *P* ke t. fu del r.
314 *P* apries
316 *P* Q. dou t.
317 *P* Ou li s. ot e. hocis
318 *P* Signor
319 *P* hõ
320 *P* De coi ke nous d. n. avon

A ma dame de son seignor
Qui si est mors a grant dolor.
Mais une cose saciés bien,
Que ne li diroie por rien,   324
Mais ci pres a un bon abé,
810   Si li disons par carité
Q'a ma dame vegne parler.«
Lors font les cevax enseler   328
Et puis lor a on amenés,
Par l'estrier est cascuns montés:
4b   Tout ensamble d'iluec s'en von[t],
En l'abeïe venu sont.   332
L'abé et trestot le covent
Ont salüé premierement;
Puis ont de lor seignor conté,
820   Coment fu mors la verité,   336
Et de çou que n'en savoit rien
La dame, ains li celoit on bien,
Et por Deu dire li alast
Et aprés le reconfortast,   340
Que ele en avoit grant mestier.
Li abes sans plus delaier
A maintenant iluec mandé
Son palefroi; s'a comandé   344
A cex que remaignent enqui
830   Tant que il ait parlé a li:
»Que jo li voel premierement
Dire et mostrer tout mon talent,   348
Et puis revenrés aprés moi.«
Cascuns respont: »Et je l'otroi.«
L'abes et dui sergant s'en vont
Et dui moine, que plus n'i ont.   352
Tant ont cevalcié et esré
Li dui moinë o lor abé

321 *P* signor
324 *P* pour
325 *P* pries
327 *P* Qua ma d. viegne
328 *P* cevaus ensieler
332 *P* En labie venut en s.
333 *P* Labeit et trestout
335 *P* signor
337 *P* chou
339 *P* Que p. dieu
340 *P* apries

342 *P* a. saut sans d.
343 *P* Et m. a luec m.
345 *P* ceus kil remaient enki
346 *P* ke
347 *P* jou
348 *L* t. son t.
349 *P* apries
351 *P* doi serjant
352 *P* Et .ii. moines ke
353 *P* cevaucie et erre
354 *P* od

Que il sont el castel venu.
840   Li doi moine sont descendu,   356
Contremont les degrés monterent;
Li serjant les cevax garderent.
La dame ont trovee a itant
En la sale en un lit gisant,   360
Et quant ele venir les vit
Encontre l'abé sus sailli
4c   Si li dist: »Sire, bien vegniés.«
Li abes fu bien enseigniés,   364
Molt belement li respondi:
850   »Cil Dex qui onques ne menti
Vos saut et gart et beneïe
Et vos et vostre compaignie   368
Et maintiegne tos vos amis.«
Lors s'est bien pres de li assis,
Et d'autre part li moine andui
Se sont assis bien pres de lui   372
El lit molt deboinairement.
L'abes parla premierement,
Si li a par bele raison
860   Comencié un molt bel sermon.   376
Ançois que il volsist parler
Li dist: »Molt par devés amer
Celui qui vos done santé,
Et vos garde d'enfermeté,   380
Et nos raienst de nos peciés,
Et fu por nos crucefiés
Et resurrexi au tier jor.
Et vos, dame, por soie amor   384
Devrïés tout adés pener
870   A lui servir et honorer

355 *P* castiel
358 *P* cevaus
359 *P* t. gisant
360 *P* lit atant
361 *L* e. les vit venir, *P* elle
362 *P* salit
363 *P* vignies
364 *P* ensegnies
366 *P* ki
368 *P* vous et v. compaignie
369 *P* tous
371 *P* monne

372 *P* pries
373 *P* debounairement
375 *P* Si a dit p.
377 *P* vosist
378 *P* p. poes a.
379 *P* ki
380 *P* denfremete
382 *L* p. vos c., *P* crucefiies
383 *P* Et resuscita au tierc
384 *P* vous
385 *P* Deveries t. adies penser
386 *P* Por l. s. et honerer

Et prendre en boine volenté,
Dame, quanqu'il vos a doné.   388
Et si verrés qe tuit morron,
Que ja escaper n'en poron,
Que il ne nos estuisse aler
La dont ne porrons retorner,   392
De quele ore que Deu plaira.
Dame, nel vos celerai ja,
Ce saciés, bien le vos puis dire:
Mors est li prodom, vostre sire   396
Qui tant fu sages et amés
De chevaliers, de clers, d'abés.
Or, ma dame, pensés de l'ame,
Que Dex vos face prodefame.«   400
[L]i dame se pasme a cest mot
Quant son seignor nomer li ot,
Qu'il estoit mors et enterrés.
Mais li abes fu molt senés,   404
Isnelement l'a relevee,
Molt durement l'a confortee,
Mais li confors li fu molt fiers.
Atant es vos les chevaliers   408
Que li abes avoit laissiés.
Lors fu li dels recomenciés,
Que li chevalier se pasmerent.
Et aprés quant il releverent,   412
Regretoient tuit lor seignor
Come se il fust mors le jor.
Mais çou saciés vos bien sans faille
Qu'en grant duel faire se travaille   416
La dame, qu'ele i met s'entente.
Sovent se pasme et se demente

4d

880

890

900

---

387 *P* bone
388 *P* doune
389 *L* morront, *P* si saves que t.
     morront
390 *LP* poront
391 *P* nous estuece
392 *P* porons
393 *P* eure qua dieu
394 *L* nen, *P* ne
395 *P* Cou
396 *P* preudom
399 *P* larme

400 *P* diex v. f. preudefame
401 *L* large initial, *P* La d. se p. a ce
     m.
402 *P* signor nomme li ot
403 *P* entieres
408 *P* vous
410 *P* dius
413 *P* tout l. signor
415 *P* ce s. vous b. s. fale
416 *P* Qual g. d. f. se travalle
417 *P* d. ki i

Et se claime: »Lasse, caitive,
Dolante! Por coi sui jou vive   420
Quant j'ai perdu mon bon seignor
Qui si me portoit grant honor?«

5a
Lors se rescrie a molt haus cris,
Ses ceviax tire et bat son pis   424
Et maudist l'ore que fu nee
910
Ne norrie ne engenree
Por sofrir si mortel dolor.
Lors oïssiés et cri et plor,   428
Qu'il n'est hom si dur cuer eüst,
S'il les veïst, dolans ne fust.
Molt i avoit duel et tristrece,
Iluec n'avoit point de leece.   432
L'abes ne volt plus arester,
Son palefroi fist aprester,
A la dame congié demande,
920
Les chevaliers a Deu comande;   436
Mais tant lor a dit et proié
Que il en ont le duel laissié.
A l'endemain, que plus n'atent,
Fait canter messes plus de cent   440
La dame, par tous les mostiers;
Assés i avoit chevaliers,
Borgois et dames, ce saciés,
Qui molt estoient corecié,   444
De lor seignor mat et dolent.
930
Isi a esté longement
La dame, si se confortoit
A son fil que molt bel avoit;   448
A lui avoit toute s'entente,
Mais de son seignor ert dolente.
Del seignor ne voel plus conter;
Ci lairai la parole ester.   452

420 *P* je
421 *P* b. ami
423 *P* Dont se
424 *P* ceviaus ront et
425 *P* leure
426 *P* nourie
427 *P* soufrir
428 *P* cris et plour
430 *P* Sil le v.
432 *P* loece
433 *P* vot p. arriester

436 *P* dieu
438 *P* il aient lor d.
439 *P* Et l. plus ni atent
441 *P* par tot ses m.
444 *P* Que m. e. corecies
445 *P* signor
446 *P* Ensi a estet
448 *P* mout *written in full*
450 *P* signor
451 *P* signor

De la dame et de son enfant
Vos conterai d'ore en avant,
Et dirai coment li avint

940 Et com ele puis se contint. 456

B ien a, ce m'est avis, esté,
Puis qu'ele sot la verité
De son seignor qui ert ocis,
La dame set mois. El païs 460
Fu tant que vint el mois d'avril,
Que la dame tenoit son fil
Dont li solas molt li agree.
Maintes fois s'estoit por[p]ensee 464
Coment ele le garderoit

950 Que ja chevaliers ne seroit,
Ne armes ne saroit porter
Ne chevalier n'oroit nomer, 468
Qu'en lui estoit tous ses confors.
Et s'il par armes estoit mors
Come sont si oncle et ses pere,
El meïsme qui ert sa mere 472
S'ocirroit tost de duel aprés,
Ne ja un jor ne vivroit mes.
Et dist, sel pooit aprester,

960 En la gaste forest ester 476
Vodra. Et s'i ira par tens,
Ja nel savra nus hom des suens
Ains que ses fix soit auques grans
Ne sages ne apercevans, 480
Si que il ne veïst nului
Fors cex qui seroient o lui.
Ensi le cuide garder bien,
Et si n'en doute nule rien 484

454 *P* Vous c. dor 474 *P* Ne jamais jor
457 *LP large initial, P* cou m. vis si e. 475 *P* p. sans fauser
458 *P* kele 476 *P* Ken la g. f. entrer
459 *P* signor ki 477 *P* Vorra et si sera p.
461 *P* ke 478 *P* sara n. h. de sens
464 *P* Mainte 479 *P* fius
467 *P* Que 480 *P* apiercevans
469 *P* Ken l. fu tous tans s. 482 *P* ceus ki
471 *P* encle 483 *P* quident
472 *P* Ele m. kert 484 *P* si ne d.
473 *P* Sociroit t. de d. apries

5c	Trestos les jors qu'ele vivra.	
970	Un suen sergant apelé a,	
	Si a mandé un suen maior	
	Que ele amoit de grant amor,	488
	Qu'i[l] estoit sages et vaillans.	
	De sa mollier ot dose enfans:	
	Huit fix et quatre damoiseles	
	Qui molt erent gentes et beles,	492
	Sages et de boine raison.	
	Li vallés entre en la maison,	
	Que la dame i ot envoié;	
980	Le maior trova apoié	496
	Par desor le dossel d'un lit.	
	Li vallés lores li a dit	
	Que il vegne hastivement	
	Et si ne le laist por nïent;	500
	Sa dame mande qu'a li viegne,	
	Que nus afaires nel detiegne.	
	Et il si fist delivrement,	
	N'i ot point de delaiement.	504
	Isi s'en vont, si con moi samble,	
990	Li maire et li vallés ensamble;	
	Tout ensamble d'iluec s'en vont,	
	En la cambrë entré s'en sont.	508
	Quant la dame vit le maior,	
	Si li a dit par grant amor:	
	»Maire, bien soiés vos venus!«	
	Et cil ne refu pas trop mus,	512
	Ains dist: »Dame, cil Dex vos saut	
	Qui par tout puet et par tout vaut,	
	Et il vos doinst joie et santé.	
1000	Dame, vos m'avés ci mandé,	516

485 *P* Trestous l. jours
486 *P* sien serjant apielet
487 *P* sien
488 *P* elle
489 *P* vallans
490 *P* moullier
491 *P* fius et q. damoseles
492 *P* e. cointes et
493 *P* bone
494 *P* varles
495 *P* envoiie
499 *P* viengne hastiument (-1)

500 *P* noient
501 *P* m. que il v.
502 *P* n. essoinnes ne le tiegne
504 *P* delivrement
505 *P* Ensi
508 *P* c. tout droit en vont
511 *P* Maires
512 *P* ne furent p.
514 *P* et par tot v.
515 *P* il nos d.
516 *P* vous

Or me dites vostre talent.«
La dame par le main le prent,
En une cambre l'a mené,
Desor un lit sunt acosté.   520
La dame tout premierement,
Qui molt avoit le cuer dolent,
Li dist: »Maire, por Deu, vos pri
Que vos aiés de moi merchi   524
Et de mon fil, biax sire ciers.

1010 Prodom estes et chevaliers
Et si m'avés esté feeus;
Por çou vos dirai mes conseus: 528
Aler m'en voel de cest païs
Que mes fix ne me soit ochis.
En la gaste forest irai
Et ilueques le garderai   532
Tant con Deu venra a plaisir.
Et se vos volïés venir
O moi, bon gre vos en sarai

1020 Ne ja de vos ne partirai;   536
Et si amenés vostre feme
O vos, por Deu et por vostre ame,
Et trestoute vostre maisnie;
Certes molt en sera[i] plus lie.«   540
Tant li a dit et tant proié
Que li maires a otroié
Que il molt volentiers ira
En quel que leu que el volra,   544
Por çou que il set bien por voir

1030 Qu'il ne porroit pas remanoir.
Lors dist: »Dame, molt sagement
L'estevroit faire por la gent,   548

---

518 *P* p. la m.
519 *P* menet
520 *P* sont acostet
523 *P* maires p. diu merci
524 *P* Ke vous a. de m. vos pri
525 *P* biaus
526 *P* Preudom
527 *P* estet
528 *P* Pour c. vous
530 *P* Ke m. fius ne me s. ocis
531 *P* le g. foriest
533 *P* T. ke dieu

534 *P* vous
535 *P* Od moi
536 *P* vous nen p.
537 *P* fame
538 *P* Et vous p. diu et p. v. arme
540 *P* Ciertes jou en
541 *LP large initial, P* proiie
542 *P* ottroiie
544 *L* l. que il, *P* quel liu que elle
     vorra
545 *P* Pour
546 *P* poroit

Por çou, se il l'apercevoient,
Ja aler ne vos en lairoient.
Mais se vos homes faisïés
Tous mander et lor deïsiés   552
Que vostre fil volés mener
A Saint Brandain d'Escoce orer,
Si lor proiés que boinement

Se contegnent et sagement;   556
Et aprés çou vos jüerront
Que la terre vos garderont
A oés vo fil, se vos volés
Qu'il en sera sires clamés,   560
Et tout a seignor le tenront,
Come seignor le garderont.
Par mon consel si le ferés
Et a tous le comanderés.«   564
La dame li dist boinement

Qu'ele fera tout son talent.
A cest mot lor consel fenirent,
Fors de la cambre s'en issirent   568
Et la dame sans nul essoine
Onques n'i ot plus quis aloigne.
Tous les chevaliers de sa terre
A fait par tout cerquier et querre,   572
Borjois et dames et sergans
Qui estoient de li tenant;
Li messagier murent ensamble.

Au quart jor vinrent, ce me samble,   576
Et quant il furent la venu,
Lors a un parlement tenu
La dame et trestoute sa gent.
Si lor dist bel et sagement: 580

549 *P* c. sil nos a.
550 *P* ne nos en
551 *P* feissies
552 *P* deissies
555 *P* ke bonement
556 *P* contiengnent
557 *P* apries
558 *P* tiere
559 *L* A vostre f., *P* se vous v.
560 *P* Qui en s. sire
561 *P* signor
562 *P* signor
564 *P* coumanderes

565 *P* bonement
567 *LP* *large initial*, *P* ce m. l. c.
  finerent
568 *P* sen alerent
569 *P* Et . . . d.
570 *P* . . . i ot p. fet daloingne
572 *P* t. cier et
573 *P* Borgois et d. et serjans
574 *P* de lui tenans
575 *P* mesagier vinrent e.
576 *P* j. murent ce
578 *P* L. ont un

»Seignor, vos estes assamblé
Et jo vos ai ici mandé,
Si ne savés encor por coi,
Mais je le vos dirai par foi: 584
Por çou que j'ai vöé pieça
1070   Cest mien fil que vos veés ça
A Saint Brandain qui est d'Escoce,
Que Dex li doinst pooir et force   588
Si le me gart et sauf et sain:
Por çou i voel movoir demain;
S'en vuel a vos prendre consel,
Sel me donés, car je le voel.   592
Et demain par matin movrai,
Le maior avoec moi menrai.
Et por çou qu'en toute ma terre
1080   Voel que il n'ait estrif ne guerre,   596
Voel jou que trestout me jurés
Que la terre me garderés
A mon fil, se il revenoit,
Que la terre soie seroit.   600
Or savés mon comandement,
Si m'en dites vostre talent.«
Quant li chevalier l'entendirent,
Saciés que tout s'en esbahirent,   604
Car li et son fil retenissent
Molt volentiers se il peuissent.
Si li ont dit: »Dame, por De,
1090   Remanés encor cest esté   608
U nostre seignor nos laissiés.
S'andui ensamble morïés,
Nos serions tout desconfit.«
La dame lores sans afit   612

Lor dist: »Une cose saciés
Que por nient m'en proierïés,

581 *P* Signor
582 *P* jou
584 *P* jou
585 *P* Pour c. q. javoie p.
586 *P* ke
587 *P* b. kest en e.
588 *P* diex li d. honor et
591 *L* a nos p., *P* voel a vous
594 *P* maieur
595 *P* tiere
596 *P* ke il

597 *P* ke
598 *P* tiere
599–600 *P* om.
602 *P* Si me d.
604 *P* ke
605 *P* reteniscent
609 *P* n. sire n.
610 *P* Se a. e. movies
611 *P* Nous seriemes
613 *P* Lors d. u. chose
614 *P* pour noient men prieries

Mais avoec moi jo le menrai,
Come mon fil le garderai.«   616
Atant l'en ont doné congié.

1100
»Qu'ira o vos?« – »Et gié et gié!«
Font et chevalier et sergant
Qui'n estoient forment dolant   620
De çou que ele s'en aloit
Et de son fil qu'ele en menoit.
[L]a dame avoit un sien neveu,
Bon chevalier et sage et preu;   624
A celui sans plus demorer
A fait la terre asseürer
As barons qui iluec estoient,

1110
Que son comandement feroient   628
Tant que Dex lor laist repairier;
A tous lor a fait afïer.
Et quant il orent çou juré,
Li chevalier s'en sont alé   632
A lor ostex por aaisier.
Un mois devant trestout plenier
Ot la dame pris son tressor
Qu'ele avoit grant d'argent et d'or,   636
De la terre l'ot envoié.

1120
Li sergant ont aparellié
Cars et caretes plus de cent;
De ble, d'avaine et de forment   640
Les font cargier et puis errer;
Cevax et bestes font mener,
Bués et vaces, motons, berbis.
Si con raconte li escris   644

6d
Que nus hom, ce saciés vos bien,
Ne s'aperciut de nule rien

---

615 *P* Car ave ... ues m. len m.   630 *P* Et tous l. a f. affiier
      (*MS stained*)   633 *P* osteus
618 *P* Kira o vous   634 *P* m. durant t.
619 *P* Montent c. et serjant   635 *P* tresor
620 *P* Qui   637 *P* tiere lont envoiiet
621 *P* Et de chou quele   638 *P* serjant o. aparelliet
622 *P* kele   640 *P* blet davaine de f.
623 *LP large initial*   642 *P* Et bues et vaces f.
626 *P* tiere   643 *P* Cevaus et moutons et brebis
627 *P* ki   646 *P* sapercut
629 *P* ke d. l. l. ... airier

Qu'el s'en alast sans repairier.

Cele ne volt plus delaier, 648
Ançois mut l'endemain al jor,
Od li son fil et son maior
Qui mena toute sa maisnie,
De coi sa dame fu molt lie. 652
Et si ami le convoierent,
Qui au partir grant duel menerent,
Mais ele les fist retorner.

Tant ont entendu a l'esrer 656
Q'a un castel vienent tot droit
Qui sor la mer de Gale estoit,
Et molt estoit biax et plaisans;
Calfle l'apelent païsant 660
Et trestout cil de la contree.
Iluec a sa gent assemblee
Que ele avoit o lui mené.
Mais n'i a gaires demoré, 664
Ançois mut atout son harnois,
Plus rice n'ot ne quens ne rois,
Et ses gens avoec lui alerent.
Onques un jor ne sojornerent 668
Tant qu'en la forest sont esré,
S'i ont bien quinse jors erré;
Ne virent vile ne maison
Ne nule rien se forest non. 672
Tant ont erré le fort cemin
Par la gaste forest sans fin
Qu'en une lande sont venu
Dont li arbre erent vert foillu. 676
Cent liues avoit bien de le
La lande, et desos ot un pre

647 *P* Que sen
648 *P* Ele ne vot
650 *P* Od lui
651 *L* Quil m., *P* tote
652 *P* c. la d. estoit m.
655 *P* elle
656 *P* a lerrer
657 *P* Ca un c. vinrent
659 *P* m. i fist bel et plaisant
660 *P* Cafle lapielent
661 *P* trestot c. de la contee (conree?)
663 *P* Q. elle a. od li

664 *P* ni ont g.
667 *P* Et si gent a. li
668 *P* O. nul j. ne sejornerent
669 *P* s. entret
670 *P* b. xii jours estet
672 *P* foriest
673 *L* e. tout fors c., *P* erret
674 *P* le g. foriest
675 *P* Ken
676 *P* v. et dru
678 *P* desous

Qui molt fu biax et avenans,
Et desos une aige molt grans   680
Qui de la forest descendoit;
Et saciés que molt bele estoit,
Et çou vos puis dire en la fin
C'om en feïst morre un molin.   684
Tout maintenant iluec descent
La dame et trestote sa gent.
Enqui so[n]t la nuit ostelé
1170   Dusq'al matin qu'il sont levé.   688
Et la damë en apela
Son maior, se li demanda
Se il faisoit bon sejorner
Ilueques por son fil garder.   692
Et li maires li respondi:
»Dame, par verité vos di
Qu'a cent liues ci environ
N'a borc ne vile ne maison,   696
N'ome ne feme au mien espoir,
1180   Et ci feroit molt bon manoir.
Une maison faisons ci faire,
Si i sera nostre repaire;   700
Et mi fil le feront molt bien
Et nos avrons assés mairien
De la forest que ci veés.«
– »Or en faites vos volentés,   704
Fait la dame, et bon me sara.«
Et li maires tant tost ala
A ses fix et si lor a dit:
1190   »Seignor, nel metés en respit,   708
7b   Mais or pensés de l'essarter
Et de[l] mairien faire aprester,

679 *P* biaus   692 *P* f. sauver
680 *P* desous   693 *P* meres
681 *P* foriest   695 *P* Que .c. l. chi e.
682 *P* ke m. biele   696 *P* Nen a ne v. ne m.
683 *P* d. la f.   697 *P* fame al
684 *P* Con en peust mioure un (Con   698 *P* boin
     written in full)   702 *P* avons
686 *P* trestoute   703 *P* De le f. ke chi
687 *P* Enki s. iluec o.   705 *P* sera
688 *P* Jusqual   706 *P* tantost
689 *P* apiela   707 *P* fius
690 *P* si li   708 *P* Signor ne m.

Que vos ferés une maison
Ici ou nos herbergeron,   712
Que ma dame le velt ensi.«
Et cil l'otroient sans estri.

Maintenant sont el bois alé,
En quinse jors ont tant ovré   716
Qu'il orent faite une maison
1200 Close de palis environ,
Que molt i fu bien herbergie
La dame et toute sa maisnie.   720
Et li sergant aparellierent
La terre si le gaaignierent,
Et quant il les orent arees,
De ble les ont molt bien semees.   724

Ensi ont longement esté,
Et la dame a son fil gardé
Tant que il sot bien cevalcier
1210 Et de gavelos bien lancier   728
Que li fil au maior faisoient,
Qui molt bien faire le savoient.
[Q]uatorse ans a la dame est[é]
En la forest et conversé,   732
C'om de mere né ne savoit
Le leu ou ele conversoit.
Et ses gens l[e] faisoient querre
Et cerquier par mer et par terre,   736
Mais rien aprendre n'en pooient,
1220 Car tout ensamble bien cuidoient
Que ele et toute sa maisnie
Fuissent en mer morte et noïe;   740
7c Si l'avoient laissié atant.
Et la dame fait entendant
A son fil que n'avoit maison,

711 *P* Car vous
712 *P* I. u nous
713 *P* Car ma d. le viut
715 *P* bos
716 *P* jours
717 *P* fait
719 *P* herbegie
721 *P* serjant
722 *P* Le tiere et si le gaaingnierent
724 *L* bien arees, *P* blet
727 *P* ke il s. b. cevaucier
728 *L* De g. sans manecier, *P* gaverlot

730 *L* f. les s.
731 *LP large initial*
732 *P* foriest et convierse
733 *LP* Que hom de m. ne (*P* nel) s.
734 *P* liu ou e. conviersoit
736 *P* cierkier
737 *P* riens
738 *P* Mais tot e. b. quidoient
740 *P* Fuscent
741 *P* laissiet
743 *P* f. quil

N'ome ne feme, s'iluec non, 744
El mont si grans com il estoit;
Et li emfes bien le cuidoit,
Qui molt avoit de sens petit.
1230 Les li l'asist desor un lit, 748
La mere cent fois le baisa,
Bel fil et seignor l'apela
Et si li dist: »Fix, vos alés
En la forest, si ocïés 752
Kevrex et cers assés sovent,
Mais une cose vos deffent:
Se vos une gent veïés
Qui sunt isi aparelliés 756
Con s'il fuissent de fer covert,
1240 C'est dïables tout en apert,
Qui sont felon et enpené;
Tost vos aroient devoré. 760
Gardés o els vos n'arestés,
Mais tost ariere revenés
Et si vos en sainiés molt bien;
Ja en tout çou ne perdrés rien. 764
Et si dites vostre credo,
Biax fix, por Deu je le vos lou,
Ja puis n'arés garde de rien.«
1250 – »Dame, fait il, jel ferai bien. 768
Saciés, se je tel gent veoie,
Molt tost ariere revenroie,
Se je m'en pooie venir
Et Dex m'en donoit le loisir.« 772
7d Atant d'ilueques se leva.
Trestoute la nuit demora

---

744 *P* fame
746 *P* enfes b. le quidoit
748 *P* sassist
749 *P* m. et .c.
750 *P* Biaus fius et signor
751 *P* fius vous
752 *P* foriest si ochies
753 *P* Cevrieus
754 *P* chose
755 *P* vous unes gens i veries
756 *P* sont issi
757 *P* Com sil fuscent (Com *written in full*)

758 *P* Ce sont li dyable en apiert
759 *P* empene
761 *P* od eus ni arrestes
762 *P* arriere
765 *P* dires
766 *P* Biaus fius p. dieu je le v. lo
769 *P* jou
770 *P* arriere
771 *P* jou
772 *P* diex men done

Dusq'al matin que se leva.
Isnelement s'aparella,   776
Au plus tost qu'il se pot haster
1260   Son ceval a fait enseler,
Puis si est maintenant montés.
En la forest s'en est entrés,   780
Ses trois gavelos en sa main,
Et cerque le bois et le plain
Trestout le jor, ainc ne fina,
Que nule beste n'encontra,   784
Et dist que l'endemain iroit
Assés plus loig que ne soloit.
Atant est a l'ostel venus,
1270   Isnelement est descendus.   788
Sa mere contre lui ala,
Qui plus de cent fois le baisa,
Et aprés li a demandé
Molt doucement et comandé   792
Que li die que trové a;
Et cil de rien menti n'en a:
»Dame, je fui en la forest,
Et saciés bien que molt me plest   796
L'envoiseüre et li deduit.«
1280   Ensi a esté cele nuit:
La mere plus ne li enquist,
Et li vallés plus ne li dist.   800

775 *P* Jusquau m. quil se   788 *P* Isnielement
781 *P* gaverlos   789 *P* encontre
782 *P* cerke le bos   791 *P* apries
783 *P* cains   793 *P* Quil li d. q. trovet
784 *P* bieste   798 *P* E. ont e.
786 *P* loing   799 *P* Sa m.

TEXTUAL NOTES

ABBREVIATIONS: (For items not in this list, see Bibliography) Bloch – von Wartburg, *Dictionnaire* = Bloch, Oscar and Walther von Wartburg. *Dictionnaire étymologique de la langue française*. 5th ed. Paris: PUF, 1968; Brunot, *Histoire* = Brunot, Ferdinand. *Histoire de la Langue française des origines à 1900*, vol. I. *De l'époque latine à la Renaissance*. Paris: Colin, 1924; Constans, *Troie* = Constans, Léopold. *Le Roman de Troie*, vol. V. Paris: Didot, 1909 (SATF, 1904, v. 2, pt. 5); Elwert = Elwert, W. Theodor. *Traité de Versification française, des origines à nos jours*. Paris: Klincksieck, 1965; Ewert, *Tristran* = Ewert, A. *The Romance of Tristran by Béroul*. 2 vols. Oxford: Blackwell, 1939–1970; *First Continuation* = Roach, William. *The Continuations of the Old French Perceval of Chrétien de Troyes*. 3 vols. Philadelphia, 1949–1952; Foerster – Breuer, *Wörterbuch* = Foerster, Wendelin and Hermann Breuer. *Wörterbuch zu Kristian von Troyes' Sämtlichen Werken*. Halle (Saale): Niemeyer, 1933; Fouché, *Verbe fr.* = Fouché, Pierre. *Le Verbe français, étude morphologique*. Paris: Klincksieck, 1967; Foulet, *Glossary* = Foulet, Lucien. *The Continuations of the Old French Perceval of Chrétien de Troyes*, ed. William Roach, vol. III, part 2, *The Glossary of the First Continuation*. Philadelphia, 1955; Foulet, *Petite Syntaxe*[3] = Foulet, Lucien. *Petite Syntaxe de l'ancien français*. 3rd ed. Paris: Champion, 1930 (Reprinted 1966); Gildea, *Durmart* = Gildea, Joseph. *Durmart le Galois*. 2 vols. Villanova, Pennsylvania, 1965–1966; Godefroy = Godefroy, Frédéric. *Dictionnaire de l'ancienne langue française et de tous ses dialectes du IXe au XVe siècle*. 10 vols. Paris, 1880–1902 (Reprinted 1969); Gossen = Gossen, Charles Théodore. *Grammaire de l'ancien picard*. Paris: Klincksieck, 1970; A. Henry, *Cleomadés* = Henry, Albert. *Les Œuvres d'Adenet le Roi*, tome V (2 vols.), *Cleomadés*. Bruxelles, 1971; Hilka = Hilka, Alfons, ed. *Der Percevalroman (Li Contes del Graal) von Christian von Troyes*. Halle (Saale): Niemeyer, 1932; Hoepffner, *Folie Berne* = Hoepffner, Ernest. *La Folie Tristan de Berne*. 2nd ed. Paris, 1949; Lerch, *Syntax* = Lerch, Eugen. *Historische französische Syntax*, vol. I. Leipzig, 1925; Littré = Littré, Emile. *Dictionnaire de la langue française . . .* 5 vols. Paris, 1885–1889; Livingston, *Gliglois* = Livingston, Charles H. *Gliglois, a French Arthurian Romance of the Thirteenth Century*. Cambridge: Harvard University Press, 1932; Morawski, *Proverbes* = Morawski, Joseph. *Proverbes français*. Paris: Champion, 1925 (CFMA, no. 47); Nyrop = Nyrop, Kr. *Grammaire historique de la langue française*. 6 vols. Copenhagen, Leipzig, New York, Paris: vol. I, 5th ed., 1935; vol. II, 5th ed., printed 1968; vol. III, 2nd ed., 1936; vol. V, 1925; Pope = Pope, Mildred K. *From Latin to Modern French with Especial Consideration of Anglo-Norman*. Rev. ed. Manchester, 1952 (Reprinted 1966); Schwan – Behrens = Schwan, E. and D. Behrens. *Grammaire de l'ancien français*. Trans. Oscar Bloch. Leipzig, 1932; *Second Continuation* = Roach, William. *The Continuations of the Old French Perceval of Chrétien de Troyes.* Vol. IV. Philadelphia, 1971; Suchier, *Aucassin*[7] = Suchier, Hermann. *Aucassin et Nicolette.* Trans. Albert Counson. 7th ed. Paderborn, 1909; Tobler–Lommatzsch = Tobler, Adolf and Erhard Lommatzsch. *Altfranzösisches Wörterbuch.* 80 fascicles *(a – servitude)* to date. Wiesbaden, 1925–; Tobler, *Mélanges* = Tobler, Adolf. *Mélanges de grammaire française.* Trans. Max Kuttner and Léopold Sudre. Paris, 1905; Tobler, *Vers fr.* = Tobler, Adolphe. *Le Vers français ancien et moderne.* Trans. Karl Breul and Léopold Sudre. Paris, 1885 (Reprinted 1972); Wagner, *Phrases hypothétiques* = Wagner, Robert-Léon. *Les Phrases hypothétiques commençant par »si« dans la langue française.* Paris: Droz, 1939; Waters = Waters, E. G. R., ed. *The Anglo-Norman Voyage of St. Brendan by Benedeit.* Oxford, 1928.

1   The large initial of ms *L* in the first line is the only one supplied by the scribe. Space (one or two lines) for an initial was left at lines 53, 119, 161, 305, 401, 457, 541, 567, 623 and 731. A small guide letter is visible in the margins at lines 161, 305, 457, 541, 567; in these cases square brackets have not been put around the letter in the text. Ms *P* has an illuminated initial at line 1 and large, decorative initials at lines 53, 161, 305, 457, 541, 567, 623 and 731. Episode divisions of the text correspond to large initials in the mss at lines 53, 161 and 457. Other episodes begin at 244, 656 and 725. The rubric of ms *P*, »Ci endroit comence li contes del saint greail«, and the rubric preceding line 69 of the *Perceval* proper and following the *Bliocadran* without a break, »Ensi come Perceval trova en la lande les chevaliers«, indicate clearly that the copyist of *P* considered the *Bliocadran* to be an integral part of the work.

2   The abbreviation *ml't* has been solved as *molt* for ms *L* and as *mout* for ms *P*. Potvin used *moult* even though the word is written in full as *mout* at lines 154 and 448. Hilka used *mout* for *L*. Although the form is not written in full in ms *L* in the *Bliocadran*, *dolcement* (154, 223) is a supporting factor for *molt* (but *doucement*, 792); also *cevalcier* in 353, 727; *els* 16, 761; *dusqu'al* 138, 688, 775; *maltalent* 192. Hilka gives *molt* in the variant for *L* in line 154.

14   *guerres:* Hilka gives an *L* variant as *gerres.* The ms reads *g're*[s] which, according to Suchier, *Aucassin*[7], p. 43, can equal *guerres* just as *q're* = *querre.* Cf. also line 596. The same abbreviation occurs in ms *P* but Hilka shows no variant.

17   *P* omits this line. In 1863 Potvin added to fill the lacuna: *De lor aventure la some;* in 1864 he left the line blank; in 1865 he added: [*De lor aventures la some;*] with a note to the line that said he was supplying a »formule de l'époque et du poète« (Potvin, I [1865], 309).

17–19   Hilka indicates that these lines are from the *Perceval* 429 [427–431] (his note to *Bliocadran* line 18). There are other examples of *mescheoir* that indicate that misfortune often befalls a good man, and the expression is used proverbially. Cf. *Perceval* 2492–96, 2776–80. In Manessier's Continuation 33486 (= Potvin, V, line 35854): »Mais a maint prodome meschiet.«

21–22   In *P* the rime *seus* : *honeurs* is an example of preconsonantal *r* ignored in rime. Another example is in *L* 587–588. For discussion see Nyrop, I, § 362 (pp. 366–367); Ewert, II, pp. 15–16; and *Second Continuation,* IV, note to 20611–12.

23 In ms *L* the adjective *toutes* refers only to the preceding *terres* and not to *aleus*. Although Old French nouns beginning with a vowel were often of unstable gender, *aleus*, »hereditary goods«, occurs only as a masculine. See Nyrop, III, § 706, p. 385; § 25; Tobler, *Mélanges*, p. 295; *Second Continuation*, IV, note to 20138. Ms *P*, however, uses *honeurs* and not *aleus*. In this case *toutes* would present no problem.

23–24 In *P* identical rime *estoit : estoit*. See Tobler, *Vers fr.*, p. 169.

25 One is tempted to emend, as Hilka did, the *sages* of *L* using *larges* from *P*. *Sages* here is most likely a dittography of the same word in line 24. Hilka's emendation, however, is more than a mere substitution, as the lines are constructed differently: *L* »Cortois, sages et emparlés«, *P* »Larges et molt bien emparlés.« Hilka thus gives a line different from both mss. The scribe of *L* may have wished to replace the colorless *molt bien* in his exemplar by another adjective. If he had not committed a dittography he might have included the adjective *larges*, thereby mentioning an attribute which was usually regarded as desirable in the courtly knight.

26 The form of the name in ms *L*, *Bilocadran*, is not entirely clear. The name appears ten times in each ms. The readings are as follows:

In *L*	26	Bilocadrã	(nom.)	In *P*	26	Bliocadrans	(nom.)
	145	Bliocadron	(nom.)		145	Bliocadrans	(nom.)
	151	Bliocadron	(obl.)		151	Blocadroon	(obl.)
	161	Bliocadrõ	(nom.)		161	Bliocadrans	(nom.)
	180	Bliocadrõ	(nom.)		180	Bliocadran	(nom.)
	186	Bliocadras	(nom.)		186	Bliocadrans	(nom.)
	194	Bliocadras	(nom.)		194	Bliocadrans	(nom.)
	205	Bliocadras	(nom.)		205	Bliocadrans	(nom.)
	214	Bliocadras	(nom.)		214	Bliocadrans	(nom.)
	219	Bliocadrã	(obl.)		219	Bliocadras	(obl.)

Hilka uses the predominant form of *P* (Bliocadrans) for the eight nominatives but retained the form of *L* for the two cases of the oblique. This edition has preserved all the forms of *L* in the text without restoring nominative -*s*. For another option see Gildea, II, note to 594. He does restore nominative -*s* to proper names: »Lorsqu'un nom est abrégé, nous avons résolu l'abréviation en accord avec la fonction grammaticale.« This solution does not appear necessary in the case of so short a text and where the syntax of the name is clear. On the breakdown of the declension system with proper names see Waters, p. clxxxix; Nyrop, II, § 275 (p. 203), V, §§ 93–95; Pope, § 806 (pp. 313–314).

29–30 *L feni : pensis, P fenis : pensis*. The scribe of ms *L* shows a preference for the nominative used predicatively, disregarding eye rime, where the scribe of ms *P* uses the accusative, which also provides eye rime. There are three other similar cases:

443–444	*L* saciés : corecié	*P* saciés : coreciés
573–574	*L* sergans : tenant	*P* serjans : tenans
659–660	*L* plaisans : païsant	*P* plaisant : païsant

In two other instances *L* shows disregard for eye rime as compared to *P*: 275–276 *L tort*: *mors*, *P tors*: *mors* and 361–362 *L venir*: *sailli* (or *vit*: *sailli*), *P vit*: *salit*. In each of these six cases Hilka used the form in *P*. It is not necessary to emend these rimes since the final consonant is *s*, *r*, or *t*. Cf. Tobler, *Vers fr.*, p. 150–154; Nyrop, II, p. 35; Pope, §§ 400–402 *(-r)*, 617–621 *(-s, -t)*; Gildea, II, notes to lines 43, 439–440, 594, 4672 (restoration of *-t*), 7378 (rime as opposed to flection); Waters, pp. cxc–cxci (fluctuation of nominative and accusative used predicatively). There are two instances where the scribe of *L* used the accusative predicatively; *L* 33–34 *lié*: *irié*, 755–756 *veïés*: *aparelliés*. Both *L* and *P* seem to disregard grammatically correct *grant* in lines 679–680 *avenans*: *grans*. This latter case is the only one where the scribe of *L* seems to show concern for eye rime only. On the use of *grans*, however, see A. Henry, *Cleomadés*, II, note to 1315, who cites fourteen cases of *grans* used as nom. f. sing. and ten cases of *grant* so used, six cases of *grans* as obl. f. sing. and eight cases of *grant* so used.

33–34 *L lié*: *irié*, *P liés*: *iriés*. See note preceding.

35–36 Scheler, who annotated Potvin's 1864 publication of the text (Jahrb. für roman. und engl. Lit., V [1864], 26–50) said in a note to line 35 »Cet *home* m'embarrasse; je le prendrais volontiers comme une reprise du pronom *on* des vers précédents, si la grammaire n'exigeait pas au nominatif la forme *hom* ou *hon*« (p. 29). In 1865 Potvin did not include any remark about these lines in his edition nor does he emend or indicate any lacuna in the text. Hilka suggested in his notes that a gap does exist »Vor oder hinter 35« (pp. 789–790) and fabricated eight lines based on the 1530 Prose (Hilka, 499, lines 15–20) to fill the gap: »Adonc se prist a porpenser Que por son duel a allever Li convenoit aucun tornoi Veoir atout son bel conroi: Trop lonc tens ot ja demoré; Tost li porroit estre atorné A vilenie duel mener Sifaitement, ains veut sambler Home ...«. Hilka's conjectural addition is of doubtful value and, in fact, rationalizes the portrait of Biocadran (see above pp. 63–67). The extreme freedom of the prose text limits its reliability as a means of reconstructing the original verse. It is significant that in ms *P* the couplet 33–34 ends the second column of page 6 and that *Home*, therefore, is the first word of page 7. The lacuna then might be due to scribal inattention in the transition from one folio to the next. In ms *L* these lines are in the middle of a column. The copyist of *L*, if he had an exemplar similar to *P*, might not have noticed the omission as the sense is clear, almost proverbial, from lines 31 to 36. The occurrence of the same lacuna in both mss indicates their close relationship. Cf. *Second Continuation*, note to lines 26355–56. There are some instances where *home* is a nominative (Hoepffner, *Folie Berne* 503, 392; Ewert, *Tristran* 188, 4205; Morawski 846, *Home mort n'a ami*).

43 The version in *P* »Remanés ci, n'i alés mie«, (Hilka's text) is perhaps more restrictive in meaning than the version of *L*. Both, however, give satisfactory meanings.

47 Hilka adds *et* from ms *P* in order to make a smoother line. Ms *P* also uses an *et* not in ms *L* in lines 676 and 749. See note to line 749 where the use of *et* creates a possible example of ἀπὸ κοινοῦ.

50   Hilka uses the singular pronoun *tout* of ms *P* where ms *L* has the oblique masculine plural pronoun *tous*. There are sixty-seven instances in the text of a form of *tout* used as a pronoun, adjective or adverb. There are two cases in ms *L* that support the use of *tous* in line 50 as a dative (in apposition to *lor*): In *L* 630 »A tous lor a fait afïer« and *L* 564 »Et a tous le comanderés«. Line 50 was probably »Qu'il lor a a tous otroié«. Either *Qu'il* became *Que il* influenced by the similar beginning of line 51 and therefore caused the scribe to omit a second *a* intentionally (synaeresis, two *a*'s combined into one) or he noticed the double *a* but not its function and left it out unintentionally (haplology). On *tot* and its forms and usages see Foulet, *Glossary*, »tot«; cf. Nyrop, V, § 25 on haplology.

54   Potvin's original error in transcribing this line from the Mons manuscript created a problem that was long in being settled. In 1863 he printed: »(Kammuëlles ert bone dame)«. In 1864 he printed it in the same way and Scheler, in a note to line 26 (not to line 54) said »D'après la version de Chrestien de Troies, le père et la mère de Perceval s'appellent respectivement *Bliocadran* et *Cammuelle* (v. 54); ces personnages sont, dans notre fragment, tout autrement mis en scène que Gamuret et Herzeloyde de Wolfram von Eschenbach.« When Paul Meyer reviewed Potvin's edition of 1865 (Rev. critique d'Hist. et de Lit., no. 35 [September, 1866], 129–137) he undoubtedly had a copy on *papier ordinaire* that retained the blunder (see pp. 58–59 above for a discussion of Potvin's editions). Meyer pointed out (p. 136): »Que M. P. veuille bien y regarder de nouveau; je suis sûr qu'il verra non pas *Kammuèlles*, mais *Kam'uelles;* ce qui doit être transcrit *K'a mervelles.*« Those copies printed later, but also dated 1865, on large paper and destined for the members of the Société des Bibliophiles belges were corrected, but not quite, so that line 54 (= 538) reads »K'a merveilles«. Hilka, using this line from *P* in his variant, still did not quite get it right: *K'am mervelles*. The spurious name Kammuelle or Cammuelle was not eliminated from the Arthurian onomasticon by Paul Meyer's correction. Heinzel referred to Kammuelles (*Über die franz. Gralromane* [1891], p. 81): »Die Mutter Percevals heißt hier auch Kammuelles, 538, ein Name, der weder bei Crestien noch bei den Fortsetzern vorkommt.« Sister M. A. Rachbauer used Camuelles in her summary of the *Bliocadran* (*Wolfram von Eschenbach* [1934], p. 6), but she never refers to the name again, referring only to »Perceval's mother« or to the »widow« in the rest of her study. As late as 1962 Flutre (*Table des noms propres*, p. 41) indexed »Cammuelle: femme de Bliocadran, mère de Perceval, *Perc. Prol.* 54«.

66   After this line *P* adds the supernumerary line, »Et tant venu et tant alé«, which gives three lines ending in *-é*. Potvin made note of this line in all three of his printings of the text. Hilka, however, does not mention it in his variants or in his notes.

79   On the abrupt introduction of *tutoiement* see Foulet, *Petite Syntaxe³*, pp. 198–201.

81   On the use of *Et* to introduce direct discourse see A. Henry, *Cleomadés*, II, note to line 1952: »Dans le discours direct *et* introduit, parfois après les termes en apostrophe, l'intervention de l'interlocuteur et souligne le lien conceptual avec ce

qui a été dit par le locuteur.« He cites twelve examples in the *Cleomadés*. Other examples in the *Bliocadran* are lines 350 and 618.

81–82 These lines are in the same order in both *L* and *P*. Potvin reversed them in all three printings of *P*. In 1864 Scheler's note to these lines said that the verses are inverted in the ms. In 1865 Potvin said in his note to these lines (= 565–566) that they are inverted in the ms but that »C'est par erreur qu'ils sont imprimés l'un avant l'autre.« This sounds as though he had changed his mind about the order except that he still calls the lines inverted in the manuscript. Does he now mean that the lines are in correct order in the manuscript (which they are) and that he inverted them »par erreur«? He indicated the use of the same formula in the *Perceval* 5971–72 (= Hilka 4593–94) where the lines appear in the same order as, correctly, they do in 81–82: *Come chevaliers esprovés* refers not to the speaker but to the one spoken to. This is very clear in *Perceval* 4593–94 where the speaker is the Queen. Hilka either did not understand Potvin's misleading note or he ignored it and therefore gives as variant *in P umgestellt*.

94–95 *Et li sire respont celui: »Mais assés«, tant con lui plaira.* Both *L* and *P* have this vaguely wrong reading. In 1863 Potvin put the whole of line 95 (= 579) in quotation marks. In 1864 he punctuated the same way and Scheler commented in his note to the line »ce *lui* pour *vous* est gênant«. In 1865 Potvin removed the quotation marks but ended line 94 (= 578) with a colon. Since elsewhere in his edition direct discourse is in quotation marks he seems to have avoided the issue. Hilka uses the same punctuation here (colon at the end of 94 and no quotation marks). Scheler's recommendation, *vous* instead of *lui*, changes the text least, but both mss have *lui*. Another solution would be to interpret line 95 as indirect discourse: ∼ Mais assés, tant con lui plaira, or »Mais assés«, ∼ tant con lui plaira. (On direct discourse see A. Henry, *Cleomadés*, II, note to 389, and Tobler, *Mélanges*, pp. 331–338.) It is also possible that *Mais = Mes* (»mets«). (See *First Continuation*, II, note to 4097; but here one ms [*U*] supports the emendation to *mes* from *mais*.) Another possibility is that there is an error in line 94: *respont* > *promet*. This latter interpretation would support the interpretaion *Mais = »mets«*. This is one of the many problems common to both *L* and *P* that suggest dependence of both on a similar exemplar.

95 For the solution of the abbreviation *9* as *com* or *con* see *First Continuation*, III, note to 5547; Gildea, II note to 324; Suchier, *Aucassin*[7], p. 44. The system used in this edition is *com* before a vowel and *con* before a consonant, unless the word is written in full otherwise in the manuscript.

96 The summoning of a *chevalier* to attend an *escuier* (so called in lines 73 and 97, but *vallés* in 83 and 136) seems at first to be a breach in protocol. In the *Bliocadran* the differences in rank between *chevalier* and *escuier* seem to be established in lines 138–142 where the *escuier* are to make the preparations while the *chevalier* are being summoned. Of a lower rank than *escuier* is the *serjant* who holds the horses (line 358) or who is a messenger within the household (lines 486–487). The rôles are less clear in lines 494 and 506 where the *sergant* is called a *vallés*. The rôle of the *sergant* is, however, confirmed by line 638, where »sergents« load the

lady's belongings and line 721 where »sergents« till the land. The *maire* is of high rank, called *chevalier* by the lady (line 526).

The meaning assigned to *chevalier, escuier* and *vallés* by the *Bliocadran* author could be a clue to his understanding of courtly protocol or even to the date of composition of the work. Foulet, in a remarkable series of articles, *Sire, Messire* (Romania, LXXI [1950], 1–48, 180–221; LXXII [1951], 31–77, 324–367, 479–528, referred to here as articles 1, 2, 3, 4, 5), has pointed out the changing interpretation of these ranks. Of the »écuyer« he says: »Au XIIIe siècle le mot a une signification assez flottante. Dès le XIIe siècle il s'était appliqué particulièrement à quelqu'un qui prend soin des chevaux. Par ailleurs l'écuyer est au service personnel de son maître; il lui porte sa lance et son bouclier et s'acquitte de ses messages; il sert et dessert à table... Bref *écuyer* et *valet* sont des termes à peu près synonymes« (2, p. 183). However: »Mais il y a écuyer et écuyer« (2, p. 184). Joinville mentions an »écuyer« whom he made knight and one who was addressed as a count (2, p. 184). Thus, by the time of Joinville the *écuyer* »pouvait désigner des gens de fonctions et de catégories sociales très différentes« (3, p. 74). Later a young noble can be called »écuyer« and by the fourteenth century »l'écuyer est un combattant qui à la bataille est l'égal du chevalier« (3, p. 74). Thus the »écuyer« is an appellation that rose in rank. In the middle of the thirteenth century there were »écuyers-chevaliers« but also »beaucoup d'écuyers étaient des plébéiens, astreints à des services domestiques parfois assez humbles« (4, p. 329). What we seem to have in the *Bliocadran* is a reflection of the »écuyer« of a »signification assez flottante«. He is firstly a messenger who brings news of a tournament, but he is secondly of high rank; but high enough to justify his being served at table by a »chevalier«?

The »chevalier« could have certain functions to perform at table. Foulet, in the *Glossary* of the First Continuation, says in the article »vallet«: »Les valets sont souvent mentionnés à côté des écuyers quand il s'agit d'aider un chevalier à revêtir son armure ... ou à enlever ses armes ... à côté des ›sergens‹ ... mais les sergents apportent les bassins d'eau chaude à laver les mains, les serviettes à s'essuyer, les tréteaux sur lesquels est posée la table, tandis qu'un valet se borne à étendre une nappe dessus...«. The *chevalier* of our poem may, then, be supervising the meal, not serving it himself.

The »écuyer« had arrived on a »roncin« which was, Foulet notes (*Glossary*, »roncin«), »un terme courant pour indiquer un cheval de charge ou une monture pour les valets et les écuyers«. The »écuyer«, then, is appropriately designated by the *Bliocadran* author, and his rank is ascending. It seems fitting then for a »chevalier« to attend to his repast, although he may not serve it personally.

The low rank of the »écuyer« is clearly evident in the *Perceval*. There is a significant passage where Gauvain, seeing a host of knights passing, enquires of an *escuier* who they are. He learns from the *escuier* about the tournament undertaken by Melïans de Lis against Tybaut de Tintagueil (Roach, *Perceval* 4816–55). Melïans is a chevalier (4826) but, to Tybaut's daughter, according to ms *T* (Roach edition), he is just an *escuier* (4852) until he proves himself. (Hilka's text does not have this scornful reference to the *escuier*.) At the end of this conversation Gauvain addresses the *escuier* as »Frere« (4879). The tone of address in this passage seems to indicate a great social distance between Messire Gauvain and his informant.

The *Bliocadran* author seems, then, to be using terms for rôles that at least reflect a period of time before Joinville but after Chrétien.

105 *L A bele ciere, P Et biele ciere.* The *Et* for *A* in *P* is a common error at the beginning of a line. *P* shows this type of error again in lines 439, 630. In 538 *P* substitutes *Et* for *O*.

106 The sporadic occurrence of the form *Asés* in this line has been corrected on the basis of the regular use of the *-ss-* form in the other instances of the word in the text, lines 95, 103, 442, 702, 753 and 786. The correction might have been omitted because of the not uncommon alternation of these forms in other Picard texts. On the confusion of *-s-* and *-ss-*, see Gossen, § 49, p. 107.

115 There are two instances of the absence of the *-i* ending of the first person singular in the future: *dira[i]* and *L* 540 *sera[i]*. On the possibility of this being a dialectal variation rather than a lapse, see Nyrop, II, p. 166; Livingston, *Gliglois*, p. 43, note 5; and Gossen, pp. 52–53.

123 The *Gaste Fontaine* is the name of a place in the verse romances only in the *Bliocadran*. See G. D. West, *Index*.

124 *Ne velt pas que en lui remaigne.* In 1863 and 1865 Potvin printed *en liu* (= 608). In 1864 he printed *enlui* and Scheler notes »Je ne comprends pas cette expression *enlui*.« The interpretation of the line depends upon the meaning of the verb. The King of Wales is holding the tournament for his own people, those of Cornwall against those of the Gaste Fontaine. *He does not want to be slow about it* so he is sending out for knights to come. For examples and discussions see Roach, *Perceval*, »Glossaire«, *remanoir*; A. Henry, *St. Nicolas*, »Glossaire«, *remaigne (remaindre)* and note to 231; Foulet, *Glossary*, »remanoir«; Constans, *Troie*, V, »remaindre«; Tobler–Lommatzsch, VIII (1971), 710.30–711.41. On rime *Fontaine : remaigne* see Gossen, § 60, p. 116.

142–143 The emendation of *L il* to *cil* in 143 (*Si* in *L* 142 remains) clarifies the situation, that it is the *escuier* who are to prepare things quickly and that the knights (= *cil*) assembled. Hilka's text with 142 *Cil* and 143 *si* makes the three lines 142–144 all refer to the *chevalier*.

145 *L Bliocadron, P Bliocadrans.* The form in *L* serves as a nominative (see note to line 26). Thompson (The Text of the *Bliocadran*, RPh, IX [1955–56], 209) declared that »It seems ... likely that the original form was *Bliocadron(s)*. It is easy to see that the ending *-ōs* could have been mistaken for *-ās* or *-as* by the copyists.« Although rime can attest form, it does not seem likely that *Bliocadron(s)* was the original form. In ms *L* the tonic vowel of the name is six times *a* and three times *o*, discounting the *o* of line 151 where *Bliocadron : maison*. In ms *P* the evidence for *a* is even greater, for *o* appears as the tonic vowel of the name only at line 151.

147 Hilka emended in ms *L* a very nice example of agreement of the p.p. of *faire* with the accusative object of the infinitive. See Tobler, *Mélanges*, 258–259, 265–266; Livingston, *Gliglois*, note to line 2325. Hilka's emendation also replaces *tos* (in apposition with *somiers*) by *tost*.

116

153 Cf. *Perceval* 366–67.

164–167 The reading of *L* is more consistent than that of *P*. In *L* the knights come to the *camp* but lodge in a *castel* where they have *bel ostel*. In *P* they come to the *castiel*, stay in an *ostel* where they are well lodged *(l'orent bon a talent)*. The state of affairs in *P* is contradicted in line 231 where both mss say that the wounded Bliocadran is carried back *El castel (P castiel) u il ont (P ot) esté*. The reading of this line in *L* also seems to be supported by line 178. The knights arm in the morning and travel to the *cité* for the tournament. *P* however had announced (164) that the knights arrived »Au castiel ou li tornois fu« before moving on to their lodgings. Either *P* identifies *castiel* with *cité* (see Foulet, *Glossary*, »cité«) or has again been contradictory. In *L* the knights could very well have passed by a *camp* that was just outside the walls of the *cité*. The 1530 Prose seems to follow both versions: the knights arrive at *ung chastel* (Hilka, 500, 10) but *»se allerent heberger a dextre le plus recelement«* (Hilka, 500, 11–12). However, the next morning »*si sortirent hors le chastel*« (Hilka, 500, 17) and go to the tourney (place not specified). As in both mss the wounded Bliocadran is carried back *»vers le chastel dont ilz estoyent meuz le matin«* (Hilka, 501, 15).

176 *Come quarriax quant il destent (P descent)*. For other examples of this figure see *First Continuation*, I, 845–847, 2392–94; II, E 5989–90.

193–194 *frosse : angoisse*. The reduction of the dipthong $oi > o$ is probably only a scribal variation in spelling. Godefroy (IV, 158) and Tobler–Lommatzsch (III, 1938) both cite the example of *frosse* from *Florimont* (Hilka, 1932, 6662). This is not, however, a case of the rime of a simple vowel with a diphthong. Cf. Gossen, p. 82; Pope, p. 488 (vii).

197–198 The expressions *contreval* and *del ceval* are in more logical order in ms *L*. A »chiasmus« of rime elements also occurs in *P* in lines 359–360 and 523–524.

204 Hilka uses the reading of ms *P* for this line. His interpretation makes a unit of lines 202–204 with the subject being *tout li autre*. The reading of ms *L* makes a unit of 204–207, with Bliocadran as the subject. It is tempting to use the reading of *P* as Bliocadran did lose something that day, his life. Moreover, line 203 is the beginning of a column in ms *L* so that the singular verb in 204 could be seen as a mistake in anticipation of the subject *Bliocadras* when the plural subject *tout li autre* was overlooked in the transition to a new column. A scribal error at the beginning of a column is commonplace (see *First Continuation*, III, note to *L* 111). There is, however, no real contradiction of sense within the unit *L* 204–207, as it is devoted to praise of Bliocadran and the »nothing lost« probably refers to booty. He did not lose any equipment during the mêlée.

208 *dansel:* This is the syncopated form of *damoisel* (Schwan – Behrens, p. 65). Foulet, *Sire, Messire* (2, p. 209; see note to line 96 above) defines the *demoisel:* »titre réservé d'ordinaire à un jeune noble qui n'a pas encore été adoubé; il sait ›d'armes et de cheval‹, il court les tournois du pays où on représente les aventures de la Table Ronde«. The 1530 Prose (Hilka, 501, 3–4) introduces a rationalization here con-

cerning the violence of the combat: the *damoisel* »vient pour venger le dommage que Bliocadras leur faict«.

210   *vassal:* As Foulet points out (*Glossary*, »vassal«), the word is used in the romance as a courtly epithet and not to designate feudal status. To his examples from the First Continuation, add Second Continuation 21280 »Car molt ierent andui vasal«.

217   Hilka replaced the reading of *L*, *li vole en clices*, by that of *P*, *vole en esclices*, both of which are acceptable versions for describing the splintering of the lance. For examples of *clices* see Micha, *Cligés* 3553; Constans, *Troie* 2516 (variants). The more common form is *esclices*. See Godefroy, II, 153 and Tobler–Lommatzsch, II, 481–482, where *clice* is given as a variant form under *esclice*. For derivation of *esclice-clice*, see *F.E.W.*, XVII (1966), 151–154, **slītan*.

219–223   The blow here is reminiscent of the one delivered by Perceval to the Chevalier Vermeil (Hilka 1115–17) with his javelin. Cf. note to line 208.

223   *Paru* in ms *L* shows the normal dropping of unsupported final *t* in the perfect tense (Nyrop, II, p. 35). By emending with the *Parut* of ms *P*, Hilka corrected his text unnecessarily. Conservation of final unsupported *t* is a feature of ms *P* especially in past participles, and is also a feature of Picard (Gossen, p. 147). Hilka, however, did not consistently choose Picard features from *P* so that his use of it here is random. See note to lines 361–362.

231   Cf. note to lines 164–167.

237   The 1530 Prose version ends with this line.

239–240   In ms *P* the rime *fisent* : *detirent (L firent* : *descirent)* illustrates the strong Picard coloring of that text. The scribe did not alter the form in anticipation of rime. There are in this passage five successive uses of the third person plural preterit of *faire* (229, 235, 239, 242, 253) all of which are *fisent* in *P*, whereas three of the five are *firent* in ms *L*.

250   Ms *L* indicates that three days after Bliocadran left for the tournament the child was born, and ms *P* says four days. It is tempting to emend the three of *L* to the four of *P*. It took Bliocadran one day to make the journey. He and his men lodged one night and fought the next day. He was mortally wounded that day and lived only two days longer. This would equal four days. If, then, the son was born on the same day the father died, pathos would be increased. The three-day unit of time of ms *L* is a commonplace that seems less a deliberate choice than the four days of ms *P*.

256–258   These lines alluding to the naming of the child are puzzling. In 1864 Scheler said in a note to 256: »Je ne pénètre pas le sens de cette allusion au nom de Perceval.« The scribes of mss *L* and *P* show their own puzzlement, the first using *seüs*, *només* and *amenteüs* and the second *veüs*, *nonciés* and *apierceüs*. Much has

118

been written about the concealment and sudden discovery of Perceval's name in Chrétien's *Perceval*. For a recent discussion of the subject see Peter Haidu, *Aesthetic Distance in Chrétien de Troyes* (Geneva: Droz, 1968), pp. 126, 177–181.

275–276   *L tort : mors:* see note to lines 29–30.

289   *respondus:* Scheler (1864) remarked in a note to this line: »Notez cet emploi transitif du verbe *respondre,* limité aujourd'hui au terme ›lettres répondues‹.« Tobler–Lommatzsch, VIII, 1068–69 gives five examples of this usage (incl. *Durmart* 13818, »Mout laidement fust respondus« [ed. Gildea, 1965]).

301–302   Self-rime *fui : fui.* Cf. Tobler, *Vers fr.*, p. 169.

304   The seven days in ms *L* must be emended to the eight days from *P* in conformity with the statement of line 314 where both *L* and *P* agree on eight days. The reading of *L*, »Devant set jors ne venront mes« is not technically incorrect, but most likely the numbers were intended to be the same in both passages.

319–320   Ms *L* reads *hom : avõ* and ms *P hõ : avon.* There seems to be no reason to prevent using the eye rime *hom : avom* (Hilka's solution), except that the first person plural appears only with *-on(s)* in the text of *L* (lines 89, 326, 389–390, 392, 611, 699, 702, 712).

339   *Et* = »alors« *(P Que).* The symbol ~ to indicate indirect discourse could be used at the beginning of this line. See A. Henry, *Cleomadés*, II, note to line 389 and I *(Texte),* 389, 4224, 5057, 5107, 5903. The sense of this line does not follow directly from 335 »Puis ont de lor seignor conté«, unless one interprets *conté* also to mean *dit.*

341   Hilka emended *LP avoit* to *av[r]oit.* There is an analogy here to those »if« clauses in which the imperfect rather than the conditional is used in the result clause. With the conditional, a paraphrase of 339–341 could read »Might he speak to her, and comfort her afterwards, for she would need it greatly«, i.e., the need would follow from the speaking to her. With the imperfect the meaning is »Might he speak to her and comfort her afterwards, for she has need of this«, i.e., her great need existed independently of and previously to her being told the news. Cf. A. Henry, *Cleomadés*, II, notes to 4433–34, 4702–03 and *Syntaxe expressive,* p. 44ff.; R.-L. Wagner, *Phrases hypothétiques,* pp. 251–256. Wagner refers to an »imparfait d'imminence« (p. 256) and Henry to an »imparfait de certitude inéluctable« *(Syntaxe,* p. 45).

350   Cf. note to line 81.

359–360   Cf. note to lines 197–198.

361–362   The error at the end of the column in *L* (cf. *First Continuation,* note to *L* 111) may have been caused by the similarity of sound elements in the couplet. The scribe wrote *Et quant ele les vit venir Encontre l'abé sus sailli.* The scribe may not have objected to the resulting assonance (cf. Thompson, *Elucidation,* p. 29, no. 13). Changing the word order of 361 to *venir les vit* (as in *P*) makes a more satisfactory line, but it is not necessary to restore -*t* of *sailli* (Hilka used *salit* from *P*; cf. note to lines 29–30 and to line 223).

375 The scribe of ms *P* wrote a satisfactory line, *Si a dit par bele raison*, but he failed to take into account the following line, *Comencié un molt bel sermon*.

386 *A lui servir et honorer:* On the disjunctive pronoun (»forme forte«) as direct object of an infinitive when the infinitive is object of a preposition, see Foulet, *Petite Syntaxe³*, p. 129.

389–390 Both *L* and *P* agree in using the third person plural form of the verbs, *morront : poront*. Potvin (1865) and Hilka emended to first person plural, bringing the lines into agreement with 391–393 with which they form a unit. Potvin did not emend in 1863 nor in 1864, but Scheler added a note (1864) to these lines: »Il faut sans doute corriger *morrons, porons*.« Potvin did emend in 1865. He made a mistake in his note, saying the ms read *morront, porront*, but he did not double the *r* of *porons* in his text. Hilka further confused the matter by doubling the *r* of *porons* both in his text and in the variant *poront*. (He also uses *savés* from *P* in his text for *verrés* of *L*, and records the incorrect variant *verrés P*.) The emendation to first person plural is a logical one. The scribes may have been led to the third person plural by the subject *tuit*. The author did not use »nos« here as his words were carefully graduated. From a generalized notion of death he gradually proceeded to the revelation of a particular death. The absence of »nos« in lines 389–390 thus leaves a measure of ambiguity. Seen in this way, it is possible that the third person plural was intended by the author. In any case, a conservative approach is to drop -*t* but not add -*s* (as in lines 320 and 712).

394 *nel:* ms *L nen*, ms *P ne:* Hilka also emends to *nel* showing only the variant from *P*. The use of *nel* is pleonastic, parallel with the use of *Ce* and *le* in line 395, all anticipating the revelation of line 396. (On pleonasms, see Nyrop, V, pp. 262–264). If *ne* is retained the syntax is altered but not the sense. In such a case lines 394 and 396 form a clause with ellipsis of *que* at the beginning of 396. Line 395 intervenes giving the effect of delay or preparation for the revelation in the following line. With *nel* in 394, there is instead a series of three parallel (paratactic) phrases that precede the revelation of line 396. This latter was probably the intended form as the verb of 394 requires an expressed direct object and its syntactic relationship to line 396 is not explicit.

407 *fiers:* Scheler, in his note to this line (the line is misnumbered: beginning at 395 the numbering skips five figures, so that 400 = 395. Thus 412 = 407.) said: »*Fier* paraît signifier ici difficile, pénible.« Godefroy (III, 788) quotes seven lines of this text (401–407) in order to discuss the meaning of this adjective: »Il s'employait encore pour signifier l'excellence, la supériorité en telle ou telle chose, et était souvent synonyme de grand et fort.« Perhaps the clue to the very different interpretations given by Scheler and Godefroy is in their interpretations of *Mais*. If the adversative sense is considered, then »pénible« is appropriate. (Tobler–Lommatzsch does not use this example from the *Bliocadran*.)

419 Hilka does not begin the quotation after *Et se claime,* but with line 420. This punctation loses the accumulative effect of the three epithets.

421 Hilka gives the variant from *P* as *signor.* Potvin had emended the ms reading *ami* to *signor* in 1863. In 1864 he restored *ami* to his text and Scheler noted that emendation to *signor* was necessary. In 1865 Potvin used *signor* in the text with no note indicating the ms reading.

439 *Et* for *A* in *P.* See note to line 105.

443–444 *L saciés : corecié.* See note to lines 29–30.

444 Ms *L Qui,* ms *P Que:* Hilka uses *Que* for his text. Since he does not record a variant from *L* it may be that he considered *Que* to be the reading of both mss. Foulet discusses *que* as a Picard relative pronoun used as subject (*Petite Syntaxe³* p. 358). Nyrop (V, p. 326) discusses *que* nom. rel. pron. as a form older than *qui.* Cf. note to 223 on Hilka's random choices of dialectal forms for his text. Or Hilka may have considered *Que* = »car«.

453–454 This couplet at the top of folio 5*b* is indented. The scribe may have considered this the beginning of the next episode, as it well could have been. He then noticed that the beginning indicated in his exemplar was at line 457 and so copied 455–456 at the center margin and indented again at 457, the correct beginning, as indicated by the guide initial »b« left for the decorator at this line.

476, 531, 674 *gaste forest.* Is this a proper name? In the *Perceval* neither Hilka nor Roach capitalizes *gaste forest* in lines 75, 392 and 451. Perceval, upon taking leave of Blancheflor, says »Ne cuidiez vos que ce soit biens Que je ma mere veoir vois, Qui sole manoit an cel bois Qui la Gaste Forez a non?« (Hilka 2956–59). It seems, then, that *gaste forest* becomes a proper name at 2959 of the *Perceval. Gaste Forest* is a proper name in the Second Continuation 23548. G. D. West, *Index,* cites the name in Manessier's Continuation 44601, 44753. The name is not listed in the Table of Proper Names of the Gerbert Continuation, compiled by A. Stanton (Gerbert as a Writer of Grail Romance, diss. University of Chicago, 1939). Nitze and Williams (*Arthurian Names in the Perceval,* University of California Pub. in Modern Philology, vol. 38, no. 3 [1955], p. 293) mention the *gaste forest* only in their discussion of *Veve Dame.* In the *Perlesvaus* there is a *Forest Soutaine* (3310) and a *gaste païs* (4908). Cf. Nitze, *Perlesvaus,* II, 96–97. The *gaste forest* is not then to be considered a proper name in a prologue to the *Perceval;* it becomes one at line 2959. In the latest edition of the *Perceval* by Félix Lecoy (CFMA, 100 [1973], vol. 1 to line 6008), the editor of B.N. 794 capitalizes *gaste forest* at lines 75 and 390, not at 449 *(forest gaste),* and capitalizes again at 2953 (= Hilka 2959).

523–524 This is the third case in which *P* shows a »chiasmus« of rime words. Cf. note to lines 197–198.

538 *P Et vous.* This kind of error, *et* for *a* or *o(d)* is a common one at the beginning of a line (see note to 105). Potvin emended *P* to *Od vous* but he made a curious error in his notes (1865). Line 535 (= Potvin 1019) begins *Od moi.* Potvin

wrote a note to this line saying the ms reads »Et moi« and that he is emending to *Od moi.* There is no such error in this line. Potvin should have written his note to line 538 (= 1022) where the same *kind* of error does occur. His text is correct for line 538 but the note is misplaced. Hilka picked up this erroneous note to 535 (1019) and records the incorrect variants 535 *Et moi P* and 538 *Od vous P.*

540 *L sera[i].* This is the second instance of a first person singular future without *-i.* See note to line 115.

551–562 These twelve lines can be considered a two-part condition of six lines each. The construction at first seems an example of anacoluthon: a hypothetical clause without a conclusion. (Cf. Livingston, *Gliglois*, note to line 1326, who cites this same kind of construction as anacoluthon, and Nyrop, V, p. 46.) However, Wagner, *Phrases hypothétiques*, pp. 463, 467, 469, discusses a less usual condition: *se + imperfect indicative* or *imperfect subjunctive ... future*. In these lines the condition is stated in 551–552, *se faisiés (P feïssiés)* and *deïsiés*, and the results are 557 *jüerront*, 558 *garderont*, 561 *tenront*, 562 *garderont*. The use of the future indicates the certainty of the speaker (the *maire*) about what the lady's people will do if she called them together and told them what he is outlining to her. Rather than put the result clauses into the conditional or the imperfect subjunctive, the speaker presents the conclusions desired by the listener as future certainties. And so she agrees at once to his plan.

554 *Saint Brandain d'Escoce.* See Introduction, pp. 46–52.

557 *jüerront:* For this Picard form of the future see Gossen, p. 114; Fouché, *Verbe français*, pp. 391–393.

559 *L A vostre fil, P A oés vo fil.* Ms P preserves the *lectio difficilior.* On this particular error see Foulet, *Glossary*, p. 201; *First Continuation*, I, note to 4315 (discussion, many examples and bibliography of the problem).

559–560 *se vos volés Qu'il en sera sires clamés.* Tobler, *Mélanges*, ch. V, discusses anacoluthon wherein the imperative or future is used instead of the subjunctive after a verb of will or command (esp. p. 34, note 1). See also Brunot, *Histoire*, I, 248–249. In this phrase *se = si* with retention of the subject *vos* and no inversion.

563–564 The two verbs in the future, *ferés, comanderés*, function as imperatives. This phenomenon is analogous to the one discussed in the preceding note.

573–574 *L sergans : tenant.* See note to lines 29–30.

575–576 The verbs of these two lines are reversed in ms P. Hilka chose the version in P for his text. According to the version in ms P the messengers are the subject until line 577 where a shift takes place, but it is not clear what happened on the fourth day: did the messengers go out on that day or did the people summoned start toward the parliament? Using the version of ms L it seems clear that the messengers went out (575), and on the fourth day those summoned arrived (576). The fourth day surely must denote when the parliament began, i.e., it took four days to assemble the parliament, from the departure of the messengers to the arrival of the people.

585 Ms *P* has a garbled line: *Pour cou que javoie pieca* which Potvin emended (= 1069) in 1863 and 1865. See Scheler's note (1864) to manuscript reading that Potvin printed in the text. Hilka recorded no variant as Potvin had no note about the manuscript reading in 1865.

587–588 *Escoce : force.* See note to lines 21–22.

599–611 In ms *P* two elements make its version differ in tone from the version in *L*. Ms *P* omits lines 599–600, in which the lady mentions the possibility that her son may not return: *se il revenoit.* In line 610 ms *P* has *moviés* instead of *L* *moriés.* Taken together these two differences make the statements in *L* more revealing of the true state of affairs in the first instance and more threatening in the second. Could the version in ms *P* be deliberate? The omission of a couplet is not remarkable in itself and the general sense is not distorted by the omission. In the second instance the difference between *moviés* and *moriés* is only the change of one letter. Even though both of these differences in ms *P* combine to affect the tone, it is entirely possible they occurred by chance. However, in the *L* version, when the lady says *se il revenoit,* she is endangering her ruse: the pretense of going on a pilgrimage in order to disguise their flight is weakened by her alluding to the possibility that her son may not return. In the second instance it would not be out of place for the knights to fear the death of anyone going on a long journey, but it is to be remembered that when Bliocadran announced his leaving for a tournament there was no mention of his possible death in their pleas (lines 42–48, 150–154) to make him stay. Their regret was only about his leaving. References to not returning and to dying seem, in *L*, not to accord with the previous text.

614 The monosyllabic form *nient* must be used here rather than dissyllabic *nïent,* as in lines 204 and 500 (*noient* in 118), since the conditional verb ending of *proierïés* must be dissyllabic, as are the other conditional and imperfect indicative verb endings in the text: *lairïés* 46, *devrïés* 385, *volïés* 534, *faisïés* 551, *morïés* 610, *veïés* 755. On *nient* see *First Continuation,* III, note to *L* 103, where Roach says: »Although *nient* is usually dissyllabic in *L* (cf. 2420, 3888), the occurrence of both monosyllabic and dissyllabic forms in the same text is not unusual.«

618 »*Et gié et gié*«. On *Et* see note to line 81. On *gié* see Anna Granville Hatcher, *From »ce suis je« to »c'est moi«,* PMLA, LXIII (1948), 1074–75; Gossen, § 64, p. 123.

629 *Tant que Dex lor laist repairier.* In 1864 Scheler commented on this line (= 632): »Notez ce datif *lor* de la personne avec *laissier,* dans le sens de permettre; il faut envisager l'infin. *repairier* comme le régime direct.« Cf. Tobler, *Mélanges,* pp. 254–268; Foulet, *Petite Syntaxe³,* pp. 146–147.

630 *P Et tous, L A tous.* In 1864 Scheler commented to this line (= 633): »Le ms. porte fautivement, ce me semble, *et tous.*« Potvin, having corrected the text in 1864, based on Scheler's comment, printed the ms reading again in 1865. See also notes to lines 105, 439 and 538.

634 *L Un mois devant, P Un mois durant.* Hilka used *P* for his text. In ms *P durant* is a relatively rare example of early use of this preposition. Cf. Tobler – Lommatzsch, II, 2109 (three examples); Foulet, *Petite Syntaxe*[3], pp. 304–305, 98–100; Lerch, *Syntax*, I, p. 39; Nyrop, III, p. 318; Bloch – von Wartburg, *Dictionnaire*, »durer«. The reading of *L* fits the context better. The pluperfects *ot pris* 635 and *ot envoié* 637 accord better with *devant* from *L* than with *durant* from *P*.

669–670 *esré : erré* is an identical rime that could have been emended by using *entret* from *P* 669 (Hilka used *entré*). This emendation would be supported by the auxiliary *sont* of lines 669. With *sont* the use of *entré* is less striking than the use of *esré*.

674 *gaste forest.* See note to line 476.

676 *L vert foillu, P vert et dru.* Hilka chose the reading of ms *P* for his text in order, perhaps, to eliminate this example of asyndeton. Cf. lines 47 and 748–749.

679–680 *avenans : grans.* See note to lines 29–30.

695 *cent liues.* Any literal interpretation of a league would render the *gaste forest* too vast. *Cent liues* also appears in line 677. Hilka used *.V. liues* for his text in the present instance, although both *L* and *P* clearly have *.C.*. Littré (III, 305) gives many examples of *cent lieues* and *mille lieues* used figuratively to mean simply a great distance. *Cent* is also used figuratively in lines 440, 639, 747, 790.

711 The future *ferés* functions as an imperative. See Tobler, *Mélanges*, pp. 34–38.

723–724 The pronoun *les* in each of these lines refers to the singular noun *la terre* of line 722. Scheler noted in 1864 (to line 726): »Ce pronom pluriel répond irrégulièrement au singular *tière.*« On collective nouns, see Tobler, *Mélanges*, pp. 290–301 (*terre* is not among his examples).

724 *L arees* is an obvious dittography from line 723 and has been emended to *semees* from ms *P*.

730 The *les* of *L* has been emended to *le* from *P*. The singular pronoun indicates that the ability to hurl the javelin is the subject matter of the line, whereas the plural *les* would indicate that the ability of the son to ride and to hurl the javelin was being compared to these accomplishments of the steward's sons. See note to line 208 for Foulet's definition of the *demoisel:* »il sait ›d'armes et de cheval‹.« The *-s* of *les* could have been added in anticipation of the initial consonant of the following word, *savoient,* beginning with *s.* Cf. Nyrop, I, pp. 328–329.

733 *LP Que hom de mere ne (P nel) savoit:* This line is an example of what Roach called »thoughtless correction made by the scribes« (*Second Continuation,* note to 27143). The expression called for here is *hom de mere né.* The haplography occurred because of inattention to the sense in conjunction with a repetition of *ne.* In 1864 Scheler (note to 736) correctly suggested: »Lisez *hom de mere net*«, but this was ignored by Potvin. Hilka used *nel* from ms *P* in his text and showed no variant from ms *L.* Ms *L* is torn and mended here but *nel* does not appear nor is there space enough for the appropriate *ne ne.*

748–749 *L Les li l'asist (P s'assist) desor un lit, La mere (P et) cent fois le baisa:* These lines as they appear in ms *P* (with *et*) and as used by Hilka in his text form an enjambement. As in lines 47 and 676, ms *P* uses *et* where *L* has examples of asyndeton. Hilka apparently rejects this effect where *P* offers an alternative producing a smoother line. In these two lines ms *L* has parallel (or paratactic) lines, or, perhaps, they are an example of ἀπὸ κοινοῦ discussed by Tobler (*Mélanges,* pp. 174–178) and Nyrop (V, pp. 28–29). If the latter were the case, then *La mere* would be the subject of both *asist* and *baisa.* There is, however, no way of ascertaining that the figure ἀπὸ κοινοῦ appears here, since the subject in 748 does not have to be expressed and the sense is in no way altered. The tonic pronoun of 748, *li,* must be taken as feminine. In both *L* and *P* the masc. tonic form is always *lui* (lines 99, 110, 124, 162, 181, 189, 228, 244, 245, 372, 386, 449, 469, 482, 789). In the case of the tonic feminine pronoun, both *L* and *P* use *li* at lines 346, 370, 501, 605; *P* uses *lui* as tonic fem. in lines 674 and 650 and *L* uses *lui* as tonic fem. in lines 663 and 667. The reflexive in *P (s'assist)* is thus an error since *li,* a possible Picard form of the tonic masc. (cf. Gossen, p. 124), does not appear elsewhere in either manuscript as a masc. tonic.

755–756 The singular *gent* takes a plural verb, *sunt,* and a masculine plural predicate adjective. The *-s* of *aparelliés* is either a sign of the accusative (although ms *L* more often uses a nominative in the predicate: cf. note to lines 29–30) or was added for the eye rime. Hilka chose *unes gens* from ms *P* for his text, a choice which makes an unnecessary »correction«. On *gens* see Tobler, *Mélanges,* p. 292 and n. 1; Foulet, *Glossary,* p. 135; Foulet, *Petite Syntaxe*[3], p. 62 *(unes);* Nyrop, III, pp. 393–394, V, pp. 74, 78–79; Livingston, *Gliglois,* note to line 2148. There is a passage in the *Perceval* for which these lines of the *Bliocadran* are a preparation and in which *la gent* also occurs with a plural verb: »Les angles dont la gent se plaignent«, Roach 399. Hilka (*Perceval* 399) uses *les janz* with the plural verb *se plaingnent.*

758 *L C'est dïables tout en apert, P Ce sont li dÿable en apiert:* Ms *L* is using a singular noun in a collective sense with the plural *sont* (line 759). Ms *P* has no such problem as it shows a clearly plural form of the noun and *Ce sont.* As with *gens* (line 755) Hilka chose the reading of ms *P* for his text. The form *dïables* in ms *L* is not so clearly a nom. sing. subject. Examples from the Second Continuation show hesitation among the scribes who used *li deables* as both a singular and plural: 24797 »Li deables vos ont gari«; 25798 »Que li deables ne deçoit«; in 28498 *KLPSTV* »Mais li deable ont Ke gari« whereas *EMQU* use *deables.* After *c'est,* however, the third person plural does not appear (see Anna Granville Hatcher,

From »ce suis je« to »c'est moi«, PMLA, LXIII [1948], 1053–1100, esp. 1054–56). See also Tobler, *Mélanges*, pp. 290–301, on collective nouns; *dïables* is not among his examples.

761   Hilka apparently regarded *arestés* as an imperative in a series of imperatives (*Gardés* 761, *revenés* 762, *si vos en sainiés* 763) rather than as a present subjunctive dependent upon *Gardés* with *que* omitted. He replaced *L vos* with *n'i* from *P*. (He does not record the variant *arrestes* from *P*.)

763   The pronoun complement *vos* of the imperative *sainiés* appears before the verb because the adverb *si* precedes the verb; cf. Foulet, *Petite Syntaxe*³, p. 124.

783   *L ainc, P c'ains:* Foulet (*Glossary*, »ains«) says: »Les confusions de graphie entre *ainc* et *ains*, et particulièrement celles qui nous présentent un emploi de *ains* ou *ainz* sont assez fréquentes au moyen âge.« Cf. also *Petite Syntaxe*³: »*mais* peut toujours remplacer *ainz*« (p. 309). In many instances the meaning of either word is possible. A. Henry studied the confusion between *ainc* and *ains* in the *Cleomadés* and presents his conclusions in a note to line 186: »on trouve 59 fois *ainc* où on l'attend (= *ainques*), 76 fois *ains* pour *ainz* (sans compter *ains que*) et 84 fois *ains* pour *ainc*. *Ainc* n'apparaît pas à la place de *ains* (= *ainz*).« *Ainc* is the *lectio difficilior* and *ains* for *ainc* the most likely error; or, when one finds *ainc* it is probably not an error but an intended form. In a random sample from the Second Continuation the same sort of confusion between *ainc* and *ains* occurs among the manuscripts; see lines 20304, 20846, 21088, 21248, 21686, 21960 and variants to these lines. In the *Bliocadran*, then, *ainc* is retained, although Hilka preferred *c'ains* from *P*.

793–794   Self-rime in *a*. Cf. Tobler, *Vers fr.*, p. 169.

INDEX OF PROPER NAMES

GLOSSARY

Words in the Glossary have been chosen generally on the basis of peculiarities of orthography, meaning or usage. The references are not exhaustive: only up to five references are given for any word, usually the first, last and three from evenly spaced intervals in the text. Verbs are for the most part listed under the infinitive, declinable words under the accusative singular and masculine in the case of words varying in gender.

aaisier *intr* 633 se reposer

abeïe *f* 332 couvent, abbaye

abes *m sg nom* 342, 364, 374, 404, 433, abé *sg obl* 325, 333, 354, 362 abés *pl obl* 398 abbé

acomencier *tr* 183 commencer

acosté *p p* 520 assis côte à côte

acoucier *tr: inf employé comme subst* 67 mettre au monde, accoucher

adés *adv: loc* tout adés 31, 385 continûment, sans interruption, pendant tout le temps

adrecier *réfl* 189 se diriger

afaires *m sg nom* 502 besogne, devoir, au sens d'empêchement

aficier *tr* 309 affirmer, assurer

afïer *tr* 630 promettre solennellement

afit *m* 612 réprimande, reproche

agreer *intr* 463 plaire

aige *f* 680 cours d'eau

ainc *adv* 204 jamais; 783 pas un instant, pas un seul moment

ains *adv* 33, 125, 277, 338, 513 plutôt; *conj* ains que 479 avant que

aïr *m: loc adv* par aïr 214 avec violence et impétuosité

aler *intr* 40, 141, 391, 529, 550 aller, s'en aller; *p p* alés 161, 277, alé 300, 316, 632, 715; *ps ind 3* vait 137, *5* alés 45, 751, *6* vont 149, 331, 351, 505, 507; *impf ind 3* aloit 621, *6* aloient 13; *prét 3* ala 249, 265, 706, 789, *6* alerent 667; *fut 1* irai 92, 531, *3* ira 51, 135, 477, 543, 618; *cond 3* iroit 785; *impf sbj 3* alast 339, 647 *impér pl* alés 43

aleüre *f: loc adv* grant aleüre 74 à toute allure

aleus *m pl obl* 22 biens héréditaires

aloigne *f* 570 retard, délai

ambedui *v* andui

ament 112, 117 *ps sbj 3* de amender aider

amenteüs 258 *p p* de amentevoir rappeler, mentionner

amer *tr* 378 aimer; *p p* amés 397; *ps ind 6* aiment 61; *impf ind 3* amoit 488

amont *adv* 283 en haut

amor *f* 384, 488, 510 amour

ançois *adv* 85, 246, 649, 665 plutôt; *conj* ançois que 377 avant que

andui *adj num* 371, 610, andoi 210, ambedui 190 tous deux

angoisse *f: loc adv* par angoisse 194 avec violence et force

anui *m* 294 peine, tourment

anuit *adv: loc* anuit mais 87 cette nuit

apaisiés 156 *impér 5* de apaisier *refl* se calmer

aparellier *tr* 38, 98, 148, 638, 721 apprêter, préparer; 756 équiper, parer; *réfl* 776 s'équiper

apercevans *adj m sg nom* 480 conscient, perspicace

aperciut 646 *prét 3* de apercevoir 549

apert: *loc adv* en apert 758 à découvert, clairement

apoiés 69, apoié 496 *p p* de apuier appuyer

aprés: *loc conj* aprés çou que 249 après que

aprester *tr* 434, 475, 710 apprêter, préparer

arees 723 *p p f* de arer labourer

as = a + les *art* 14, 70 aux; 627 par les

asseoir *réfl: p p* assis 370, 372; *tr: prét 3* asist 748

assés *adv* 103, 106, 442, 702, 786 beaucoup; 95 jusqu'à satiété; 753 très

asseürer *tr* 626 guarantir

atant *adv* 72, 136, 208, 408, 787 alors

atorner *réfl* 142 se préparer à partir

atout *prép* 665 avec

aüner *intr* 144 se réunir

auques *adv* 479 assez

aus *v* els

ausi *adv: loc* ausi . . . come 175 aussi . . . que, de la même façon que

autre *pr m pl nom* li autre 202

avaine *f* 640 avoine

avant: *loc adv* d'ore en avant 454 désormais, dorénavant

avenans *adj m sg nom* 679 agréable

avenir *impers* 455 arriver, advenir

avis: *loc* ce m'est avis 457 il me semble

aviser *tr* 188 apercevoir

avoec *prép* 181, 594, 615, 667 avec

avoir *tr* 56, 65, 294 avoir; *p p* eü 57, 60, 263; *ps ind 1* ai 421, 582, 585, *3* a 50, 158, 288, 510, 798, ra 188, 219, *4* avon 320, *5* avés 296, 516 527, *6* ont 49, 231, 438, 638, 725; *impf ind 3* avoit 187, 409, 522, 663, 747, *6* avoient 57, 741; *prét 3* ot 19, 273 (venu), 490, 570, 678, *6* orent 167, 631, 717, 723; *fut 4* avrons 702, *5* arés 88, 767; *cond 6* aroient 760; *ps sbj 3* ait 346, 596, *5* aiés 524; *impf sbj 3* eüst 298, 429; *inf employé comme subst* avoir 8 richesse, biens; *loc* avoir le cuer dolent 522 s'affliger; n'avoir garde 767 ne pas avoir de raison de craindre; avoir mestier 341 avoir besoin

balancier *intr* 224 être ébranlé

bel *adv* 580 bien; *v* bien *adv*

belement *adv* 365 en termes précis, dûment, doucement

beneïe 367 *ps sbj 3* de beneïr bénir

berbis *f* 643 brebis

bien *m* 36 bien, qualité morale

bien *adv: loc* et bien et bel 207 suivant toutes les règles en usage (dans le monde des chevaliers)

boinement *adv* 555 dûment et courtoisement; 565 courtoisement et gentiment

bon: *loc* estre bon 705 plaire; *impers* faire (molt) bon 691, 698 être bon

borc *m* 696 bourg

borgois *m* 443, borjois 573 citoyen, habitant d'une ville

bués *m pl* 643 bœufs

ça *adv de lieu* 586 ici

caï 226 *prét 3* de caoir tomber

caitive *adj f sg nom* 419 malheureuse, infortunée, chétive

camp *m* 164 champ de tournoi

canter *tr* 440 chanter

caretes *f pl* 639 charrettes

cargier *tr* 147, 641 charger

carité *f* 326 charité

cars *m pl obl* 639 chars, chariots

cascuns *pr indéf m sg nom* 330, 350 chacun

castel *m* 166, 355, 657, *pl obl* castiax 9 château

ce *pr dém neutre* 44, 90, 443, 576, 645 il (*impers*), ceci, cela; *v* çou

cel *adj dém m sg obl* 97, *m sg nom* cil 366, 513, *f sg obl* cele 203, 798 cet, ce, cette

celer *tr* 338, 394 cacher

celui *pr dém m sg obl* 94, 379, 625 celui; *v* cil

cerquier *tr* 3, 126, 572, 736 chercher; *ps ind 3* cerque 782 fouille

cers *m* 753 cerf

cest *adj dém m sg obl* 401, 529, 567, 608, *f sg obl* ceste 125 ce, cet, cette

cestui *pr dém m* 293 celui-ci

ceval *m sg obl* 78, 198, 209, 778, *m pl obl* cevax 39, 173, 328, 358, 642 cheval

cevalcier *intr* 353, 727, cevaucier 178 aller à cheval

ceviax *m pl obl* 240, 424 cheveux

ci *adv de lieu* 87, 244, 325, 516, 703, ici 582, 712 ici

cief *m: loc* el cief premier 184 en tête

ciere *f* 221 visage, figure; *loc* a bele ciere 105 à bonne chère

ciers *adj m sg nom* 83, 525 cher

cil *pr dém m sg nom* 37, 80, 191, 265, 794; *m pl nom* 60, 150, 174, 285, 661, 714; *m pl obl* cex 71, 120, 123, 345,

482; *f sg obl* **cele** 648 celui, ceux, celle; *v* **celui**

clamer *tr* 560 nommer, appeler; *ps ind réfl 3* **claime** 419 se plaindre

clers *m pl obl* 398 membres de clergé

clices *f pl* 217 éclats; *v la note à ce vers*

close 718 *p p f* de **clore** entourer

coi *pr interr* 420, 583 quoi; *pr rel* 652 dont

comander *tr* 436 recommander

combatant *adj* 12 combatif

conduie 160 *ps sbj 3* de **conduire**

confaitement *adv* 262 de quelle manière, comment

confés *adj pris subst:* **faire confés** 235 faire confesser

confors *m sg nom* 407 réconfort; 469 consolation

conforter *tr et réfl* 406, 447 réconforter, soulager

congié *m* 435, 617 permission de partir

conquester *tr* 15 gagner, rapporter

consel *m* 563, 591 conseil, indication donnée à qqn sur ce qu'il doit faire; 567 entretien privé; *pl obl* 528 **conseus** secrets, plans, projets

contenir *réfl: prét 3* **contint** 456; *ps sbj 6* **contegnent** 556 se comporter

contre *prép* 110, 789 au devant de, à la rencontre de

contree *f* 3, 661 région

contremont *adv* 357 en haut, vers le haut

contreval *adv* 197 en bas, vers le bas

converser *intr* 732, 734 demeurer

convoier *tr* 653 escorter

corecié 444 *p p m pl nom* de **corecier** affliger

çou *pr dém neutre* 45, 102, 308, 590, 764 ce, ceci, cela; *conj por çou que* 309, 545, 585, 595 parce que; *conj après çou que* 249 après que; *v* ce

coucier *tr* 233 coucher

covent *m* 333 couvent, abbaye

creés 86 *ps ind 5* de **croire**

cremoit 294 *impf ind 3* de **criembre**, **cremir** craindre

crestïenés *p p m sg nom* 255 baptisé

cri *m sg obl* 428, *m pl obl* **cris** 423 lamentations, cris de douleur

crupe *f* 198 croupe

cuer *m* 429 cœur; *loc* **avoir le cuer**

dolent 522, **de cuer dolent** 153 (être) affligée, désolée

cuidier *tr* croire, penser; *ps ind 3* **cuide** 483; *impf ind 3* **cuidoit** 306, 746, 6 **cuidoient** 738

dalés *prép* 282 à côté de

dansel *m* 208 jeune noble non armé chevalier, forme syncopé de **damoisel** 251, *f pl* **damoiseles** 491 jeune femmes non mariées de naissance noble

deboinairement *adv* 373 gentiment, poliment

dedens *prép* 241 à l'intérieur de

deduit *p p employé comme subst* 797 plaisir, joie, divertissement, amusement

deffendre *tr* 274, 311, 754 interdire

del = **de** + **le** *art* 710

dela *adv* 174 de l'autre côté

delaiement *m* 504 retard, sursis, remise

delaier *intr* 37, 342, 648 faire du retard, s'attarder

delivrement *adv* 503 sans perdre un instant

dels *v* duel

demener *tr* 32 manifester, montrer (deuil)

dementer *réfl* 418 se lamenter, se désoler, se désespérer

demorer *intr* 108, 237, 250, 314, 625 tarder; 664, 774 demeurer, rester

departir *réfl* 136 s'en aller, partir; 157 se séparer

descendre *intr* 76, 282, 356, 685, 788 descendre d'un cheval; 681 descendre

descirier *tr* 240 déchirer

desconfit *p p* 611 confondu

desconfort *m* 19 découragement, inquiétude, chagrin

desconsellie *adj f* 47 affligée, sans direction

desmentir *intr* 216 se désagréger

desor *prép* 173, 520, 748 sur; *loc* **par desor** 497 par-dessus

desos *adv* 678, 680 dessous

destent 176 *ps ind 3* de **destendre** *intr* filer dans l'air, s'élancer

detiegne 502 *ps sbj 3* de **detenir** retenir

devant *prép* 76 devant; *prép* 304 avant; *adv* 634 auparavant

devoir *tr* devoir; *ps ind 3* **doit** 31, 33;

cond 5 **devrïés** 385; *impér pl* **devés** 378

dïables *m sg nom* 758 diable; *v la note à ce vers*

dire *tr* 17, 265, 348, 395, 683 dire; *p p* **dit** 49, 320, 510, 607, 707; *ps ind 1* **di** 88, 297, 694, 6 **dïent** 42; *prét 3* **dist** 79, 140, 475, 751, 800; *fut 1* **dirai** 115, 128, 455, 528, 584; *cond 1* **diroie** 324; *ps sbj 3* **die** 793; *impf sbj 3* **desist** 275, 277, 307, 310, 5 **deïsiés** 552; *impér* **disons** 326, **dites** 517, 602, 765

dognon *m* 282 donjon, réduit de la défense dans un château-fort

dolcement *adv* 154, 233, **doucement** 792 avec douceur, avec tendresse

dolent *adj m sg obl* 153, 522, *m sg nom* **dolens** 28, **dolans** 430, *m pl nom* **dolant** 620, **dolent** 445, *f sg obl* **dolante** 48, *f sg nom* **dolante** 420, **dolente** 450 attristé, accablé de douleur

dolor *f* 322, 427 douleur

doner *tr* 91 donner; *p p* **doné** 199, 388, 617; *ps ind 3* **done** 103, 379; *impf ind 3* **donoit** 772; *ps sbj 3* **doinst** 515, 588; *impér* **donés** 592

dont *adv* 392 d'où; *pr rel* 463, 676 dont

dose *num* 2, 490 douze

dossel *m* 497 chevet d'un lit paré de tenture ou de rideau

douter *tr* 484 craindre, redouter

dras *m pl obl* 240 vêtements

droit *adv* 260 immédiatement; *loc adv* **tout droit** 73, **tot d.** 657 promptement, directement; *loc adv* **n'a droit n'a tort** 275 ni directement ni indirectement

duel *m sg obl* 156, 416, 431, 438, 473, *sg nom* **dels** 410 douleur, chagrin; *loc* **mener duel** 228, 654, **demener d.** 32 manifester ouvertement de la douleur

dui *num* 351, 352, 354, **doi** 356 deux

dur *adj* 429 insensible

durement *adv d'intensité* 406 de toutes ses forces

dusque *prép* 138, 200, 688, 775 jusque

el *pr pers f* 472, 544, 647 elle

el = **en** + **le** *art* 27, 195, 355, 461, 745

els *pr pers m pl obl* 16, 761, **aus** 157, **eus** 23 eux

emfes *m sg nom* 746 enfant

emparlés *adj m sg nom* 25 qui parle bien

empris 119 *p p* de **emprendre** entreprendre (un tournoi)

en *pr* 763 contre eux; 689 lui, à elle

encontre *prép* 362 à la rencontre de *v* contre

encontrer *tr* 285, 784 rencontrer

endemain *m* 169, 439, 649, 785 lendemain

enfermeté *f* 380 maladie

enfoi 266 *p p* de **enfouir** enterrer

enmi *prép* 221 au milieu de

enpené *adj m pl nom* 759 ailé, empenné

enquerre *adv* 345, 687 là

enquist 799 *prét 3* de **enquerre** demander, s'enquérir de

ensamble: *loc* **tout ensamble** 738 après tout, en fin de compte

enseigniés *adj* 364 plein de tact et de savoir-faire, préparé

enseller *tr* 328, 778 seller

ensi *adv* 276, 483, 713, 725, 798 ainsi; *loc* **n'ensi n'ensi** 51 ni d'une façon ni de l'autre, en tout cas

entendre *intr* 656 s'appliquer, mettre son effort; 603 entendre dire, comprendre; *loc* **faire entendant** 742 donner à entendre, faire comprendre

entente *f* 417, 449 pensée, désir, effort; *v* metre

entreferir *réfl* 190, 213 frapper de grands coups de part et d'autre

entrepris *adj* 318 tombé dans l'embarras

environ *adv* 695, 718 à l'entour

envoiseüre *f* 797 plaisir, gaîté, joie

errer *intr* 73, 280, 641, 670, 673, **esrer** 353, 669 aller, cheminer, voyager; *inf employé comme subst* **l'esrer** 656

es *interj:* **es vos** 72, 184, 408 voilà, voici

esbahir *tr et réfl* 158, 604 étonner, être éperdu, stupéfait

escaper *intr* 390 éviter, échapper

escris *m sg nom* 644 écrit, histoire, conte (source de l'auteur?)

escu *m* 192, 220, *sg nom* **escus** 215 bouclier

escuier *m* 73, 97, 140 écuyer; *v la note au vers 96*

esgarder *tr* 70 voir, regarder

esperon *m:* *loc adv* **a esperon** 281 en piquant le cheval de l'éperon

esperoner *intr* 186, 212 piquer le cheval de l'éperon

esprovés *adj:* **chevalier esprovés** 82

chevalier éprouvé, qui a fait ses preuves

esrer *v* errer

essarter *tr: inf employé comme subst* 709 défricher la terre en arrachant le bois

essïent *m: loc adv* mien essïent 6 à mon avis, à ce que je crois

essoine *m* 569 empêchement, difficulté

esté *m* 608 été

ester *intr* 231, 457, 476, 725, 798 rester, demeurer, se tenir; *ps ind* 6 estont 169; *loc* laissier ester 452 renoncer à

estevroit 548 *cond* 3 de estovoir falloir, être nécessaire

estre *intr* 90, 182 être; *p p* esté 317, 527; *ps ind* 1 sui 420, 3 est 32, 161, 322, 779, 788, rest 189, 4 somes 318, 5 estes 526, 581, 6 sont 29, 166, 508, 675, 759, sunt 270, 520, 756; *impf ind* 3 estoit 4, 84, 225, 489, 745, ert 26, 54, 450, 459, 472, 6 estoient 1, 210, 444, 620, 627, erent 316, 492, 676; *prét* 1 fui 301, 302, 795, 3 fu 59, 164, 255, 652, 719, refu 512, 6 furent 20, 171, 269, 577; *fut* 1 serai 116, 540, 3 sera 560, 700, sara 705, ert 122, 6 seront 133; *cond* 3 seroit 44, 466, 600, 4 serions 611, 6 seroient 482; *ps sbj* 3 soit 33, 479, 530, 5 soiés 81, 511, 6 soient 129; *imp sbj* 3 fust 257, 276, 414, 430, 6 fuissent 740, 757; *loc* estre bon a 705 plaire

estri *m: loc* sans estri 714 en bon accord; estrif 596 dispute, querelle

estrier *m* 330 étrier

estuisse 391 *ps sbj* 3 de estovoir falloir, être nécessaire

faille *f: loc adv* sans faille 122, 415 certainement, à coup sûr

faindre *tr* 33 faire semblant

faire *tr* 229, 548, 699, 710, 730 faire; *p p* fait 205, 207, 238, 572, 630, faite 717, fais 147; *ps ind* 3 fait 83, 117, 319, 440, 768, 6 font 254, 328, 619, 641, 642; *impf ind* 3 faisoit 691, 5 faisïés 551, 6 faisoient 729, 735; *prét* 3 fist 38, 145, 279, 503, 655; 6 firent 235, 239, 242, fisent 229, 253; *fut* 1 ferai 768, 3 fera 566, 4 ferons 89, 5 ferés 563, 711, 6 feront 701; *cond* 3 feroit 698, 6 feroient 628; *ps sbj* 3 face 400; *impf*

sbj 3 feïst 684; *impér* faites 91, 98, 704, faisons 699; *impers* faire (molt) bon 691, 698 être bon; faire et bien et bel 207 se comporter très vaillamment; faire grant feste de 89, 145 acueillir avec empressement; faire joie 271, 284 manifester de la joie

fait *m* 206 acte, action

feeus *adj m sg nom* 527 fidèle

felon *adj m pl nom* 759 méchant, redoutable, dangereux

fenir *intr* 29 mourir; *tr* 567 terminer

ferer *tr* 39 garnir de clous

ferir *tr: p p* feru 219; *ps ind* 3 fiert 191, 195, 214 frapper

fermetés *f pl* 9 forteresses

fers *m sg nom* 223 fer, pointe en fer qui est au bout d'une lance

fier *adj m pl nom* 12 violent, fort, *m sg nom* fiers 407 pénible; *v la note au vers* 407

fierement *adv* 203 farouchement, violemment

fin *f* 674; *loc* en la fin 683 en fin de compte

finer *intr* 212, 783 cesser

foi *f: loc* par foi 584 vraiment, par la foi que je vous dois

foillu *adj* 676 garni de feuilles

fois *f: loc adv* a cele fois 203 à ce moment-là; maintes fois 464 plus d'une fois, souvent

folie *f* 32 chose déraisonnable

force *f* 588 puissance, vigueur

forment *m* 640 froment

forment *adv* 620 fortement

fors *prép* 482 sauf; fors de *prép* 109, 568 hors de

fort *adj* 209 puissant; 673 difficile, pénible

frain *m* 201 frein; la bride, le mors et les rênes

front *m: loc adv* el premier front 180 au premier rang

frosse 193 *ps ind* 3 de frossier casser, briser, rompre; *v la note à ce vers*

fuer *m: loc adv* a nul fuer 64 en aucune manière

gaaignier *tr* 722 labourer

gaires *adv de quantité* 664 guère

garde *f: loc* n'avoir garde 767 ne pas avoir de raison de craindre garder *tr* 358, 465, 598, 616, 761 garder, protéger, préserver; *ps sbj 3* gart 135, 367, 589

gaste *adj* 476, 531, 674 désert, inhabité, inculte

gavelos *m pl* 728, 781 javelots

gent *f sg obl* 48, 234, 287, 662, 769, *f sg nom* 168, 579, 686, *f pl nom* gens 667, 735, *f pl obl* 27; *nom collectif au singulier avec le verbe au pluriel* 548, 755; la grant gent 132 les gens de marque, les hauts personnages

gentes *adj f pl* 492 gentilles, nobles

gesir *intr: p ps* gisant 360; *impf ind 3* gisoit 283, 305 être couché

gié *pr pers* 618 je, moi; *v* jel, jo, jou

gre *m: loc* savoir bon gre 535 être reconnaissant

greignor *adj comp f sg obl* 64 plus grande

harnois *m* 148, 200, 665 équipement, armure

haster *réfl* 174, 777 se hâter

hastivement *adv* 499 promptement

haterel *m* 222 nuque

herbergier *tr et réfl* 166, 712, 719 loger, héberger

honor *f* 422 honneur

iluec *adv de lieu* 232, 343, 507, 685, 744, ilueques 532, 692, 773 là

irié *adj m sg obl* 34, *m pl nom* 270, *f* irie 48 fâché, mécontent, chagriné

isi *adv* 256, 446, 505, 756 ainsi

isnelement *adv* 142, 405, 776, 788 rapidement, vite

issir *intr et réfl: p p* issus 109; *prét 6* issirent 568 sortir

itant *adv* 91 tant; *loc* a itant 359 alors, tout de suite

ja *adv* 116, 390, 474, 550, 767 jamais; nel vos celerai ja 394 je ne puis plus vous le cacher

jel = je + le *pr* 768; *v* gié, jo, jou

jo *pr pers* 115, 347, 582, 615 je; *v* gié, jel, jou

joie *f* 295, 515; *loc* faire joie 271, 284 manifester de la joie

jor *m: loc adv* le jor 204, 414 ce jour-là; al jor 649 à l'aube

josté 202 *p p* de joster jouter

jou *pr pers* 420, 597 je; *v* gié, jel, jo

jüerront 557 *fut 6* de jurer *tr* 597, 631 promettre par serment

kevrex *m* 753 chevreuil

la *adv* 179, 308, 392, 577 là; *conj* la u 179 lorsque

laissier *tr* laisser: *p p* laissié 165, 438, 741, laissiés 158, 409; *ps ind 3* lait 138 diffère; *fut 1* lairai 452; *cond 5* lairïés 46, 6 lairoient 550; *ps sbj 3* laist 500, 629; *impér* laissiés 609; *loc* laissier ester 452 renoncer à

lande *f* 675, 678 terrain en général plat, non cultivé, mais qui peut être agréable d'aspect

laniers *adj m sg nom* 84 lent, hésitant

lasse *adj f* 419 malheureuse, misérable

le *pr pers f sg obl* 340, 653, 722, 735 la

le *art f sg obl* 195, 518 la

le *adj m* 677, *f* lee 4 large

leece *f* 432 gaîté, liesse

les *prép* 104 près de, à côté de

leu *m* 544, 734 lieu

lever *intr et réfl* 688, 773, 775 se lever; *tr* 254 tenir sur les fonts baptismaux

li *art f sg nom* 305, 401 la

lié *adj m sg obl* 33, liés *m sg nom* 292, lié *m pl nom* 52, 269, lie *f sg* 540, 652 heureux, joyeux

lé *f pl* 677, 695; lieue; *v la note au vers 695*

loënt 206 *ps ind 6* de loër approuver, louer

loig *adv* 187, 234, 786 loin

longe *adj f* 4 longue

longement *adv* 446, 725 longtemps

lors *adv* 199, 229, 328, 423, 578, lores 498, 612 alors

los *m* 15 renommée

lou 766 *ps ind 1* de loër conseiller, recommander

lui *pr f obl après prép* 663, 667; *v la note aux vers 748–749*

main *f: loc adv* a destre main 165 à droite

maintenant *adv de temps* 101, 343, 685, 715, 779 sur-le-champ, immédiatement

maintiegne 369 *ps sbj 3* de maintenir 23, 248, 262

maior *m* 487, 509, 650, 690, 729, **maire**
sg nom 506, 511, 523, **maires** 542, 693,
706 majordome
mairien *m* 702, 710 bois à bâtir
mais *conj* 16, 165, 407, 551, 754 mais;
adv 95 bien sûr; **ne** ... **mais plus** 146
ne ... plus; **ne** ... **onques mais** 264,
292 jamais auparavant, jamais encore;
ne...mes 304 ne...pas, 474 ne...plus;
loc **Il n'en puet mais** 224 Il n'y peut
rien; **anuit mais** 87 cette nuit; *v les*
notes aux vers 95 et 407
maisnie *f* 539, 651, 720, 739 l'ensemble
de ceux qui forme la maison
maltalent *m:* *loc adv* par maltalent 192
avec colère
mangier *tr* 103 manger; *p p* **mangié** 106;
prét 1 **manjai** 93, *3* **manja** 100; *inf*
employé comme subst 68
manoir *intr* 698 demeurer, rester
mat *adj* 445 triste, désolé
matin *m* 688; *loc adv* **par matin** 593 de
bon matin, dès le matin
meïsme *adj* 472 même
mençoignieres *adj m sg nom* 116 men-
songer
mener, amener *tr* 101, 162, 329, 537, 663
mener, conduire, emmener; *fut 1* **men-**
rai 594, 615; *loc* **mener duel** 228, 654
manifester ouvertement le deuil
merchi *f* 42, 524 »expression de recon-
naissance pour une faveur accordée
ou que vous priez qu'on vous accorde«
[Foulet]
mervelles *f* *pris adverbialement* 54 re-
marquablement
mes *v* **mais**
mesciet 18 *ps ind 3* de mescheoir *impers*
arriver du mal, du malheur
messagier *m pl nom* 575 messager
mestier *m:* *loc* **avoir mestier** 341 avoir
besoin
metre *tr* 197 mettre; *loc* **metre s'entente**
à 417 s'adonner à; **metre en respit**
708 différer, reporter à plus tard
mi *adj poss m pl nom* 701 mes
mie *renforçatif de la nég* 31, 43, 84
mien *adj poss m sg obl* 6, 586, 697 mon
mollier *f* 490 épouse
mont *m* 745 monde
morir *intr:* *p p m pl* **mort** 266, *m sg*
mors 237, 276, 322, 403; *impf ind 5*
moriés 610; *fut 4* **morron** 389 mourir;

tr: *p p m pl* **mort** 20, *m sg* **mors** 470
tué(s)
morre *tr* 684 moudre
mostier *m* 238, 253, 441 église
mostrer *tr* 348 montrer
motons *m pl* 643 moutons
movoir *intr* 590 partir, s'en aller, se
mettre en route; *prét 3 mut* 649, 665,
6 **murent** 575; *fut 1* **movrai** 593
muevre *intr* mouvoir: *inf employé*
comme subst 302 départ
mus *adj m sg nom* 512 muet

navrés 225 *p p m sg nom* de **navrer**
blesser
né 733 *p p m, f* **nee** 425 de nestre naître
nel = ne + le *pr* 394, 478, 502
nïent *pr indéf* 204, 500 rien, néant; *loc*
adv **por nient** 614 en vain; **de noient**
118 pas du tout, aucunement; *v la*
note au vers 614
noïe 740 *p p f* de noier noyer
nons *m sg nom* 256 nom
norrie 426 *p p f* de **norrir** élever (un
enfant)
nostre 177 *pr m pl nom* **li nostre** les
nôtres
nul *adj m sg obl* 7, 57, 293, 569, *nom*
nus 252, 478, 502, 645, *f* **nule** 484,
646, 672, 784 aucun
nului *pr indéf* 481 personne

o *prép* 53, 354, 482, 535, 761, **od** 162,
650 avec
ocirre *tr et réfl* tuer: *p p* **ocis** 317, 459,
ochis 530; *ps ind 5* **ociés** 752; *cond 3*
ocirroit 473
oés *m:* *loc* **a oés vo fil** 559 dans l'intérêt
de votre fils, pour votre fils; *v la*
note à ce vers
oïr *tr* entendre: *p p* **oï** 52; *ps ind 3* **ot**
402; *cond 3* **oroit** 468; *impf sbj 5* **oïs-**
siés 428
onques *adv* 252, 264, 366, 570, 668
jamais
or *adv* 399, 517, 601, 704, 709 maintenant, à l'heure présente; *loc* **d'ore**
en avant 454 désormais, dorénavant
ore *f* 34, 425 heure; *loc* **de quele ore**
393 du moment
orer *intr* 554 prier
orle *m ou f* 220 bordure
osté 201 *p p* de oster 107 ôter

ostel *m* 248, 787, *pl obl* ostex 633 maison, logement; *loc* avoir bon ostel 88, 167 se loger bien

ostelé 687 *p p* de osteler loger, héberger

ot 402 *ps ind 3* de oïr

otroier *tr* 50, 350, 542, 714 octroyer

ou *v* u

ovré 716 *p p* de ovrer travailler

païsant *m pl nom* 660 paysan

palefroi *m* 344, 434 cheval de promenade ou de voyage

palis *m* 718 palissade

par *adv servant à renforcer un verbe, adv ou adj* molt par devés amer 378 vous devez aimer beaucoup

par *prép: loc* par tout 514 partout, en tout; 572 partout; par tens 477 bientôt

parfaire *tr* 36 mettre à l'exécution

parmi *prép* 196, 198, 221 à travers

parole *f* 452 récit

part *f: loc* d'autre part 371 de l'autre côté

paru 223 *prét 3* de paroir paraître; *v la note à ce vers*

pasmer *réfl* 226, 401, 411, 418 perdre connaissance, s'évanouir, se pâmer

passet *m: loc* tout le passet 179 tout tranquillement au petit pas

peçoie 215 *ps 3* de peçoier se briser en morceaux

pener *intr* 385 s'appliquer, mettre toute son attention

penser de *tr* 99, 399, 709 s'occuper de

pensis *adj m sg nom* 30 triste, préoccupé

peril *m* 295 péril, danger

pieça *loc adv* 585 il y a quelque temps

pis *m* 195, 424 poitrine

plain *m* 782 plaine, terrain plat

plaire *v* plaisir

plaisans *adj m sg nom* 659 agréable, qui plaît

plaisir *intr* plaire: *ps ind 3* plest 796; *prét 3* plot 106; *fut 3* plaira 95, 393; *inf employé comme subst* 533

plenier *adj* 634 entier

plor *m sg obl* 428 pleurs, action de pleurer

pooir *intr* pouvoir: *ps ind 1* puis 395, 683, *3* puet 90, 224, 514, *6* pueent

271; *impf ind 1* pooie 771, *3* pooit 475, *6* pooient 737; *prét 3* pot 64, 102, 777, *6* porent 56, 211; *fut 4* poron 390, porrons 392; *cond 3* porroit 546; *impf sbj 3* peüst 3, 297, *6* peuissent 606; *inf employé comme subst* 127 a lor pooir avec leurs gens; 588 puissance, capacité; *loc* il n'en puet mais 224 il n'y peut rien

por *prép: loc* por soie amor 384 pour amour de lui

por çou que *conj* 309, 545, 549, 585, 595 parce que

porpenser *réfl* 464 songer, réfléchir

porveü 58 *p p* de porveoir *tr* veiller à

prendre *tr* 387, 591 prendre; *p p* pris 635; *ps ind 3* prent 518; *impér* prendés 97

preu *adj m sg obl* 624 qui a du mérite; vertueux, honorable, distingué

preudome *m* 18 homme digne et loyal

pris *m* 7, 15 estime, réputation

prodefame *f* 54, 400 femme honorable

proier *tr et intr* supplier, prier: *p p* proié 49, 150, 437, 541; *ps ind 1* pri 523, *5* proiés 555, *6* proient 159; *cond 5* proieriés 614

puis *adv* 243, 329, 349, 641, 779 après, ensuite; 456 depuis

puis que *conj* 458 depuis que

quanque *loc conj* 388 autant que, tout ce que

quarriax *m sg nom* 176 carreau d'arbalète, grosse flèche

quart *adj* 576 quatrième

que *conj* 100, 182, 250, 352, 784 car

quens *m sg nom* 666 comte

querre *tr* 126, 572, 735 chercher, chercher et trouver, vouloir; *p p* quis 570

qui'n = qui en 620

ra *v* re

radement *adv* 175 rapidement

raienst 381 *prét 3* de raembre payer la rançon de, racheter

raison *f: loc* par bele raison 375 avec de belles paroles, d'une belle façon de parler; de boine raison 493 de bon sens

randoner *intr* 185 courir impétueusement

re *préfixe répétitif ou réciproque avec* avoir *et* estre *auxiliaires:* ra 188, 219, rest 189, refu 512

remanoir *intr* 546 rester; *p p f* remese 247; *prét 3* remest 21, 53; *fut 5* remanrés 87; *ps sbj 3* remaigne 124, 6 remaignent 345; *impf sbj 3* remansist 152; *impér pl* remanés 43, 608; *impers* Ne velt pas que en lui remaigne 124 il ne veut pas tarder

repaire *m* 700 refuge, maison, domicile

repairier *réfl* 272 s'en revenir; *intr* 629, 647 revenir

reproier *tr* 154 supplier, prier à son tour

respit *m* 708 ajournement, délai; *v* metre

respondus *p p m sg nom* 289 accueilli

rest *v* re

resurrexi 383 *prét 3* de resurrexir *intr* ressusciter

retenissent 605 *impf sbj 6* de retenir

retraire *réfl* 35 se retirer

revenir *intr* 599, 762; *fut 5* revenrés 349; *cond 1* revenroie 770

riche *adj m sg obl* 8, rice 666 riche; *sg nom* rices 319 puissant, formidable

roncin *m* 72 cheval de charge ou une monture pour les valets et les écuyers

sailli 362 *prét 3* de sallir se lever avec empressement

sainier *réfl* 763 se signer: Et si vos en sainiés Faites sur vous le signe de la croix contre eux

salus *m pl obl* 290 salutations

saut 367, 513 *ps sbj 3* de salver sauver

savoir *tr* 261 savoir; *p p m sg nom* seüs 257; *ps ind 3* set 545, 5 savés 114, 583; *impf ind 3* savoit 337, 733, 6 savoient 730; *prét 3* sot 458, 727; *fut 1* sarai 535, 3 savra 478; *cond 3* saroit 467; *impér* saciés 62, 323, 443, 645, 796, savés 601; *loc* savoir bon gre 535 être reconnaissant

se *conj* 45, 414, 430, 549, 771, si, en cas que, pourvu que; se ... non 672, 744 sinon, sauf, excepté

sel = si *adv* + le *pr* 233, 254, 592; se *conj* + le *pr* 475

semedi *m* 129 samedi

senés *adj m sg nom* 85, 404 sensé, sage

sergant *m* 351, 486, 619, 638, 721, serjant 358, *pl obl* sergans 573 serviteur domestique

sermon *m* 376 discours

serré *p p m pl nom* 177 en rangs serrés

seus *adj* 21 *m sg nom* de seul

si *adj poss m pl nom* 41, 149, 239, 303, 471, 653 ses

si *adv* 7, 84, 292, 422, 429 si, tellement; 11, 76, 140, 487, 700, 779 aussi, ainsi, et; *devant le pr pers* li *cet adv peut s'écrire* se *par dissimilation vocalique:* se li 690

sien *v* suen

sofrir 427 supporter, endurer

soie *pr poss f* 600 la sienne; *adj poss f:* por soie amor 384 pour amour de lui

sojorner *intr* 668, sejorner 691 demeurer, rester

solas *m* 463 plaisir, divertissement, distraction

soloir *intr* 786 avoir coutume

some *f: loc* en la some 17 en deux mots

sor *prép* 72, 192, 658 sur

sos *prép* 195 sous

sovent *adv* 418, 753 souvent

suen *adj poss m* 486, 487, sien 623 son, sien; *pr m pl nom* li suen 227, *m pl obl* suens 478 les siens

sus *adv* en haut: sus sailli 362 se dressa d'un bond

taisiés 155 *impér pl* de taisir se taire

talent *m* 348, 517, 566, 602 envie, désir, volonté, opinion; *loc* à talent 167 comme on désire, à (leur) gré

tans, tens 313 temps; *loc adv* par tens 477 bientôt

tant *adv* 66, 161, 252, 541, 716 tant; *conj* de tant com 211 tant que; tant come (con) 4, 95, 106, 533 autant que; tant que 58, 313, 346, 461, 629 jusqu'à ce que

tel *adj f sg* 769, tele 34 telle

tenant *m pl nom* 574 tenanciers

tenront a 561 *fut 6* de tenir a considérer comme

termine *m* 312 terme, période de l'accouchement

tier *num* 383 troisième

tort *adj: loc adv* n'a droit n'a tort 275 ni directement ni indirectement

tost *adv* 80, 185, 473, 762, 777 vite, promptement

tout *pr m pl nom* 206, 269, 561, 604, 611 tous; *v* tuit

travailler *réfl* 416 se peiner, faire tous ses efforts

tressor *m* 635 trésor

trestot *pr* et *adj m sg obl* 333, trestout 137, 783, *m pl nom* trestot 300, trestout 597, 661, trestuit 143, *m pl obl* trestos 120, 485, *f* trestote 287, 686, trestoute 168, 539, 579, 774 tout

trestot *adv* 177, trestout 634 complètement, entièrement

trover *tr* 81, 266, 308, 359, 793 trouver; *impf sbj 3* trovast 6

tuit *pr m pl nom* 133, 171, 389, 413 tous; *v* tout

u *adv* 179, 231, 283, 300, 317, ou 164, 712, 734 où

u *conj* 609 ou

vaillans *adj* 489 digne, honorable

vassal *m pl nom* 210 hommes courageux

venir *intr* 77, 208, 361, 534, 771 venir; *p p* venu 133, 170, 273 (ot venu), 355, 675, venus 110, 511; *ps ind 6* vienent 657; *impf ind 3* venoit 74, 6 venoient 71; *prét 3* vint 461, 6 vinrent 175, 213, 576; *fut 3* venra 533, 6 venront 304; *ps sbj 2* vegnes 79, 3 vegne 327, 499, viegne 501, 6 vegnent 127; *impér pl* venés 130, vegniés 363

veoir *tr* voir: *p p f* veüe 299; *ps ind 3* voit 208, 5 veés 586, 703, 6 voient 218; *impf ind 1* veoie 769, 5 veïés 755; *prét 3* vit 77, 252, 361, 509, 6 virent 671; *fut 5* verrés 131, 389; *impf sbj 3* veïst 430, 481

vergier *m* 104 jardin

vers *prép* 178, 189 vers; 123 contre

verté *f* 65 *autre forme de* verité 279, 307, 336, 458, 694

vesqui 236 *prét 3* de vivre

vis *m* 221 figure, visage

viser *tr* 187, 211 voir, apercevoir

vive *adj f* 420 vivante

vo *pr poss m sg obl* 559 votre

vöé 585 *p p* de voër promettre par un vœu

voir: *loc por* voir 128, 302, 545 en vérité, vraiment

voires *adj f pl* 114 vraies

volentés *f pl obl* 704 volonté; *loc* en boine volenté 387 en bonne part

voloir *tr* vouloir: *ps ind 1* voel 16, 244, 451, 592, 597, vuel 591, 3 velt 35, 40, 124, 141, 713; *impf ind 3* voloit 108, 182, 261, 5 voliés 534; *prét 3* volt 37, 433, 648; *fut 3* vodra 477, volra 544; *impf sbj 3* volsist 377